Rebel, Rogue, Mischievous Babe

Sharlene Azam

with girls and young women from across Canada

Rebel, Rogue, Mischievous Babe

Stories About Being a Powerful Girl

Illustrated by Alicia Glavac and Olga Ryabets

HarperCollinsPublishersLtd

Rebel, Rogue, Mischievous Babe:
Stories About Being a Powerful Girl

For information address HarperCollins Publishers Ltd.,
55 Avenue Road, Suite 2900,
Toronto, Ontario, Canada M5R 3L2

http://www.harpercanada.com

HarperCollins books may be purchased for educational, business, or sales promotional use.
For information please write:
Special Markets Department,
HarperCollins Canada,
55 Avenue Road, Suite 2900,
Toronto, Ontario, Canada M5R 3L2

First edition ISBN 0-00-638604-0

Canadian Cataloguing in Publication Data

Azam, Sharlene
Rebel, rogue, mischievous babe : stories about being a powerful girl

ISBN 0-00-638604-0

1. Teenage girls. I. Title.

HQ798.A92 2000 305.235 C00-930093-7

---

01 02 03 04 05 PCC 6 5 4 3 2 1

Printed and bound in the United States
Set in Franklin Gothic and FF Quadraat

The opinions expressed throughout this book are those of the contributors.

This book is dedicated to my wonderful parents.

Contents

Introduction

Because Image Is Everything, Silly

Her scuffed-up army boots look good. They don't seem one bit heavy for her tiny frame. Two brownish-gold plaits, held at the ends and the tops with pink and yellow barrettes, swing as she moves. Her velvet baby doll dress is drenched from dancing in the tight spaces of this airless basement. With her guitar, with the mirror leaning against the wall that slightly distorts her view of herself because of the web-like scratches inside, she is rebel, rogue, mischievous babe.

When Juliette's not here belting it out, the feeling carries her. It's the image in her head of who she is, of how she wants to be seen, and it makes her feel tough and in control. She'll tell you she's Goodwill, Army Surplus, and retro. She's every powerful girl she's ever seen on MuchMusic and MTV, even though she knows such creatures are rare. She's sexy like Drew Barrymore and in your face like Madonna.

Yeah, she knows she's one of the lucky ones. She knows what she likes and she's not afraid to tell you. When she stands in front of her bathroom mirror, she smiles at what she sees. A tummy that's soft and squishy. Breasts. Whatever! Nobody cares about size, at least no one worth knowing. And the whole day rocks.

But then, there are days when she can't see herself. When the mirror keeps showing her what she's not; when she can't find that natural high; when no one notices her as she walks down the street; when glitter just looks bad and blue nail polish makes her feel like she bought what the advertiser was hawking.

Does body image determine how we act? Do we limit ourselves without even knowing it? It's probably not just the stuff we put on our bodies that bugs us so much on days like these. It's more that the feeling of being completely in the groove—when everything is humming—sometimes evaporates, with no explanation. I've felt it as a void in my centre, an empty black space that even mochaccinos, flip-flops, and Ani DiFranco's music can't fill.

I think it sometimes comes from the desperation of recognizing that I am nothing but the sum of music videos, sucky magazines, fashion, and the daily paper's astrological forecast. Ahhh, it's like being Hobbes in a "Calvin and Hobbes" cartoon and asking, "Who am I?" "Where am I?" only to realize that the shiny yellow tendrils of pop culture have me in their mighty grip and I am no one and nothing without it. Why? Because image is everything, silly. Heh heh, time for a Slurpee.

How you feel about your body, how your friends make you feel, where you find happiness—a lot of these things take time to reveal themselves to you. In part it's because if you want to know who you are, you need to be out in the world doing things and meeting people and experiencing life.

I'm curious to know about you and what you think. What influences your image of yourself? As much as everyone says young people are slaves to the media, let's get something straight: you're not a passive consumer. You don't accept everything you're given.

I think most people are willing to believe that the media do have some influence, but hey, parents and friends also have a big impact on personality, likes, dislikes, the whole gamut. As a polymorphous being, I think you'll agree, you're influenced a little bit by everything out there, depending on your mood, of course.

So why am I telling you this? In part because these are the questions that come up over and over when I talk to girls. It seems as though you are acutely aware of influences and care enough to ask: How much control do I have over my decisions? How much control do I give to others? How much should I care about what other people think? How often, and when, do I take action?

Those are the bigger questions, and maybe you'll answer them eventually. I'm still working on the answers for myself. I've learned that it helps to also look at a lot of the little, seemingly inconsequential things in your life for clues. Why do you pick Fubu over Reeboks? Why do you smoke? Why do you smoke up?

How much of your life do you imagine in your head, and how much of who you are is real because of the stuff you do and say? Sometimes when I'm in my shiny yellow pants, strutting down Queen Street hauling my guitar case, all of a sudden, out of the blue, I feel like a fraud, like this is just dress-up for me and real for everyone else. Has that ever happened to you? That feeling of things not being real?

And then what about the very real way our bodies get in the way of being magnificent? Why do we spend so much time primping and preening and squeezing our bodies into sizes that just don't suit, when we know jumping it around is a much better idea, and the effects last longer?

Why do we spend hours going through racks at vintage stores? Why wash your hair with grape-flavoured Kool-Aid? Hairy legs may not attract flies, but try washing your hair in Kool-Aid—swarms! You have to bleach your hair anyway before the Kool-Aid will take, but if you're making that kind of commitment, you might as well just dye it.

Pleasure is always the goal for me, and I've done some very silly things to make myself feel good. Nothing terribly harmful, just wacky. Over and over, though, I've found that the things that make me feel good, the natural highs, come from creating. I know that because the one thing I can count on—the one thing that never changes—is how proud I feel of calluses that finally appear on fingers that have been pressed down on steel strings for hours.

Creating or making stuff is actually what brought me to write this book. Several years ago, I started publishing *Reluctant Hero*, a magazine written by and for teenage girls because they told me that magazines like *Seventeen* and *Cosmopolitan* didn't accurately reflect their lives.

In the handful of years since I've been publishing it, I've met hundreds of girls between the ages of eleven and eighteen. When they started to tell me about their lives and their relationships at school, at home, and with their friends, I was surprised to learn that being a teenager hasn't become any easier since I was one. It's tougher—even though there are many more choices, even though you have more disposable income and cash on demand than any previous generation, and even though you're the next "it" generation where technology is concerned.

It seems that the pressures and expectations at home and school have quadrupled, and being a teenager has become one of the toughest times you'll go through. The golden time of being a kid and just hanging out on the porch with your pals eating Mr. Freezes is shorter, and there is more pressure to perform, to excel, to succeed right away.

As a kind of response to the fact that being a teenager isn't easy, being a girl isn't easy, this book was written. I'm hoping it might serve as a guide for girls, parents, or really anyone who cares about girls. Don't misunderstand, I'm not trying to say that I have the answers. But I do want to tell you about a few of the things I've seen and observed, give you a few things to think about, and take a look at some of the myths that teenagers are asked to accept. Mostly, though, I want you to know that it gets easier, and that you are already powerful and amazing, even if you don't always know it or feel it.

It was only after I graduated from university that I realized how valuable it would have been to have had a guide or mentor to help me navigate my way during my four years there. At the time, I was too busy struggling to stay on top of the workload to notice that there is a method to getting through school and that it can be less overwhelming if you have a little help. The same is true for life in general. It was with that in mind that I finally began to write pieces and stories that eventually became chapters.

Writing this book has been among the hardest things I've ever done, and that surprised me, for a number of reasons. First, I write a weekly column for a newspaper, so the discipline of sitting down to put words on paper is something I've learned. And although teenagers aren't some kind of homogeneous, Borg-like group to be analyzed, I felt as though I knew enough about girls to write something meaningful for them. Finally, here was my chance to share ideas, feelings, experiences that might inspire, and that's the biggest thrill—so what was stopping me?

I guess I was afraid. After all, who am I to tell girls anything? If I hate being told what to do, or how to behave, or how to act, wouldn't you, too? And then of course I was just plain scared that the book would fail and that somehow that would mean that I had failed. I know failure is supposed to be the greatest teacher, but I prefer to think of action as the teacher I want to learn from.

Although I'm the kind of person who doesn't like to be told stuff, sometimes I need things spelled out for me. Strangely enough it's the glaringly obvious truths that I miss. For times when you might want a little bit of guidance, turn to the myths. Myths are things I've noticed that keep the truth from us. The myths explore the idea that the world is not as it seems.

My favourite stories, newspaper articles, and novels are those that incorporate elements from the writer's personal experience, which is why every chapter begins with a piece about my life. It seemed only fair that if I was going to ask young people to share their stories about school, family, friends, violence, that I should do the same.

The stories and submissions by girls (and a few guys) will, I hope, show you that you are not alone. We almost all have similar hurts, feelings of fear, and lots of toe-curlingly good things that happen to us, we just don't share them often enough with others to be able to take comfort.

Surviving the bullies, school pressures, and the demands placed on you by your parents has a lot to do with figuring out how to handle those things, and it's not something you're born knowing. Coping with stress, learning how to negotiate with your parents, getting out of sticky situations with guys and girlfriends—these are skills that have to be developed. Figuring out the options for a situation ahead of time will allow you to assess how you feel and how you're going to feel when you're in the thick of it.

While being a girl is tough, it is, of course, more often a blast. I hope this book will help you explore some of the messy things you're feeling, but also celebrate many of the fantastic things about being a girl.

How much you accomplish, what you can make, how far you push and challenge yourself out in the world—a lot of it has to do with how you see yourself. Maybe this book will get you to shift your perspective just enough to change the movie that plays in your head and turn it into one that is more fun, dynamic, romantic, and silly.

In the movie that plays in my head, in my imagination, I am like a roar. One big glass of effervescence that spills everywhere and is delicious. Sip me. Drink too much of me. Instead of just plain walking, I saunter, or sashay, or bounce (hence the spilling, I guess). I imagine that when you see me and stand next to me, you will want to reach inside and grab handfuls.

It's what I imagine I am like, and if you could step inside of me, it's what you would see, too. But I don't always know how to say it out loud; there isn't a clear passage from imagining to being. So I just keep all of these images of me, and who I think I am, or who I dream I could be, swirling in my head.

I hate it when people don't see me in the same way. My parents used to think of me as small and quiet, and they were right for a while; with them, my voice used to be a whisper. I've now found a way to tell them how I feel without offending or being disrespectful.

When I was in my teens, a lady sitting next to me on a train to Montreal told me that she couldn't see me ever being loud or silly. "You should meet my daughter. My daughter is so wild. She's crazy." I wanted to scream, "That's ME! I'm wild. I'm crazy." I wish it. I want it. Maybe one day someone will say, "She's crazy." Crazy like unstoppable and unpredictable and the kind of person who makes you laugh so hard, laugh SO hard, laugh so HARD you notice the room is quiet when I'm not in it, even though it's full to bursting.

That's the kind of person I am inside, and on the outside too, sometimes. Is that you, too?

Chapter 1

Image

Symbols and Talismans

The Indian classical dancers are sprawled in their colourful saris along the freshly swept wooden floor. Their hair is wound with flowers, gold bangles cover their arms, and their eyes are lined with kohl.

On the straw mat next to each woman is a bell-wrap, a long piece of cloth that is tied around the dancers' ankles before the bells are tied on. This is the final preparation for the dance. The bells do not seem to have any particular power, beyond being decorative and musical. Yet dancers will tell you that they call the dancer to the dance. They have the power to transform an ordinary person into someone who will tell the story of Rama and Sita, and in that way they hold a certain magic.

The sound of tablas being drummed can be heard in the background. The last of the bells has been wrapped around slender ankles. "There is a very intense psychological experience in putting on the bells," explains Joanna Das, an Indian classical dancer. "For me, the dance has already begun just by putting the bells on."

Das also says that power is found in the elaborate make-up that is part of the costume. "Kajal, or kohl, is used around the eyes as a form of protection to the inner spirit. Traditionally, mothers have used it on their babies to create a blemish on an otherwise perfect being. The belief is that if there is a blemish, the child will be spared the evil eye from those who might be jealous."

"There is an innate power in clothing, ornaments, make-up, even colours," says Del Ashkewe, a native Indian healer. "Colours are basically symbols, and every conviction has a colour. The conviction of love is red. The conviction of spirituality is white. When you understand your convictions, you wear the colours that go with them," he adds.

His partner, Paula Johnstone, explains that the jewellery she wears on her fingers has power. "People stop me and ask me about my rings all the time. The ring I wear on my soul finger happens to be a great big spider. This spider tells about my relationship to life. The spider has a lot to do with being a mother."

"The jewellery you wear, the symbols you are attracted to or repelled by, all say something about you and your relationship to the world," Ashkewe adds.

I know that some mornings, before heading out the door, I have to put my watch in my knapsack because I just can't bring myself to put it on. It's hard to explain, but it's as though the watch has its own vibe, and for whatever reason it doesn't always click with mine.

A girlfriend of mine can't wear the beautiful velvet choker her boyfriend gave her because she feels as though it's "pressing down on my pulse and makes me feel like I'm suffocating." Yet she has no problem wearing little silk scarves around her neck.

The consideration given to the power inherent in clothing or ornaments is not limited to any one particular ethnicity, culture, or domain. Athletes often wear lucky socks or tie their laces a certain way for success on the field. Almost every businessperson has a lucky suit, and most women have a ring or bracelet they wear for power or confidence, or to enhance their luck.

Clothing, jewellery, make-up can all influence how we feel. They can make us feel good, strong, capable. They can also have the opposite effect. Continuing to wear the sweatshirt you wore the night your boyfriend broke up with you might make you feel sad, and although it might be your favourite article of clothing, you're probably better off tucking it away somewhere.

Gifts, too, have power. They can help us build our identity, or they can keep us trapped in an old image of ourselves. If your grandmother insists on giving you a stuffed toy reptile when you'd really rather have faux-reptile pants, you might want to let her know that your tastes have changed over the last few years, and although you love her for thinking of you, you really need her to see the person you are becoming. If you can't make any headway, you might want to just tuck the gifts that don't reflect who you are away in a box in the basement, or donate them to a charity.

Keeping things around that don't reflect your emerging identity, or that make you feel six years old when you want to feel sixteen, can have a negative impact on you. This is true not only of gifts, but also of your personal space. Look around your bedroom and ask yourself if that frilly white bedspread reflects who you are and who you want to become. Does it? Or does it make you feel like a baby? How about those Holly Hobby curtains?

Your bedroom is one of the only really private spaces you have in your house, and while your decorating budget might be limited or nil, you can still take stock of the things in your room to see how they make you feel about yourself, and what they say about you.

Your room is sacred, and unless you share it with someone, you shouldn't have to keep anything in it that doesn't suit your current tastes. If, when you wake up, the first thing you see is something that stresses you out, like photos of you and your ex-best friend, you might want to remove them from view, at least until you patch things up.

The power that clothing, make-up, gifts, and furniture have is present at an innate level, and also in a more conspicuous way. Why else would people talk about their "power suit"? The quick summing up of someone's wealth or position is often based on their clothing and sense of style. People drive fast, flashy cars because they want to be perceived as having financial power. Then again, there are guys like Bill Gates who dress like schleps because they know they are powerful enough to dress badly and still be treated with deference. Gates inverts the conspicuous consumption model. Instead of wearing his wealth on his sleeve, so to speak, he seems to make a conscious effort to dress badly, knowing that he can count on being taken seriously, no matter what.

I think most things have their own innate power, kind of like my watch. I'm sure those quartz crystals have some kind of force. Or maybe I'm wrong. Maybe they acquire their power through traditional practices that have been passed down, or as a result of the way we perceive value in society.

What items of clothing make you feel powerful? Do you wear kohl around your eyes for protection? Are there any rituals that go into becoming you? Do you ever wonder why certain colours make you feel more powerful than others? The clothes and jewellery we wear can really reveal our convictions to those who are watching and listening. Do you know what you're saying?

Myth:

If you're smart, you can't also be pretty

For some strange reason, if you're smart, you're expected not to be interested in your appearance.

At my high school, there was a tendency to categorize people and put them in neat little boxes. A person's appearance and the amount of time they spent in front of the washroom mirror before class let us know if they thought they were smart, funny, pretty, or none of those things.

There was the occasional pretty girl who was smart, but she was an anomaly.

You might say that smart girls pride themselves on looking slightly nerdy. They understand the deferential way in which teachers, parents, and peers sometimes treat them if they are seen to be preoccupied with the mind rather than the body. Too bad. It encourages the stereotype that any kind of thought about clothing, hair, or make-up is nothing more than blatant vanity.

People don't necessarily want to stop boxing you in as you get older. If you have manicured nails and shiny hair, people will sometimes assume that you couldn't possibly be interested in conflicts in the Middle East, or anything they might consider a "serious issue."

Sometimes the assumption or myth is really just a chip they've been carrying around. Maybe they've fought really hard to be taken seriously and expect you to do the same, or to fit the mould they thought they were expected to fill. There was a time when women were told to modulate the way they spoke, to sound more like a man, in order to be heard.

The myth has a slightly different twist when it comes to men. Smart, powerful men sometimes deliberately want to be seen as not caring about their appearance, to make the statement that they are too important to care, or that, regardless of how they look, you have to take them seriously anyway. Woody Allen dresses in sloppy cardigans and baggy pants because he knows he has enough clout to make the films he wants to make. Yet, when you learn that all of his clothes are handmade and not the sort of bargain-basement stuff they look to be, you realize that he does care.

For women, it seems a little more difficult to get away with looking terrible and being taken seriously. Maybe that's why intellectual feminists such as Naomi Wolf and Gloria Steinem also spend time making themselves look beautiful. They understand that the power available to them through their sexuality and appearance—coupled with a killer intellect—slays.

Veiled Not Silent

Sultana Yusufali, 16*,
Eastern/Central Canada

I probably do not fit into the preconceived notion of a "rebel." I have no visible tattoos and minimal piercing. I do not possess a leather jacket. In fact, when most people look at me, their first thought usually is something along the lines of "oppressed female." The individuals who have mustered the courage to ask me about the way I dress usually have questions like: "Do your parents make you wear that?" or "Don't you find that really unfair?"

A while back, a couple of girls in Montreal were kicked out of school for dressing like I do. It seems strange that a little piece of

* All ages throughout this book refer to the contributor's age at the time of writing.

cloth would make for such controversy. Perhaps the fear is that I am harbouring an Uzi underneath it. You never can tell with those Muslim fundamentalists.

Of course, the issue at hand is more than a mere piece of cloth. I am a Muslim woman who, like millions of other Muslim women around the globe, chooses to wear the hijab. There are many different ways to wear it, but in essence, what we do is cover our entire bodies (including our hands and faces).

If you're the kind of person who has watched a lot of popular movies, you'd probably think of harem girls and belly-dancers, women who are kept in seclusion except for the private pleasure of their male masters. In the true Islamic faith, nothing could be further from the truth. And the concept of the hijab, contrary to popular opinion, is actually one of the most fundamental aspects of female empowerment.

When I cover myself, I make it virtually impossible for people to judge me according to the way I look. I cannot be categorized because of my attractiveness or lack thereof. Compare this to life in today's society: we are constantly sizing one another up on the basis of our clothing, jewellery, hair, and make-up. What kind of depth can there be in a world like this?

Yes, I have a body, a physical manifestation upon this Earth. But it is the vessel of an intelligent mind and a strong spirit. It is not for the beholder to leer at or to use in advertisements to sell everything from beer to cars. Because of the superficiality of the world in which we live, external appearances are so stressed that the value of the individual counts for almost nothing.

It is a myth that women in today's society are liberated. What kind of freedom can there be when a woman cannot walk down the street without every aspect of her physical self being "checked out"? When I wear the hijab, I feel safe from all of this. I can rest assured that no one is looking at me and making assumptions about my character from the length of my skirt. There is a barrier between me and those who would exploit me. I am first and foremost a human being, equal to any man, and not vulnerable because of my sexuality.

One of the saddest truths of our time is the problem of the beauty myth and female self-image. Reading popular teenage magazines, you can instantly find out what kind of body image is "in" or "out."

And if you have the "wrong" body type, well, then, you're just going to have to change it, aren't you? After all, there is no way that you can be overweight and still be beautiful.

Look at any advertisement. Is a woman being used to sell the product? How old is she? How attractive is she? What is she wearing? More often than not, that woman will be no older than her early twenties, taller, slimmer, and more attractive than average, dressed in skimpy clothing. Why do we allow ourselves to be manipulated like this? Whether the woman of today wishes to believe it or not, she is being forced into a mould. She is being coerced into selling herself, into compromising herself. This is why we have thirteen-year-old girls sticking their fingers down their throats and overweight adolescents hanging themselves.

When people ask me if I feel oppressed, I can honestly say no. I made this decision of my own free will. I like the fact that I am taking control of the way other people perceive me. I enjoy the fact that I don't give anyone anything to look at and that I have released myself from the bondage of the swinging pendulum of the fashion industry and other institutions that exploit females.

My body is my own business. Nobody can tell me how I should look, or whether or not I am beautiful. I know that there is more to me than that. I am also able to say no comfortably when people ask me if I feel as though my sexuality is being repressed. I have taken control of my sexuality.

I am thankful I will never have to suffer the fate of trying to lose or gain weight or trying to find the exact lipstick shade that will go with my skin colour. I have made choices about what my priorities are and these are not among them.

So next time you see me, don't look at me with pity. I am not under duress and I am not a male-worshipping female captive from those barbarous Arabic deserts. I've been liberated.

"Everybody in" ... the Same Clothes

Tema Smith, 16,
Eastern/Central

It's Saturday night and, like many of my friends who just aren't in the mood to go out, I'm lying on my bed, channel surfing. I turn to a station just in time to catch a Gap commercial. The expressionless faces of twenty or so young adults sitting in a white room, all of them wearing cords and singing "Mellow Yellow," stare out at me. Instantly recognizing the design signature of this clothing store, I await the catch phrase that I know is coming up. Sure enough, the words "Everybody In ..." grace the screen, followed by a white screen with only the navy and white Gap logo, capping off the commercial.

I stare at the screen, puzzled, thinking. As far above this susceptibility as I like to believe I am, no one really is. Corporations spend millions of dollars paying psychoanalysts and researchers to figure out how to influence the most people. They pay "cool-hunters" to find out what the target audience is interested in so that they can address these interests in their advertising campaigns and win over the most consumers.

The Gap has successful marketing under its belt. Its commercials have been ingrained in the minds of those who have seen them, most notably its holiday commercial featuring the skaters and dancers frolicking to a medley of the well-known Christmas song "Sleigh Ride" and the pop song probably better known to the teenagers of today, Vanilla Ice's "Ice, Ice, Baby." Because of the commercials, when people think of Gap, they think of cords, and vice versa.

Many people are disgusted with the Gap's method of appeal. "I really don't see what they're trying to show. It's like they're promoting a lifestyle dependent on material goods rather than the clothes themselves," says Robert Whillans, fifteen. Others do not see a problem with the advertising at all. Jay Torres, sixteen, states, "Gap is like any other brand. There are many designers and they all want people in their clothes. They all just want to make money and there's nothing wrong with that."

Apparently, a large company, such as the Gap, has adjusted quickly and used the influence of advertising to its advantage.

Coinciding with the increase of money dispensable for promotion and a revamping of their ads' images, their sales have soared. Sales increased by close to 50 percent for the holiday season of December 1999. A single store can sell more than $50,000 of merchandise in a ten-and-a-half-hour day, and employees are expected to sell more than $150 worth per hour worked, selling on average three units per transaction. Shockingly, these are the minimum sales goals and are considered to be easy to meet and even surpass on a half-decent day.

Exemplary of the far-reaching influence of the designation of some items as "hot" is what happened with the Gap's Crazy Stripe items for the holiday season. The sweater sold out soon after every shipment was received; the scarf was out of stock at the supplier. GapKids at the corner of Bay and Bloor was down to three extra-smalls with no chance of replenishing them, even though the sweater—made of lambswool, requiring hand washing, and costing $54—was impractical for children. Furthermore, the warmest jacket, the season's line of bomber jackets, was sold out at Gap in every size but extra-large. By the time many of the items went on sale for Boxing Day, there were few sizes left.

The Gap offered promotions on nearly all of their Pro-Fleece items over the holiday season. Employees were apparently informed that, over the weekends during the holiday season, they would be required to wear Pro-Fleece items. Incentives such as prize draws for people selling the most Pro-Fleece were occurring on an almost weekly basis. Promotion prices were in effect on at least one Pro-Fleece item from each section of each store, including Gap, GapKids, and BabyGap. Drawn by the illusion that Pro-Fleece items were the most economical and popular in the store, many holiday shoppers purchased them for gifts.

The Gap has been successful in manufacturing the desire for many products. By telling us that everyone should be wearing leather, vests, or cords, they are creating an ideal image for teenagers who are desperate to fit in. They have made their products affordable, so as to appeal to teenagers on limited budgets, and they have hired themselves a young, energetic staff to appeal to people much the same. By clothing their employees in Gap items, they have created a desire to look "just like that person" and adapt personal style to fit into their standards.

We have been trained to associate products with brands, and the Gap has benefited from this through catchy advertisements. They have been fortunate enough to be accepted into the everyday culture of today's youth and will continue to be provided they keep their name known and respected. Today, though, we need to ask: "Everybody in" what?

48 Inches, Baby

Denise Williams, 20,
Atlantic Provinces

I go jogging. Even more strange, I like to go jogging. I am a former Highland dancer, volleyball-soccer-hockey-and-more player, downhill ski racer, and actress. I've always read more frequently than anyone else I know, ever since pre-school. My preferred style of clothing could be characterized as casual prep.

Nobody has ever had a problem with any of these things. So why oh why must people react to such extremes when they see me on my skateboard?

I get stares, I get whistles. Even when longboarding with my boyfriend, I get whistles.

I get comments. Oh, the comments.

I received my absolute favourite comment from a guy who was, apparently, so offended and bent on saying something that he leaned his Tommy Hilfigered frame out the window of his cute little car and yelled at me. The problem was, his rage (and remarkably low IQ) stopped up the lines of communication between brain and mouth, and all that came out was a bellowed "Lalalalala!" (I went home and thought long and hard about what he'd said, let me tell you.)

Less ridiculous and more frightening, another guy detached himself from his group of bar-going friends to run up behind and grab my waist as I passed. "I'll give you a push, I'll give you a push!!" I dispatched him with a shot of ire, but the brazenness of the assault shocked me. People actually think they have the right to get away with that.

Personally, I don't understand where these people are coming from. I don't dress like a skater, so maybe I look like a poser. My femaleness is obviously an issue, as my boyfriend gets about one-tenth of the hassle that I get. But I have always been one to try every new challenge or sport I can get my hands on. I don't skate to make a fashion statement. I don't skate to impress boys. But the issue seems to be my attempted infiltration of a culture—a male-dominated culture at that.

Now, this social aspect of longboarding hasn't been a completely alienating experience. (I was going to write unpleasant, but I have to admit I kind of like being alienated from some kinds of people.) There are very few longboarders in Halifax, period, and I haven't seen a single other girl longboarder. The trend hasn't really caught on yet, even though the city has a lively skateboarding community. So we raise a few eyebrows of skaters and non-skaters. We elicit the same lame jokes every time we leave the house. ("If you take the wheels off, can you use it as a surfboard?")

But it's a sure conversation-starter when you run into people who don't assume you want to beat them with your board, even if you're wearing a skirt. I get random positive comments on the street regarding how rare it is to see a girl on a skateboard. Even the police seem to frown a little less on Sean and me when we're caught on the street. I've met a lot of cool people already, and these open-minded people tend to react very enthusiastically towards me. I still don't really understand what the big deal is, but this kind of attention is a lot more pleasant than the other.

In fact, I was having a beer with some cruise-ship musicians from Michigan and Toronto whom I'd met when they saw me longboarding and accosted me in excitement. Good friends already, one guy told me what the big deal was. "In your case, I think zipping around on a longboard actually does say a lot about you. It tells me that you're adventurous. But more importantly, it shows that you are comfortable enough with yourself that you're not scared of being different."

Umm, okay. Sounds kind of like an excerpt from a guidance counsellor's manual. To me, the attraction will always be that longboarding is a lot more fun than biking in the city. The attraction will be that I can pick up a new sport and learn it and have fun with it. But I guess it makes me happy that it sends positive signals about me to like-minded people.

And besides the jerk who grabbed me, I'm beginning to enjoy the situation as a whole. My new hobby tends to weed out the kind of people I'd just as soon not be talking to anyway. I was at a wedding in Ontario, being hit on by one of the groom's ultra-smooth engineering school friends. I was trying to figure out how to politely get rid of him when he asked me how I'd scarred my shoulder. "I fell," I told him, standing there in my formal dress and fancy shoes. "Off my skateboard." His face took on a look like he'd just swallowed a bug, and that was the last I saw of engineer-boy.

Images of a Poet

Heather Sonser, 15,
Eastern/Central

Rebel, Rogue, Mischievous Babe

Typical, eh? She sits in her room sipping milk and eating oatmeal cookies.

She's not popular. But she's not alone. She's not *too* bright. But highly intelligent in a way that is beyond the average man. Often she's alone as she scrawls in a dog-eared notebook that she keeps hidden away from the REAL world. A vast pool of innocent queries, unmistakable knowledge, and naive hope.

Often a pair of nondescript glasses adorns her face. For she has forgone the recommended contacts. Believing her sight to be a gift. She believes that the eyes *are* the window to the soul and that man cannot be bothered with such trivial things as abused animals and world hunger. Therefore she has made it her mission to get men to notice this. She'll even try to save the world by herself. Though she knows this is entirely impossible without a *little* help.

Not well known. Not necessarily the *picture* of fashion. Hers is a style made up of a patchwork of many others. She is reclusive. Often preferring the company of a good book to that of a group of gregarious friends. But she harbours in her heart the hopes and dreams of a millennium.

And if she spends one waking moment not pondering, then that will be one moment lost to the universe. Which she is in a constant battle with, of course. She is grateful for her inspiration, but hates the fact of her limited existence.

Therefore, she has resolved never to let it take over. For if it did, worlds would be lost and times destroyed. She is one who will cry at lovers as she sees them separate, lost worlds, each not knowing if in the next life they will meet.

And, oh, the tales she will tell and the yarns she will spin as she regales her grandchildren with stories of old.

So keep an eye out for her.
For all too easily is she missed.
And all too easily is she lost.
The Poet.

Chapter 2

The Body

Weight and Weightlessness

Sometimes the way we use our bodies is directly related to the place women are supposed to occupy in society. Before the suffragette movement, women were expected to stay home, to make the family their focus, and were excluded from many "public" places—especially those related to government or commerce. The function of a woman's body was childbearing and decoration. And so, to keep women from moving their bodies too quickly or going too far, the fashion of the day required women to be draped in heavy fabric that restricted movement and was exhausting to carry.

World War II, and the serious fabric shortage that came with it, meant that women had to drop those cumbersome dresses and head to work. They were needed to run the economy while the men went to war. A single taste of the freedom to move without hindrance, to run companies because we were capable and not weak of mind (as had been supposed), and we fought to never go back. I don't think women have ever been quite as powerful as they were in the 1940s.

When the men got back from fighting the war, they wanted their jobs and their place at the head of society back. They wanted women to leave the running of the economy to them and return home to bring up baby. Most women did—which explains the postwar baby boom. And interestingly, the "ideal" shape of a woman's body at that time reflected the place she held in society. A strong female body meant wide hips and big boobs, perfect for our image of women as mothers and caregivers.

In the 1960s, the introduction of the birth control pill gave women greater control over their bodies. We could now have sex without fear of unwanted pregnancy. Getting an abortion back then was very dangerous and difficult. First of all, it was illegal, which meant that if discovered, both you and the doctor performing the abortion could be charged. And the risks of a backroom abortion—sometimes performed with a clothes hanger or knitting needles—included death.

Freedom from unwanted pregnancy gave us the opportunity to decide whether or not to have children. And if we did raise a family, we could decide when our childbearing years were over; when it was time to define ourselves in a different way out in the world. That gave us an economic freedom we had never enjoyed before. And since any perceived differences between men and women were used to oppress us, the fact that we could now conduct ourselves more freely in the sexual arena meant that we could claim more social liberties and begin to define ourselves as people on a more equal footing with men.

Our body image changed, too. Women in the 1960s embraced a boyish look. Instead of the 1950s' torpedo bras and cinched waists that accentuated our stereotypically female features, we decided to blur the lines between the sexes and wear our boyfriends' jeans. I think we believed that looking too female was detrimental to our progress at work and in our attempts to be taken seriously as women.

In the 1970s, women realized that being powerful also meant being physically strong. We started running, en masse, for the first time. It's funny to be able to actually pinpoint a line or a time when women abandoned the notion that running was somehow unladylike and instead fought to run right next to the men in the Olympics.

The 1980s were about being powerful in a squishy body. Along with MTV came Madonna, who showed us that you could have fun in your curvy body, render patriarchal symbols powerless, make loads of money, make things, make fun of things, and not be afraid of the power of your sexuality as a woman. Of course, at the same time women were going to work in suits with square shoulder pads. I think the shoulder padding also bore a symbolic message: "I have wide shoulders and I can carry the load."

The 1990s were a bit of a disappointment since it was really a fall-back decade. The great leaps women made in terms of economic power and control should have taught us that we can have any kind of body and still have power. But we don't believe it. We're still striving for an ideal body type that eludes us, no matter how smart we are or how much we know.

We still seem to be trying to figure out which shape, what clothes, what image makes us powerful at work, in our personal lives, to ourselves. The consensus right now seems to be that thin is powerful. Maybe that's because being thin means you have discipline, willpower, money to work out. And that's all fine, except when we take it to an extreme and thin becomes frail and weak and just ends up looking bad.

Why can't thin just mean a body that's physically fit and healthy? Why is it better to be *too* thin? Why do we strive so hard to disappear? Maybe it's because we are still unsure of ourselves and we can't believe that the warmth of our personalities, the originality of our thoughts, the scope of our accomplishments could possibly make us as desirable as the circumference of our waists. Is that it?

Sometimes I think the preoccupation with being fit and slender is used as a distraction from doing work that is actually meaningful, satisfying, important, and probably challenging, and that's when the effort to be thin becomes dangerous. We should all strive to take good care of our bodies, but when it goes over the top, it's like any other obsession that prevents us from functioning and moving forward in our lives.

Striving to be thin, for me, is often a symptom of a larger problem. Sometimes, I focus on working out and losing weight when I'm unhappy in other areas of my life. To help me stay healthy, I have a few friends who will tell me if they think I'm not eating well, or if I seem too thin. I can then look at the stuff that is going on in my life and see if there is a problem that I should confront.

I'm also smart enough to know that if I looked at my body as the temple of my soul, or someone I should be kind to, I would never starve it, or punish it, the way I sometimes do. When I think of my body as a good friend, I know how to act. I remember how to be kind, and the results are discernible in my work, in the way I relate to others, in where I place my energy, and in the progress I make in my life.

Myth:

No pain no gain

We seem to believe that girls with strong, muscular bodies are healthier than those who are thin, or average, or a little chunky. That buff, gym-rat physique is something we're shooting for, we say, all in the interests of our health. Yet sometimes, in our desire to be fit and strong, lines get crossed.

It is important to jump your body around, but when getting in great shape becomes an obsession, it is as unhealthy as dieting to be too thin.

You know you're headed for obsession when you stop seeing your body the way it really is and begin to see fat that's not really there, or calves that could just be a little more shapely if you only exercised some more.

If the idea of a toned body drenched in sweat appeals to you, how far will you go to get it? Will you exercise for hours every day? How much time will you spend at the gym, and how much time will be left for your friends, or studying?

Becoming a toned goddess can be just as hard as getting skinny. It requires the same kind of discipline and deprivation. You have to be able to control your need, ache, or hunger for anything other than fitness. And if you're shooting for some ideal that doesn't come naturally for your body type, it might be like trying to force yourself to get taller, or make your feet smaller—it's just not going to happen. After all, look at Olympic athletes—they're fit and healthy, but do they all look the same?

The fitness obsession is in many ways similar to anorexia. It's not always about health. It is a desire to control the one thing you can tame or bend: your body. But be aware of your reasons for spending extra hours working out or doing aerobics. Ask yourself: are you trying to direct your energy into an activity to ignore the thing that is really bothering you?

My Soul Is Delicate

Nina Aning, 18,
Eastern/Central

Growing spurts confuse my soul. They make her angry, frustrated, and annoyed. My soul hates its capsule. The capsule is taking over, and that isn't right. The capsule is pulling strings, making strange changes.

My soul doesn't want to change; she's not going to take it.

It started when I was eleven. The capsule began to grow in places that did not need any more attention—in this case, the African belly that was passed down to me through generations.

My soul was furious and could no longer think straight. She started to believe that being perfect was possible, if only she could do everything the infomercials and magazines told her to do.

The capsule was growing, but it didn't look like them. There was nothing haute couture about it.

She was going to take action. Plans, plans, plans and ideas to blanket the truth.

During the day, my soul forced my capsule to exercise all the time. At night, my soul said beauty prayers, and when they jumped into bed, they reached for the duct tape and the dumbbells and fastened both to the capsule's African belly. The soul was convinced that not a moment should be wasted. The capsule could do push-ups even while she slept. Breathe in. Breathe out. Tight abs. Great idea.

Fabricated ideals of beauty blind you when you are weak, but I didn't know that until I met the true goddesses of beauty. They taught me that there is beauty in imperfection. I am beautiful.

Now my soul and the capsule laugh.

I know my soul is delicate and it loves my tummy.

Today I Ate

Erin McCallion, 22,
Eastern/Central

They were stored away in the bottom of my closet. Friends and family members smuggled them in for me. I swapped them in secret with my partners in crime, away from the staff. I clutched them in my sweaty and nervous palms in the night, their glossy photo spreads illuminated with the beam of my Itty Bitty Book Light, while I gazed at them from under the covers.

No, I was not an incarcerated porn fiend. I was an inpatient at Homewood Health Centre's Eating Disorder program, where fashion magazines were prohibited. This is not surprising because as a group, those of us in treatment at Homewood probably possessed the most distorted body images of any group of women. Yet, as a member of this group (when I was admitted, I weighed 66 pounds and didn't think that there was anything wrong with that), I can say that my distorted body image was not the product of the fashion industry—to say that would be too easy.

So where did my pathetic body image come from? All around me. I honestly can't pinpoint the sources of my own distorted body image. As a child and a teenager, I was never overweight. No one in his or her right mind would have teased me for being "fat." I have never looked at a model and said to myself, "Gee, I wish that I was as skinny as her." I never thought that if I just lost *five more pounds* then I would have a boyfriend. Society—the media, popular culture, and supermodels—certainly did not give birth to my eating disorder. But society did provide a safe nursery for it in which to grow.

Eating disorders are addictions. They are a set of self-destructive behaviours that a person engages in to soothe or medicate themselves. Anorexia distracts me from my problems (family problems, academic/job stress, failed relationships, self-hatred, and I could go on but I'm sure that you get the idea).

Dieting is my drug. My nutrient-starved mind is numb, and compulsive exercise feeds me endorphins. Everything in my life is simplified. I am fearless except for the overpowering fear of becoming fat. Controlling my weight becomes the most important thing in my life, and like a junkie, I will do anything to get my fix: lie, induce vomiting, exercise to the point of exhaustion, swallow packages of Ex-Lax. My health does not figure into the picture.

So what do my personal problems have to do with society? After all, the media never forced my last boyfriend to dump me, or told me that I was a dumbass who would never amount to anything. But after years of seeing Jenny Craig commercials, watching my mother measure out a half a cup of skim milk for her cereal in the morning and my sister cry because she had to shop in the "Pretty Plus" section of Sears, I picked up the idea that being skinny was good, wholesome, and desirable. The media gave me the *best* idea for an addiction. Who could condemn me for wanting to lose a little bit of weight? In fact, if I lost weight, I would even be *envied*. No, I wasn't going to be some wino, some strung-out junkie, or some pathetic loser who lost everything at the craps table. Instead, I would hear "I *so* wish that I were as skinny as you!"

And I did. When I was under 70 pounds with clumps of hair falling out, I got a pass from the hospital where I was being treated so that I could hand over my "First Princess of the Welland Rose Festival 1997" title to one of the girls in the 1998 crop. Just before I went on the stage to be announced, one of that year's contestants looked at me and said, "God, I wish that I was as skinny as you!"

Something is profoundly wrong when a person who looks like a concentration camp inmate is the subject of envy. Constantly, women (and increasingly men too) are bombarded with an image of the "perfect body" that only about 3 percent of the population actually possesses. These fantasy images may not be harmful in themselves, but we as a society have determined that not only are those body shapes desirable, they are also obtainable.

We have come to this sad conclusion through our roles as consumers. Without demand, there would be no supply. We enjoy the fantasies that the fashion industry sells us. The danger stems from the dieting industry, an industry that makes obscene profits from telling us that not only can we achieve these fantasies, but we are obligated to.

The dieting industry has indocrinated us with its dogma that we can shape our bodies into any form we choose simply by purchasing their products or services. If we should fail to do so, it is entirely our fault. As a result, our worth as human beings becomes tied to our ability to shape and mould our bodies. I dieted myself into emaciation not to look like a model or fit into size 1 jeans, but to be what I thought was a successful woman.

Yes, much to my mother's chagrin, I still read *Cosmopolitan*. And no, I never once consciously made the decision to look like Kate Moss. But somewhere along the line I got the idea that I could look like that, and that I should look like that. That if I did look like that I would somehow be a better person—decisive, hard-working, successful—and becoming a better person was worth certain sacrifices.

Unfortunately, instead of challenging my delusions, society fed them. My individual problem grew more acute and entrenched, because society never told me that there was anything wrong with starving my body. Instead, I got compliments for doing so. And those compliments came mainly from other women.

It is us women who have the power to stop eating disorders before they start. Once, I worked with a woman who had two preteen daughters. She asked me what she should do to try to prevent an eating disorder from happening. I told her that when I was their age, no one ever told me that I was fat. I saw my mother look at herself in the mirror with disgust and call herself fat.

Our bodies are not supposed to be simply objects to be viewed. They are tools to be used. When your jeans feel too tight, think about how wonderful it is that you can *feel* the denim waistband cutting into you. Think about the feeling of swimming through cool water on a hot sticky day. Think about how an orgasm ripples through your body when you climax. Think of having your child nurse at your breast. Think about how women can survive longer in subzero temperatures and times of famine because of our higher percentage of body fat. (Bet you didn't think there was an upside to fat, eh? Just wait until World War III, and we'll see who survives.)

Today I ate. I ate not because I was hungry, or felt that I had exercised enough, but because I wanted that damn chocolate-chip muffin.

Mirror Image

Shannon Elliott, 16,
Prairies

Most girls remember their early school years as a time of easy laughter, skipping, and whispered secrets. I remember these years as a time of relentless teasing and isolation. What was the crime that made me an outcast? I was larger than everyone thought I should be. I was teased by my classmates and by older children as well. I loathed school and didn't want to be in this tormenting place. This continued until our family relocated to a new town in northern Manitoba.

I felt good. I thought that maybe I could have a new start in a new school with new friends. I had a hopeful feeling about this new town. However, in September I became very ill and the doctors didn't have any idea what was wrong. They decided to fly me to Winnipeg where I could be treated by specialists. My mother flew with me and stayed by my bed in the hospital. It was a difficult time to be so far from my family.

When I was released two months later, I was a lot thinner. People couldn't believe what they saw. In fact, I couldn't believe what I saw reflected in the mirror: I was skinny! I began to make lots of friends who were also thin, but I decided that maybe I was too thin. I ate and ate and ate some more until I gained a lot of weight.

After two years, we packed up our family and moved farther north. By this time, I had gained all the weight back plus some. Can you imagine a young girl starting fifth grade who weighed more than her teacher? It was depressing. Again, I had no friends and I lived at home with the comfort of food to soothe me.

I returned to the specialists in Winnipeg for check-ups, and they would say that I was too big and had to lose weight. They suggested that I visit a dietician or walk every night. I would return home and eat and eat. As I gained, I became less happy. I had no one to turn to. Even my family would tell me the truth about how big I was and how I needed to lose weight. I felt like they were picking on me and I hated them for that.

I woke up one day after my doctor weighed me. I was twelve years old and weighed 260 pounds! I was shocked. How could I let myself go like that? I started to blame other people for the way I looked and felt. I had no friends and it seemed like the whole school was laughing at me, so I didn't object when my parents decided to move to Winnipeg. I was excited, but in the back of my mind I thought that maybe the city kids would treat me worse than what I was used to. That June we moved. The summer flew by and it was time to start school. I was so nervous on the first day. I entered the classroom with trepidation. Kids are kids I thought, but in fact these kids turned out to be very different.

From the moment I walked into the room, all the kids introduced themselves and asked me questions. Gee, was this different! I not only made friends, I made lots of friends. We did everything together. I knew that these friends would stick by me. They didn't care what I looked like. The funny thing was that because of this support, I started to lose weight. I eventually lost over 100 pounds and felt great. With my new confidence inspired by my new friends, I now weighed less than I had at twelve.

Not all my problems vanished with the weight. Although I am ecstatic at the loss, sometimes I think that I went overboard. I am always looking in the mirror, and the reflection I see is of someone who is fat with bulging thighs. I can never see what I have become. I only see the need for change. I look at magazines and watch movies, but it seems that dreams only come true for those who are a size 5. I know this is not true, and yet I find myself never satisfied with my looks. The weight is gone, but the poor self-esteem remains.

This year I moved back to the small northern town where I once lived. I see the same people who were here before, the same people who taunted and teased me. These people, whom I once hated, flock to me for friendship. I want to scream at them that I'm the same person. The only difference is my size.

Though I sometimes bear the scars of my childhood, overall I have been positively influenced. I don't look at people from the outside but get to know them and value their personality rather than their looks. There will always be people who judge you by what you look like. You have to ignore our weight-obsessed society and its crazy House of Mirrors that make the beauty think she's a beast.

Rebel, Rogue, Mischievous Babe

Bras

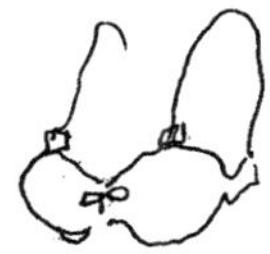

Take the escalator to the fifth floor of almost any department store and you will probably find yourself deposited in the middle of a sea of bras and underwear. Bras fashioned from flimsy nylon materials in neon pink, yellow, and green line the racks off to the side. Silky ones with French names in dark, mysterious colours trimmed with lace and bows are usually up front.

Fingers tug at straps and snaps, sometimes recoiling in horror at the prices. Boyfriends and husbands try to look casual, standing off to the side, while their girlfriends and wives hold up see-through black panties for their assessment. Slightly embarrassed younger girls searching for their first training bra slink along behind their mothers, who are somehow too loud and obvious even when they appear to whisper and simply hand things over to the fitting room attendant.

Buying a bra for the first time is a kind of rite of passage—after that it's just a pain.

Bras rarely fit me properly. In fact, of the ten or fifteen bras in my drawers, in the laundry, and dangling from the door knob in my bedroom, only two feel comfortable. I'm pretty sure I've got the size right, but inevitably if the cup fits, the strap around my torso is too tight and leaves marks.

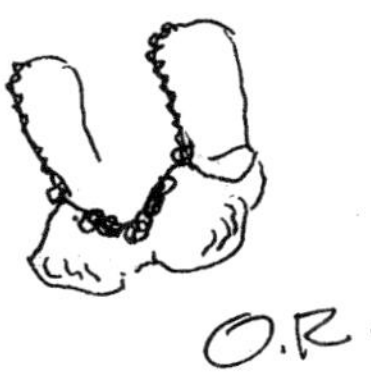

Getting fitted is actually a very good idea, I just always thought I was too small to bother. Every bra and make is different. Finding a bra that provides support and comfort requires a trip to a place that specializes in lingerie, no matter how big or small you are.

Until I get fitted, I'll stick with the two that work. I have two others in blue and silver that are more like tight-fitting camisoles. They're perfect for those times when I want the straps to show.

I'm not sure when we became so casual about letting our underwear be seen, but the visible bra strap phenomenon is a fairly new thing. In the past, if you purposely let your strap show, you risked being thought of as a tramp. "Ladies," young and old, were careful to keep prying eyes from seeing their undergarments.

Today, of course, that's all different. Or at least, it's different for younger women. Now, the more bold and provocative your bra colour, the more reason to let your straps flash in full view.

I think it might have started with Madonna, who first piqued our interest in letting our underwear show when she wore a bra and nothing else under a fishnet T-shirt in the movie *Desperately Seeking Susan*. Or maybe it was Jean Paul Gaultier who helped us lose our last inhibitions about underwear when he designed the torpedo bra Madonna donned as outerwear during her *Blonde Ambition* tour.

Either way, in the 1980s, Madonna was the most exciting, irreverent woman to hit newly launched MTV, and we wanted to bridge the distance between her behaviour, actions, style and our own. Madonna look-alikes, sporting black bras or fishnet T-shirts and ripped stockings, Boy Toy chains, and dark-red lips, were everywhere.

Madonna gave us permission to be daring and to let our parents know we had desires that couldn't be hidden or suppressed. Maybe that meant "turning the gaze" and looking at boys and men the way she did, instead of always being on the receiving end. Or maybe it meant letting that red, hot, lacy strap say everything for you, simply by letting it show.

When Victoria's Secret opened its first stores in 1982, stylish bras, underwear, and lingerie became affordable for the masses. The advent of their mail order catalogues, filled with pages and pages of well-known models wearing cheap-looking satiny red, blue, and pink lingerie, meant that regular girls were going to see this stuff and buy it. The catalogues normalized the wearing of lingerie, so that it wasn't reserved exclusively for the daring, or left in the drawer for special evenings. Sexy lingerie was now for every girl, every day.

We girls have always worn some kind of underwear. It hasn't always been comfortable, or something you would want anyone to see you in, but how we strap our boobs down or prop them up has always been a preoccupation.

In the early 1900s, women had a "mono-bosom": there was a poof, but no division between the breasts could be seen. In the 1920s, the look became boyish and flattened as flappers were the rage. In the 1940s and 1950s, the cone-shaped bullet bras could pop your eyes out. Today, choices range from sports bras, which first made an appearance with the jogging and fitness craze in the 1970s, to bras you can pump up for day or evening push-up appeal.

The first modern push-up bra was the "Rising Star," designed in 1948 by Frederick Mellinger of Frederick's of Hollywood. Today, Wonderbras seem to be every flat girl's secret weapon. Even waif model Kate Moss has fuelled their popularity by saying, "They're so brilliant, I swear, even I get cleavage with them."

Even though many bra designers and manufacturers today are men, it was an American debutante, Mary Phelps Jacobs, who designed and patented the first bra in 1914. She was getting ready for a dance, and instead of wearing the usual corset, she fashioned a bra out of two handkerchiefs and pink ribbon. She engaged a dress-maker and soon began turning out the new bra for purchase.

Given the petite size of most handkerchiefs, she too must have been tiny. Right now, when big boobs are in, it's kind of a drag to be small-breasted. It's not that I would trade mine for a much bigger set, especially when I hear about how hard it is to run up stairs or exercise if your breasts are very large. It's more that our current ideas of womanliness include having a Maidenform out front as part of your management team, rather than a couple of Bing cherries you have to keep warm lest they shrink and let your strapless dress down.

I have to admit, growing up it was nice to be flat-chested. I didn't have to wear a T-shirt that read "Look Up." I knew boys weren't interested in dating my breasts when they did, on occasion, ask me out. I could go without a bra if I wanted to. I never accidentally slipped out of my bathing suit. And I never suffered from the bruising caused by underwire.

Sometimes, I'm reminded of how tiny I am, and it's just funny. Usually it's when my mom mails me a bra. It often ends up being big enough to turn into a couple of hats with chin straps for me and a friend. Ah, well, when you read on, you'll discover that girls with big boobs have it much harder than I do.

Chest-Level

Rachael Pleet, 16,
Eastern/Central

I've been trying to find an introduction for days. But thinking about something that is such an essential part of yourself and taking it out of context, putting it on paper, really is difficult. Because the context of our subject is breasts, probably the most appropriate analogy is being dissected, examined. It's something all women are familiar with. Being spoken to at chest-level. Catcalls and stares. It comes from all sides, and recognizing it does not necessarily mean being used to or accepting it.

Acknowledging harassment does not mean appreciating it. I know I don't find being leered at the least bit pleasant, but some days I feel as though I ought to. Girls are taught from an early age that male attention is valuable—any attention. Magazines show endless pictures of women hanging helplessly at the sides of strong men, or being gazed at by men: images of women that the vast majority of mainstream media repeat and exploit. Images of women gaining their only strength from men. It follows, then, that we are taught to seek out male attention in any form. As beliefs are conditioned so that woman plus man equals strength/merit/validity, it follows that women are also taught to accept comments about their appearance, their bodies, with gratitude. Accept the stares, calls, winks, and whistles. Feel lucky. You're beautiful. Nowhere are we taught to feel outraged or violated, to curse and tell this darling man just where to shove his little comments. It would be ungrateful. More than that, it would be unladylike.

I guess that's where I'm the queen of the hill. I don't believe in society's false ideals, in which beauty is defined as shaved legs and a sturdy bra. My breasts might move when I walk, my hair might need brushing, and I might not smell of Lady Speed Stick, but I'm not hurting for it. I feel comfortable knowing that whatever beauty I have was not bought at the mall. Yet my own self-acceptance is overshadowed by the constant actions of complete strangers. Strangers with the capacity to make me feel small, to make me feel afraid on my own street. And until we evolve to a point where value is not centred at the chest, it's something I'll have to live with. We all have to live with it. It's up to each of us as women, unafraid of our strength and beauty, to make known that this is not something we will live with complacently. This is not something we will live with forever.

Rebel, Rogue, Mischievous Babe

Being Rated by the Boys

Trish Bitaxi, 14,
Eastern/Central

Our physical education program at school includes swimming once every two weeks. The first week the grade sevens go, then the grade eights. We alternate like that throughout the school year. But fewer and fewer people have been going, and the swimming program needs some serious resuscitation.

The problem is that when the girls come out of the change room, the guys are already waiting to start their lesson, and they stare at us and make snide comments and stupid remarks like "Look, it's thunder thighs." It might seem like a small thing, but it's hurtful, and it makes us feel inadequate and uncomfortable.

There are a few girls that they like, however. One of them seems practically perfect, except she doesn't really have any breasts. Everyone is constantly compared to her and put down, but when the guys are finished comparing us to her, they turn around and make fun of her by calling her "flat." There is another girl who is equally pretty, but because she doesn't shave, she is harassed by the guys, who call her "a hairy beast."

It's not just at the pool that they make these comments, but also in the hallways at school and during gym. I guess since you don't wear that much to swim, you're much more self-conscious and vulnerable.

To be fair, it's not only the guys who comment on physical appearance. The girls do it too. They say things about the guys like "He's got hips!" Or "Ew, nasty, you can see his ribs!" This makes the guys feel uncomfortable as well. The problem has gotten to the point where no one ever wants to go swimming any more and the program is about to be cut. I didn't want that to happen, so I decided to speak up.

I told my teachers that because people at this age are developing at different rates, we all feel uneasy with co-ed swimming. I suggested that the girls go one week and guys go the next. I thought everyone would be happier this way, but some people didn't like the idea at all. After a lot of discussion, it was changed. More people have started swimming again, and it seems that when we don't have to worry about how we look, we actually relax and have fun in the pool.

Frankenboobs

Audra Estrones Williams, 21,
Atlantic Provinces

"I don't know," grinned my friend Amanda, "I think you've got a half-decent chest."

Half-decent indeed. When I was fourteen, I realized that only one of my breasts was developing. I supposed it would work out eventually. At seventeen, I realized that it wouldn't. I had one D-cup breast and one A-cup breast. Imagine, if you will. I was a dancer. I was sexually active. I had to do something about the problem.

Having said that, I'm pleased to report that I was not utterly mortified. I felt no shame or self-disgust. This was an era in which women with lousy taste bought blouses with shoulder pads. Some of these blouses came my way. I happily ripped out the pads and used them to stuff my bra, which gave me a pretty convincing two-boobed look. Having one breast just didn't seem that big a deal. Probably because it was a gradual development (and lack thereof), as opposed to a sudden loss. Probably also because I hung out with the most supportive group of friends on the planet. The boy I was dating, a tortured, self-styled artiste, most likely considered himself avant-garde to have a monoboobed girlfriend.

But I can't deny the disadvantages. I couldn't go swimming. It was hell to find a leotard under which I could wear a bra. And it was hard to sleep comfortably. When I was fully clothed, however, covering up my asymmetry was a piece of cake.

I would awaken fourteen minutes before the school bell rang, look on the floor for clothes, look on the floor for a bra, and look on the floor for the two shoulder pads wrapped in pantyhose that had become my left breast. I'd throw everything on and fly out the door with uncombed hair and four layers of lipstick. Eventually I just started to wear a bra all the time and it became as though that were my body, as though that were me, naked. When I was without clothing, I sort of didn't pay attention to my chest, the same way I ignore my lips if they are bare. It didn't really occur to me that it would ever be any different. I always had bigger fish to fry, and I figured that if someone was going to see me without clothing, that person had better like me enough not to care.

In many ways, I had fun with my asymmetry. It was a novelty, and I made the most of it. In Grade 11, for example, I did volunteer work for the local AIDS committee, and each day, I wore a red ribbon to promote awareness. My friend Mike and I used to pull this routine to alarm substitute teachers.

Audra: "Hey, I dropped my ribbon. Could you grab it for me? It's under your desk."

Mike: "No problem. Here it is."

Audra: "Damn, my hands are full. Could you pin it back on?"

Mike: "Whatever. This okay?" At this point, he would plunge the pin deep into my shoulder-pad-stuffed left bra cup.

Audra: "Jesus, Mike. Can you watch it? That hurts, you know."

Mike: "Sorry." He would slowly remove the pin, and try again.

Another time, at a party, a really annoying Eurotrash guy was groping me with his girlfriend ten feet away. I yanked out the shoulder pads, left them wrapped in the nylon, handed them to him, and suggested that he take them elsewhere and leave me alone. The look on his face was priceless.

When I was nineteen, I started to get fed up with the situation. I was living on my own in Windsor, learning to be an interpreter for the Deaf, and beginning to feel off kilter all of the time. It annoyed me that some clothes never hung right on me. I hated having constantly to abandon sexy underwear in favour of training bras that offered maximum stretch room for stuffage. I decided to see if there was some way that I could become even chested.

I went to speak to my doctor about it. In the midst of my explanation, the doctor cut in:

"Everyone has one breast a little larger than the other, you know."

Well, of course I knew that. Had I not read countless advice columns in *Young Miss* magazine?

"Can I just show you?" I asked. I did, and she did a double-take.

"I see what you mean," she said. We talked about plastic surgeons. My friend Mike Pierson's father was a plastic surgeon, but still wanting to be able to enjoy future meals around the Pierson dinner table, I chose not to have this man revamp my boobs. Instead, I chose a plastic surgeon in Oshawa, Ontario, where my father and stepmom lived, and had to wait three months just to see her. When we finally met, I asked if she could bring the larger breast down to the size of the tiny one. She ruled that out—taking a breast down four sizes would leave too much scarring. Heavens. That meant that we were talking implants. This was an entirely different ball game. What about leakage? What about Pamela Anderson? What about my feminism?

She told me that implants weren't made of silicone any longer. They were made of saltwater. If the implant did leak, I would just pee it out. My implanted breast would have a natural-looking, small shape—no gargantuan orb for me. I certainly didn't want both breasts as large as my bigger one, so I chose to have an even B cup for both. I was told that I would be able to breast-feed out of the enlarged one, but not the reduced one. I had visions of my breasts turning into saltwater taffy if over-manipulated. I put the image out of my mind and agreed to the procedure. I went back to college in Windsor and imagined making the same trip after Christmas, with a huge collection of foxy bras. I told no one except my roommates.

About a week before I was supposed to go back to Oshawa for Christmas and the surgery ("What did YOU get for Christmas, Audra?" "THESE!"), I called the plastic surgeon's office, just to make sure all was well. Good thing I called. Some genius working for the Ontario Health Insurance Plan decided that the government health plan would cover the enlargement of my left breast, but not the reduction of the right. (Didn't you know all along that underneath every sober, quietly dressed, inoffensive bureaucrat is a major breast ogler?) Terrific news. I called my friend Mike, son of the plastic surgeon. He wasn't home, so I spoke with his very cool mom. "Don't worry!" she said. "You'll get your surgery even if Don [Mike's father] has to do it on our pool table!"

After Mike's father intervened on my behalf, OHIP finally agreed to pay for the reduction of my left breast. Gives a new meaning to the term "government downsizing," wouldn't you say? I was relieved, major big time. I was on my way to symmetry!

The morning of the surgery, I was a bundle of nerves and exhausted incoherence. Standing in front of my closet, I couldn't decide what to wear to the hospital. I finally settled on a sort of "June Cleaver Summer Picnic" dress, took out my six earrings, picked off the last of my nail polish (not allowed in the operating room), and set off for the hospital. My fashion crisis was perhaps fruitless, because as soon as I got in the pre-op part of the building, I had to strip down and put on a fetching little hospital robe. I took off my bra and quickly wrapped it around the shoulder pad and pantyhose "breast," without it really registering that this was the last time I would have to do this. Everything seemed sort of a few layers removed from reality. I had never been under anesthetic before! I had never been cut open before! In order to bring down the size of my left breast, they were going to have to remove my nipple and then re-attach it!

This was way worse than the pre-haircut jitters I always got in the salon waiting room.

I was wheeled into the operating room. The woman in whose hands I was entrusting my bosomy beauty said: "We'll cut here [she drew a circle around my nipple] and here [a line under each breast] and stitch you all up as good as new." They put a mask over my mouth and nose and told me to take deep breaths. I felt like I was suffocating. I started to freak out. Then I was out. Gone. Under.

The next thing I knew, I was foggy-headed and I needed to puke. This, I knew for certain. A nurse was pushing me down the hallway on a stretcher. She asked, "Did you have a breast reduction or enlargement?"

"Both," I answered.

She clucked her tongue. I could imagine her thoughts. Hoo boy, they overmedicated this one!

My family was waiting in my room. I'm sure I was a charming hostess! I was stitched up, with plastic tubes draining blood from my incisions, and vomiting. The sheer glamour of it all. I got some sleep, woke up in the middle of the night, and dragged my IV along on the trip to the bathroom. While there, although I had been warned against this, I peeked into the bandages.

That was my body, in there, and I wanted to know what was up. I had what a friend would later dub Frankenboobs, but they more or less matched. Wow. Two breasts, the same size, and both attached to me. This was beyond exciting. The implant felt sort of slushy, and the reduced boob was bruised and cut up, but I thought it looked cool.

I was sent home the next day, and told to keep my chest dry for three weeks.

I don't imagine it's the easiest thing in the world for a parent to observe a daughter going through reconstructive breast surgery. My doting father and stepmother often asked how I was doing, but we didn't really talk about what had happened until my friend Trevor came to visit. He burst into the room and called out: "SO! How're your tits?"

Gay men can get away with this stuff; you don't even want to kill them. I laughed and laughed, and told him that my boobs were great, thanks very much.

My first trip out, after lurking around the house for three weeks, was to The Bar, Whitby's creatively named gay bar. Upon entering, I was descended upon by a drag queen, who shrieked my name and whirled me around in a bear hug and didn't stop until he realized that I, too, was shrieking—but in agony. "New boobs," Trevor explained. He and the drag queen nodded sagely. I had a great evening. I was the talk of the town.

By the time my stitches came out and I was back at college in Windsor, I was feeling quite pleased with myself. I was in love with my naked body. I had cartoon boobs. They were funny and perfect and perky and very scarred. I went on the wildest bra-buying binge since my bi-polar roommate dropped her lithium, grabbed my hand, and set out to spend $650 at La Senza. But this was my bra-buying binge. I wasn't bi-polar—just bi-breasted, finally. I bought push-up bras. I bought corsets. I bought lace and velvet, in every imaginable flavour. Black, beige, pink, red, you name it.

Soon after that, I attended an opening at an art gallery. I had on my new velvet bustier and a tiny sweater. When someone ogled me, I stood up straighter and declared for all to hear: "Your tax dollars at work." One night, while I was out at the Eclectic Cafe, I spilled tea on myself. When I got home, my roommate opened the door and let out a scream. "OH my God. Audra sprung a leak!" I got the feeling that having a saline breast might end up being even more fun than having one boosted by shoulder pads.

Rebel, Rogue, Mischievous Babe

Actually, it is a lot more fun. Four years have passed since the surgery, and it is hard to remember the body I used to have. I now wear whatever I like, and as little as I like. I rarely feel self-conscious about my naked body. Indeed, I feel much better about my body than a lot of women seem to. Truth be told, I'm quite pleased with myself. After ignoring my breasts for so long, these days I'm checking them out all the time. To touch, you can tell which one is fake, but who cares? I sure don't. I can wear leotards and V-neck shirts and bathing suits with glee. I lounge around undressed longer than I have to, and my collection of fancy underwear is growing exponentially. I wouldn't have done it if it had cost me a lot of money and I would never have done it for a boy, but I sure am glad I did it this way.

For free and for me.

Roundtable

Some are small. Others are big. Sometimes one is big and the other is small. Breasts come in all different shapes and sizes. Once a girl reaches puberty, chest-level concerns suddenly present themselves, including fear of the department store bra section and rude comments from immature boys (don't worry, they're just intimidated by you).

What's a girl to do?

Stacey Stein, a *Reluctant Hero* contributing editor, put this roundtable of six girls from Toronto together to talk about breasts, bras, and boys.

The names of the girls have been changed at their request. Janet, Cindy, and Heather are fifteen. Erica, Lois, and Greta are fourteen.

Have you ever been harassed in school about having big breasts or for being flat-chested?

Janet: I've heard rumours that some guys only go out with certain girls because they have big breasts or something. That's an easy thing for guys to think. Instead of just judging a person by their

personality, they say, "She has big boobs and that's why he's going out with her."

Lois: I mean, it's possible that a guy might go out with a girl because she has big breasts, but it also depends on the type of guy he is.

How do you feel about developing? Do you want to have big breasts? Do you care?

Lois: I know that a lot of my friends have small breasts, and they seem really self-conscious about it. For instance, I've noticed that they notice the size of other people's breasts. Whereas to me, it's not an issue.

Erica: I developed really early, and I started taping down my chest so the guys wouldn't notice. I just used regular tape, but then my mom found out. I wanted to keep wearing T-shirts and hanging out with my guy friends and not be treated differently.

What about friends who have bigger breasts—do you think they get more attention?

Janet: Yup.

Greta: One of my friends, whenever we used to go out places, guys on the street used to always notice her. We would always joke about it.

What do you think of implants?

Heather: They're so fake. I don't see why anyone would do that, unless they were completely flat and really self-conscious about that.

Cindy: I don't see why everyone's so preoccupied about it. Maybe if I was, like, really abnormally large, or really abnormally small, then maybe.

What about buying a bra? Is that an embarrassing thing to do? Or are you totally comfortable with it?

Greta: When I was young, I was preoccupied with it and I would get my mom to go to the cashier, as if she was buying them. But they were tiny, so everybody knew that they couldn't be for her. Now, I'm not really preoccupied with it. I guess, if it was a guy at the cash ... but usually it's not, so I don't care.

Would you ever leave the house without one on?

Heather: I think it's really uncomfortable if you don't wear one. I have a friend who's obsessed. She always has to have it on. We were watching a movie with Cindy Crawford and she wasn't wearing one. My friend was annoyed the whole movie.

Lois: I think it's better if you are wearing one. I feel more comfortable wearing one. For me, it's comfort, but if you don't like it, then don't wear it. My sister hates wearing them.

Are you surprised when you see a woman in a tiny T-shirt without a bra?

Janet: I think it's gross.

Why?

Cindy: I think that my opinion sort of changes. I have friends who don't wear bras because they don't want to. Then there are people who wear tight shirts and high heels and they don't wear a bra. And I don't like that, because it's just, like, all over the place. And then there are people who are just very natural. I think there's a difference.

What about the court ruling in favour of Gwen Jacobs, who walked down the streets of Guelph, Ontario, topless?

Erica: I don't like it because it's just not the way I was raised. I grew up with the idea that you clothe your body to cover yourself, and that's the way it is. Like, I just think of it as a respectable thing. I guess if they allow it now, then in a couple of years, it will be just the normal thing. I'm not ready for that!

Heather: I don't think it should be a problem because it's the media that makes it such a big deal. Like, oh, boobs, breasts, they're sexual. But they don't have to be. It's the media and society that have made them into objects. And so I think maybe that the ruling that women can walk around without tops on is a good thing, because then people won't think of breasts as sexual things, but as a part of a woman's body, like an arm or a leg or something.

Cindy: I think that as long as men are allowed to go topless, women should be allowed to. But if there was a woman walking down the street topless, I'd be really shocked at first, because I'm definitely not used to that. I guess in time we might get used to it. They do it in Europe and it is not a big deal.

Janet: I understand what she's saying, but I also think it's sort of a personal thing. If this goes on, then maybe in six years they'll say, "Okay, now no one has to wear any clothes at all."

To Shave or Not to Shave

I grew up thinking that body hair had no business being on my body. I knew that the hair on my arms and elsewhere was there to keep me warm, and to provide protection, but, because I don't live in an unheated cave and because I rarely go without clothes, all that fuzz seemed useless and ugly. Besides, there were lots of girls who didn't seem to have any body hair at all—except on their arms and in other hair-acceptable areas, like underarms, and of course pubic hair—which meant I was unfairly blessed with this cursed hair suit.

Here's the thing: I don't actually have an excessively hairy body, I just thought I did. As a kid you're influenced by your parents' actions and words. And when it came to beauty, I noticed that my mom was concerned about her body hair, which meant that I became acutely aware of mine.

I'm sure you've heard that if your mom has a bunch of weight-loss calendars and diets that she's following, you're more likely to develop an eating disorder. Well, I developed a sort of body hair fixation.

Now here's the irony: although my mom has always been concerned about body hair, she doesn't seem to have even one hair on her body. Okay, slight exaggeration, but all in all she's pretty darn hairless, as far as I can see. But I guess she never thought so.

My mom noticed and compared the hair on her legs and arms to anyone who came in sight. We regularly talked about electrolysis, hair-removal creams, and bleaching potions. And there were always tweezers close at hand, ready to pluck any pesky hair that dared to make an appearance.

I'm not sure at what precise moment my mom's preoccupation became my own, but it might have been when she told me, at the tender age of ten, that when my aunt came to visit me at the hospital soon after I was born, she was concerned that I was too hairy. It's funny and annoying how a few ill-considered words from a family member, or even a stranger, can have a huge effect—good or bad—on a young person's life and neuroses.

I'm not sure why body hair was such a bad thing in my mom's eyes. Maybe it had something to do with a sense of refinement. My mom is trim and ladylike, so anything as unfeminine as a garish laugh or unsightly body hair would have made her cringe. Or perhaps body hair was *her* mom's preoccupation, and like me she just inherited it. Maybe it has something to do with the way women are portrayed in the media. Ever see a hairy woman sell anything? There's also a link between hairlessness and a kind of nubile youth. Going through puberty and all of the changes that characterize it is a rite of passage that takes us from being girls to being women. Wanting to be hairless is considered by some to represent the desire to remain a girl, and perhaps also to be treated like a child.

Dark-haired women are still portrayed in popular culture as devilish and untrustworthy vixens. In Hollywood movies, an olive-skinned, dark-haired beauty is certainly dangerous, compared to the all-American male or female with skin like milk and honey and hair the colour of sunshine. Clearly, a flagrant display of hairiness is frowned on.

Advertisements for razors and shaving cream have also probably had an effect on my ideas about the connection between beauty and hairlessness. The idea of shaving as a rite of passage into adult life certainly had some bearing on my desire to acquire my own pink razor and shaving lotion. Of course, when you discover razor-burn from shaving too often, or when you have sharp stubble on your legs because you decided to skip a few days, you soon discover that the soft hair on your legs didn't feel so bad.

I didn't learn that hair was political until after high school. At that point, some girls chose not to shave because they didn't think they should have to alter their bodies to make themselves fit anyone else's notion of attractiveness. I think feminism today is more about action than appearance. Hair or lack of hair doesn't make you any more or less political, or interesting. I think you should shave or not shave depending on how it makes you feel.

Now that I'm older, and so much *smarter*, and I know many of the reasons why I'm concerned about what people will think if they see that I have body hair (ack!), I'm no less preoccupied with lightening it, or simply getting rid of it. And that's with the certain knowledge that the more I tweeze, lighten, wax, and Nair it, the more it comes back. Hey, I never said I was perfect!

Big Hair

Kate McGee, 17,
Eastern/Central

I'm a girl with big hair: I can make it poof to three times the size of my head, or let it curl, or smoosh it flat by pulling it back.

I dye it blonde now, but it was auburn for the first few years. I only get to see a few centimetres of natural hair colour at a time. I haven't seen my real hair colour since I was fifteen, and I have no idea what it's up to now.

When I let my hair fall around my shoulders, I feel powerful. When I let it fall into its curls, I walk around thinking, BIG HAIR. I feel all-natural and wild-womany. I feel like a roar.

Sometimes I use my hair to hide my face. Sometimes it's a tool of submission, like when I'm having a bad face day, when my acne gets borderline cystic, and I think, I do not want people to look at this face! Sometimes I think about shaving it off to avoid this. Other times, it just reminds me of my dermatologist.

I shave my legs and armpits. ("Armpits" is an ugly-sounding word, but "underarms" is sterile and lame.) I like shaving because after I get a really smooth shave with my moisturizing conditioner—for my BIG HAIR—I love the smooth feel against my sheets or pants or brushing legs in a pool with a girlfriend. I try not to think of the politics of shaving and oppression, but at the same time, it sucks to avoid semi-intelligent thought.

I don't really understand pubic hair. I think it's pretty ugly. I didn't like it poking out when I wore my little boy-cut bathing suit, so I bought one of those depilatories. It served its purpose, but I feel kind of dumb. For one thing, I barely ever go swimming, and who's looking at my crotch anyway? For another, it's funny to have it growing back. But the weirdest thing is how I feel so bald. I didn't remove all of it, just the edges, but when I look in the mirror and there's a bit missing, I feel ashamed, kind of stupid and incomplete. And now I've got myself in this vicious stubble cycle. I'm not going to let this lack o' hair drive me insane, but thank God for my big head of hair. It makes me feel powerful.

One of my favourite books, *The Female Eunuch*, talks about how hair is connected to power and how women with bald legs and privates are just being childlike. I felt a little bit sick after reading that because I agree, and yet, here I am: a woman who's pretty well baldy-bald from the neck to the toes. The conflict between *The Female Eunuch* and the fashion magazine where I selected the perfect depilatory represents this crazy clash in my ideas.

I'm still not sure how to deal with it, grow it out, and grow out of it, but I'm glad I'm a feminist from the neck up. At least it's a good place to start.

All Things Foul

Catriona McEwan, 16,
Eastern/Central

Just off the top of my head, I can't think of a single girl I know who doesn't shave some part of her body, be it her legs or underarms or even toes. The second our mothers gave us permission to use that pink razor, we couldn't lather up our legs fast enough. I guess it's some sort of rite of passage. Remember the historic day when you proudly revealed your bare, hairless legs for the first time during gym class in junior high? Then as soon as the hair started to grow back and you were introduced to the horrors of ingrown hairs and tiny nips that spurted blood like mini waterfalls, the novelty faded. Soon after the practice of shaving your lower limbs had begun, you moved on to removing those little baby hairs that seemed to sprout overnight from under your arms. Soon you discovered that underarm shaving was a tad more difficult to manoeuvre than you once imagined, but eventually persistence paid off and now you can handle all sorts of hair removal with your eyes closed.

So, for the majority of adolescent girls, removing most visible body hair has become a familiar routine ritual. One we're almost proud of. Part of our right and design as a gender, like we are all members of a secret society automatically entered into after purchasing that first razor. And the funny part is that most girls don't even question why we all continue to do it or why we started in the first place. After the first time, it becomes practically automatic, and by the time you're sixteen, you feel embarrassed to even wear a tank top if you haven't shaved beforehand. The girls who refuse to practice this rite of passage are usually labelled deviants or rebels and sometimes ostracized for their obvious disrespect of gender rules. It's almost a crime to not follow this rule, and our punishment is an uncomfortable pressure to conform. Although men shave at a certain point in adolescence, it's not the same for women. Hairless legs and armpits are dubbed a feminine quality, an ideal. I, myself, shave my legs and underarms, saying it's mostly for my personal comfort when in reality it has more to do with being accepted. I really don't want to be singled out as unattractive or offensive by refusing to remove the "unfeminine" hair that arrived along with puberty. It's something I've learned to accept because it feels normal and natural even though I often resent feeling like I should, just because I'm a girl.

Most boys grow up expecting their companions to be smooth and hairless even though it's biologically unnatural. Girls may prefer their mates to be clean-shaven, but it's usually not the deciding factor or even an issue where preference is concerned. I think that if boys are allowed to demand that we use that razor without question, then we should be allowed the same right, be it on his legs or underarms or even toes.

Not Afraid to Bleed

By Corinne Alstrom aka Mophead, 14, Eastern/Central

Tuesday, April 18—10:19 p.m.

I remember my menarche (first period) vividly. It was an unseasonably warm September day, and I was in the seventh grade. I don't remember getting any kind of stomach ache ... well, except when I went to pee, pulled down my pants, and WHAM. Then I got a stomach ache of horror. Not that I didn't know what it was: I knew full well that my period would start soon. I was just hoping it would happen the day before I died or something.

So there I am, sitting there, staring at this ... brown ... staining ... I wanted dearly to believe I had inadvertently crapped myself or something. But I knew.

I went into the other bathroom, where the supplies were kept. The bulky-ass pads intimidated me, so I grabbed a pantyliner and used that. Luckily, I was the only one home. I walked dazedly around the house, in a state of disbelief. I knew that from that moment on, I would have to deal with all the stuff that my sister dealt with when she was on her period. NOOOOOOOOOOOO!!! Never mind all that talk about "becoming a woman" and "entering a new stage in your life." I was ready to throw a hissy fit. I told my sister on my way to bed that night. She reacted as if I'd let her in on the fact that I was failing math or something. I changed my underwear, used a new pantyliner, bleached the old underwear, and went to bed. The next morning before leaving for school, I told my mother that I had my period. "Oh. Well ... I guess this means you're growing up ..." "Sorry mom, gotta go to school! Bye!"

I used to think that all my periods would be that light. After a few "Oh-dear-God-the-crimson-tidal-wave-will-kill-us-all" accidents, it occurred to me that my menses were getting heavier and heavier. I decided that my period was a horrid curse that God had put on women because he didn't like us. I wondered why the suicide rate among women was so low. And it continued that way for ... hmmm ... I've been menstruating for only three years now. That's approximately 36 periods. I've spent about 28 of those crying, wishing I were dead, trying to ignore the crimson tide and massive clots rushing out of my vagina, and tolerating horrid pain. And only now have I begun to tolerate it ... even almost enjoy it.

"What?" you say. How could anyone possibly enjoy that kind of punishment? Well ... honestly, I dunno. Now that I'm almost clockwork regular, my period gives my days a better internal timing system than sunrise and sunset alone ever could. Sure, there are cramps, blah blah blah, but in comparison with knowing that all your girlfriends have this internal thing happening too—and that none of your guyfriends will ever understand—cramps and sore tits are nothing. In this world of gender equality, I want to feel different sometimes. My blood makes me different. It makes me a female.

When my period is late, I genuinely miss it. I know that blood should be cascading out of me, but it's not there. This leaves me crabby, disagreeable, and screaming at my uterus, "Bleed, damn you! Bleeeeeeeeed!!!" (Hence the overused term PMS!)

While we're on the subject of PMS, let's get one thing clear: not all women experience it. If you're a jackass/bitch/moron 24-7, it has nothing to do with PMS when a woman happens not to like you. PMS makes me depressed: that's all. I don't become unreasonably angry or mean during that time. Just a little detached. Every woman expresses herself differently, and many women don't experience any kind of PMS at all! So leave your stereotypes at the door.

I will be happy to menstruate this month, again. Menstrual blood produces an excellent fertilizer for my plants. A tampon soaked in water then wrung out will leave your plants radiant. Think about it. That blood would have nourished an egg, and then helped out a baby—plants will like it. And no, it doesn't make the plants smell. Duh.

Sorry about the harsh words.

Live long and bleed!

Pay Attention to My *Underpants*?

Kim Martyn

O.R.

Kim Martyn is a sexual health educator and co-owner of sexscape.org website. We asked her how a young woman is supposed to know when her period is going to begin.

I am often asked a lot of questions that begin with "How do you know ...?" Among them are "How do I know when I am going to get my period?" "How do I know what size my breasts will be?" "How do I know when someone likes me?"

For many things, you can't know for sure. However, when it comes to body changes, there are signals that you can watch for.

You think to yourself, "Sure, I'm between the ages of nine and sixteen, but that doesn't tell me when I'm going to get my first period!" Well, start paying attention to your underpants.

From six months to two years before your period starts, you will notice a white film that has dried on the inside of your undies. (One student I spoke to started wearing dark underwear so that she'd be sure to notice any change!) This film is caused by a sticky fluid that your vagina and cervix (which is up inside your vagina) start to produce as your body matures. You will probably also start to get some underarm and pubic hair, a height increase, as well as breast buds, before that first period.

So, you've already started your period and you'd like to know whether or not you're going to need to take pads or tampons with you on your weekend away. One clue is that about two and a half weeks before your menstrual cycle begins you might notice a clear, wet, slippery mucus flow from your vagina. Yuck? No way! This is powerful sperm-friendly stuff. Be aware, you are now very fertile for the next six or so days. Beyond this mucus, many young women feel no change in their bodies, and so each time their period begins it's a surprise. For others, just before they menstruate they have cramps or a headache or sore breasts. The only good news for this group is that they usually know their period is on its way. In either case, if your cycle becomes very regular, meaning that there is the same number of days between when one period starts and when the next one starts (it might be 21, 25, 35 ...), then keeping track on a calendar helps you avoid those "Uh-oh, wearing light pants" moments!

Chapter 3

The Family

No Place Like Home

I live 8,000 kilometres away from my family. We speak almost daily. I see them at least three times a year, and we know all about each other's lives. We are close, despite the distance.

We've lived apart for many years now, and it's only lately that I've begun to realize how much I would love to live in the same town as my parents and brothers. It's the comfort of being able to drop by for dinner, or hang out with my mom some Sunday morning, that I seek. The phone just doesn't cut it when a day has gone awry and I feel as though everything would be better if I didn't have to explain or talk about it, but could instead just curl up and be safe in the middle of the noise and endless comings and goings in my parents' home. Apart from the familiarity and ease of being together when the world outside seems harsh, I like my family, and we laugh a lot together, so sometimes it would be nice just to be able to be with them on a whim.

I left home in order to grow into my own skin. I travelled away from my family because I was eager to figure out who I was without them. The easiest way to leave the nest, for most people, is when university or college beckons. Though your parents might be afraid to let you go, when you're leaving to go to school, they know that you're going not because you don't like living with them, but because you have to go in order to start the next phase of your life. Of course, your reasons for leaving might have less to do with higher education and more to do with establishing your own rules in your own place, and seeing if the ideas you have about the world are true by experiencing it in a way that you can't always under your parents' gaze.

When I was growing up, I recognized that my family was made up of five people who were almost always engaged in five completely different activities, which meant there was lots of separation even within the family unit. My dad enjoys making things, so in his spare time he's usually tinkering in the basement. My mom is a painter who is often in her studio. My brothers have their own friends and interests. It takes some effort for us to do things together as a family.

When I say the word *family* I think about a lot of different things. I think about the way my parents brought me up, and how the ideas they had about parenting varied from child to child. My parents seemed to mellow by the time my little brother was born. All the arguments about curfews and clothing became less fierce; they gave in more often. As the only girl, I was also subject to a different set of rules than either of my brothers. My parents were much more strict with me. Although I thought this was grossly unfair, complaining about it actually made it worse, so most of the time I didn't say anything about how wrong, wrong, wrong I was sure it was.

There are lots of studies that reveal that each child's experience of the family is unique and different from that of their siblings. The experience you have can, in fact, be so unlike that of your brothers and sisters that you can feel as though you were brought up in entirely different families. This is a weird notion to wrap your head around. I think the difference is linked to birth order and expectations. Parents have specific ideas about success for their eldest child, which can mean that there is a predetermined path that older kids feel they have to take. Youngest children are often thought to be the most creative or artistic, because they are left to their own devices and allowed to follow dreams of their own making. As a middle child myself, I like to think this position allows for the most balance—a little direction from Mom and Dad, coupled with a sense of purpose that stems from our own unique interests, makes us quite lucky to have been born in-between.

The word *family* also makes me think of a safety net. My parents still provide a physical safety net that I can rely on. Knowing that I can move back home at any time is very reassuring. Right, Mom? Also, my younger brother is my best friend, and he is always in my corner. He provides me with a kind of emotional safety net. As someone who is sure of himself, and very level-headed, he advises me and still manages to make me feel smart.

Living far away from my own family, I have tried to create surrogate families, sometimes without even knowing it. In every city I have lived in there have always been older people in my life who have looked out for me. As a starving student, I lived in an apartment across from an elderly widow. Every week she would invite me over for dinner or for cookies. She made sure I was okay and even lent me a bed when I moved in and didn't have one. Having an older confidante means that conversations about guys, career, and friends benefit from the additional dimension of age and experience. As a woman living alone, having a surrogate family is also important because you should have people who check in on you from time to time.

I suppose, though, that there are some dangers in creating a makeshift family. One of those is that you can create the shell without having the substance. By substance, I mean unconditional love. I know that it probably doesn't always feel as though you have your parents' unconditional love, because they get mad at you, and because they have expectations that you sometimes can't fulfill, but you probably do.

In the surrogate family relationships I've created, no matter how close or loving, there has always been a certain amount of tit for tat. I have always been aware of the need to repay favours or kindnesses, or at least to be sure not to take those things for granted. This isn't entirely a bad thing. In fact, most families could do with more reciprocal kindness, and less taking each other for granted. Nevertheless, though some parents have all kinds of strings they like to pull to make you do their bidding, in my experience, it's only my family that would do anything for me and not expect a thing back, except maybe a thank you.

Because families are so powerful, they can give you strength and support, but they can also tear down your confidence by not listening to you, or by being too critical, or by expecting too much of you. You need to be able to determine when to move in close and listen and when to follow your own lead.

I've been lucky. My parents have almost always wanted me to

make up my own mind about my work or studies. In fact, my parents are so "do whatever you want" that sometimes I wish they would be more involved in helping me make choices. But I suppose that would come with a kind of interference that I would probably hate.

Over the years I've noticed that my parents have all kinds of foibles and shortcomings, just like regular folk. Now that I'm older, though, and I don't mind being seen traipsing around with my parents, I actually love our family outings. Maybe that's because I don't see my parents often enough, and now that they're getting older it has become more important to me to spend time with them. I know we're supposed to believe that our parents have it all figured out and are more "Brady Bunch" than "Roseanne," but knowing that they too face challenges and difficulties just makes the ebb and flow of being a family that much more real and enduring.

Myth:

Father knows best

Fathers want you to believe that they know what is best for you. And when I say "father," I suppose I really mean anyone in your life who is older, an authority figure, the kind of person who wants to keep you safe from harm.

Fathers might keep you from falling prey to schemes and time-wasting ventures, but they might also teach you caution where maybe audacity and risk-taking would have been better skills to learn. It takes courage to pick your own path, or to do things that your "father" disagrees with.

It's wasteful to refuse to listen, to reject out of hand someone else's hard-earned experience. It's easier to listen with an open mind. Hear what "father" has to say, consider your options and the possible consequences of your actions, and then make up your own mind. When you begin with the premise that the outcome of taking action and gaining experience is often positive, you will learn how capable and smart you really are.

Excerpts from a Diary with Penguins on the Cover

Anna Humphrey, 20,
Eastern/Central

Twelve—when I bought my first stick of deodorant and it was an event so monumental that I wrote about it in my diary—baby-powder scented, and it lasted me through that whole year when everything was "so." So cute, so depressing, soooo embarrassing, like when Shawna called Blake and told him I liked him, but not to tell me that he knew, and then he called me at 9:40, but my mother said I'd already gone to sleep, because I had, and I could not believe she would be so insensitive.

I'm not gonna make my kids go to bed this early when they're twelve—the stupid cow. She's so dumb and she doesn't understand at all what it's like. I'm going to remember for when I have kids what it is like to be twelve.

The dramas that shook my life and filled my head and kept me up late at night thinking about what I should have done—would have said. Like the time I had a party and invited boys and we went down to the pond and some punks bothered us, and they were at least fourteen.

Blake was shaking and so was Emily but not as much. He said they were going to beat him up for his Docs (shoes). He said, "Is there any way to get out of here, Anna, those punks over there know I have Docs and they'll beat me up for them." I showed him an escape route. Then the rest of us tried to walk around them to get back to my house. Four of the punks ran up to us. One had a broom. One had a baseball. One had a green mohawk, and the other was fat. The fat one put his hands around Adam's neck like he was going to strangle him, but then he let go. Then my mom showed up and dragged us home saying how she was going to phone the punks' parents.

How everything was about me, and just thinking about myself, was almost too much to handle; just too many disappointments, like how I couldn't clear the bar in high jump, and my mother cut my bangs crooked so I looked "retarded." And when Raphael and Mark asked if they could copy my homework I let them, because I was sure it meant they liked me. All the ink smudged from tears and all the times I talked myself into thinking I was nothing. "Total nerd. Total loser."

Maybe Blake likes me

Good #1 – He talks to me at school

Good #2 – He said he wants to come to my party

Good #3 – He gave me a 45 on my speech and an average speech gets 31

Good #4 – He asked Emily about my family

But:

Bad #1 – He's a megaflirt (flirts with every girl, even Coreen)

Bad #2 – Nearly every girl likes him

Bad #3 – I think he likes Brandy and she's sooo pretty

Bad #4 – A lot of people think I'm a nerd

Bad #5 – Why would he like me anyway?

Or the time I stole a picture of mom's boyfriend from the album and stabbed it with scissors, poked both his eyes out, poked a hole through his pants, then cut him up in a million pieces. My mother yelled and then cried when she found it in the garbage can. She said, "Al would never do this to a picture of you." That night I wrote in big letters and so hard I ripped through the page:

I Hate Al

Everything seemed bigger than life, and I couldn't wait for my period to come or for hair to grow on my legs so I could shave it off. One day a man in a white minivan tried to kidnap Wendy Loelle and the idea fascinated me to no end. Did he have a trenchcoat and no clothes on underneath? And if so, what did *it* look like? Where was he going to take her? What was he going to do with her? And was it sex?

Oh it's so freaky, okay. Wendy was walking home and this guy blocks her path and rolls down the window and says "I'm a school police, I'd like to ask you some questions, get in the car please." She screamed "No" and she ran into the community centre. She looked through pictures at the police station, but she didn't find him. I wonder if he has kidnapped a lot of kids.

A single line devoted to my grandfather, hoping for a fast recovery after eye surgery, following three pages about Jeremie coming to my house after school on a day when I was sick, and how I almost didn't change out of my pyjamas at three o'clock and thank God I did. My vague and occasional concern about the war in the Persian Gulf.

I don't know really who they are, but they sent five missiiles down on Israel and they were toxic too. Now all the people have to wear gas masks and they showed it on TV.

On the next page, big loopy letters of joy because I came third in the class for French public speaking, and a boy had offered me his chair when we were copying notes from the bulletin board. Drawings and photographs and the program from the Grade 6 musical, pasted in. Big pink hearts with initials printed inside, scratched out later. Endless heartbreaks, a new one for each day.

I'm crying again! It's not just because I want to, it's because my life sucks! For real. Will I ever be popular at school? Will I ever have a boyfriend? Alexandra has everything she could ever want, and now she won a gold medal for her grades. What more could you ask for? Alexandra and Alison are both in enrichment too and I'm just stupid I guess.

Strange how my best friend is mentioned only on days when she made me angry (though I loved her completely). I guess there was just no room for her in the diary with the penguins on the cover. The weight of my twelve-year-old grief and joy was all it could take.

You're So Mean to Me

Daryl Elliott, 15,
Prairies

First there was one. About a year and a half later there was another. Life became bearable, and even a little fun. But, alas, six years later, yet another was born. That would be me.

There are some advantages and disadvantages of being the youngest. Here are my experiences.

Okay, alright, sure. The idea of having a younger sibling around probably seemed cool to six- and eight-year-old kids. They've even admitted to saying "Aw, what a cute little baby." That was all before they brought me home. There would be many sleepless nights with endless crying, and not a thing they could do about it. Don't worry though. About five years later, they found many ways to get their revenge.

I can't really remember for sure, but I think it all started with horseradish and Tabasco sauce. Did you know that when force-fed to you by spoonfuls at a time for many years, you actually build up a tolerance to these condiments? Well, that's one of the many things we learned over the years.

I can remember the feeling I used to get every time the phone rang. I would be hoping that it wasn't the hospital calling mom back to do an ECG or X-ray or something. It usually was though. The minute the door closed behind her, my sisters would get this evil look in their eyes and a sly grin would spread across their faces. "TORTURE TEST!" And then I would run. These "torture tests" would usually consist of various punishments depending on my age. For example, if I was six years old, they would feed me six tablespoons of horseradish or Tabasco sauce; they would hold me down and tickle me for six minutes (which is very painful); I would get six slaps across the face; and they would stretch me by pulling on my arms and legs for six minutes. This was the regular session that I would experience. Every once in a while, they would get creative.

Once, while I was sleeping, they took the doorknob from the bathroom door, which was a locking knob, and switched it with the doorknob of my bedroom door. Then they locked me in from the outside. A little while later, I woke up. Naturally I walked over to my door, grabbed the knob, and turned. Actually, I tried to turn. This is when I realized I was locked in. Well, my sisters thought this was hysterically funny, or something, so they went outside my bedroom window and howled with laughter for about an hour.

Another "good one" was to pick me up and throw me outside when I was wearing just my pyjamas. Of course, they'd lock the doors. Hey, I could've handled this okay, but the fact that it was usually about –20 degrees Celsius, well, that was the bad part. These were all of the "non-violent" methods.

They weren't always so nice though. When they had friends over, they'd actually get violent. Perhaps their favourite violent game was to give me an airplane ride. You're probably thinking to yourself right now, "How can an airplane ride be violent? All little kids get them and I've never seen anyone get hurt." Well, believe me, this was no ordinary plane ride. They'd pick me up by the feet, and swing me round and round. Now, listen up, because this is the best part—they'd let me go. And fly I would. Right into the trees. This was their idea of a crash landing.

You're probably wondering why I would never tell on them. This would only have resulted in fierce retaliation. I usually just kept my mouth shut. Not saying I didn't bring it on, because I did. I would eat all the cookies, bug them when they had friends over, always ride shotgun, and I had my pick of the restaurants. Oh, and of course, I always got the best presents.

I'm afraid I'm giving you the wrong impression though. Sure, they sometimes relentlessly tortured me, but we also had good times. Like joking around at family gatherings, cruising around on the trike, playing catch, and going to the lake. Now that they're gone, I always look forward to them coming back to joke around with me, reminisce, and have the occasional scrap. I'd never trade my childhood for anything. Besides, anyone else who is the youngest child will agree—the fringe benefits are just way too good to give up.

Finding Strength Through Cancer

Siku Allooloo-Laraque, 13,
Northern Territories

My mother always taught us to pray at night before we went to sleep. We'd start off by saying "Thank You" for all that we're grateful for. I'm grateful for a lot, I have all that I need, but when I go to bed, and when I pray, I always want to say: "Dear Lord, thank you for all that you've given me. Thank you for my mom's health. Thank you for taking the cancer away and bringing her back to normal.

She is the strongest person I know, and now even stronger, because, with your help, she has beaten cancer."

But I can't say that. I want to believe that she's healthy, and everything's like it was before. When I was little, I remember mom and I skipping down the street singing "Skip to my loo." She'd tickle us, and tell us stories in the mornings. When we were sick, she took care of us, and when we were sad, she made us laugh. I feel I took her for granted.

She's been through three marriages, and is raising four children alone. One child was negligent to all but his friends, another was into parties, drinking, and drugs by the age of twelve, and the other two (my brother and myself) were too young to understand what was really going on.

It's only in the past couple of years that I've begun to understand all that she's been through, and still managed to put us through school and make us do our best. She made sure we were happy and had everything we needed. I did my best in school (I've always been a top student in my class), I helped out at home with housework and helped my little brother understand many things. I'm also very sporty and I love writing. I guess I'm like my mom in many ways, I just hope that I'll be as strong as her when I'm older.

We found out that she had breast cancer last June. It was in her left breast, but had spread to her bones and bone marrow. When I talked to her on the phone after I found out, she sounded so strong and confident. There was no fear in her voice, even though she admitted that she was scared. I told her that she sounded so strong, even stronger than before, and she said, "Well, there's been a lot of tears, but I am in good hands."

Right now, she's in a hospital room, all alone, but with much love and no loneliness. I curse myself because she's healed my every wound, and cured my every sickness, but I can't do anything to help her fight this thing, this cancer. What is cancer anyway? It doesn't live, breathe, still it takes over and kills.

I've never known hate, but I do now. I hate the thing that's killing my mother, taking her away from me. I hate how it brings me pain, and disables. She has trouble walking, standing up, and basically moving her whole body. I hate how it makes me hate, when all I've ever done is love or, at most, dislike. But most of all, I hate how it's ripping me apart. I now hate.

I really want to help her, but I can't bear to see her in such pain. She's so thin, and so weak, but her spirit is strong and unbeaten in every way. She's stronger than I am, and she's the one with the disease. I try to go on living life and being happy, but I can't keep my mind off it. It haunts me no matter where I go, or what I do. I'm not sick, but it's killing me too.

I'm usually never mad and very forgiving. I'm not easily offended; I'm tough, but sensitive. You rarely see me pissed off, and I'm always having fun. This cancer is beating me, of all people, but somehow, it hasn't come close to my mom's soul. I've never known someone so loving, kind, peaceful, all together, and with such a strong spirit.

She's not lonely in a bland hospital room all by herself. She's peaceful and brave. All of the hurt has only made her stronger, and I wonder why I'm so scared. Why do I fear and stay away from her? Why don't I have strength like her?

But I guess it's God's way of telling me to follow her example. I guess she needs strength, and if it's not found physically, then I know it's definitely found in her spirit.

My mother's aunt invited me on a cruise to some of the Caribbean islands. When I visited my mom, we discussed it for a long time. It was the longest I've stayed to visit her, and the most comfortable I've felt. I told her about this book, how it's looking for true, personal stories. I told her that I didn't want her to read what I had so far, and that it didn't have an ending yet.

I also thought about all the love she was surrounded by, all the good memories in life that she had. I remember a past conversation when I asked her, "If you had a chance to live life all over again, and go through all the pain, would you do it just to know the happy moments?" I remember her hesitating, thinking, then finally saying, "Yes."

I started walking away, but I turned and said, "I finally know why you're not lonely here." She asked why, and I answered, "Because there are so many beautiful things in life not to worry about." I finally am at peace and unafraid because I have love in my heart that has surpassed my hate. There's not a day that goes by when I don't think of my mom. But now, I have her bravery to take place of my fear. After I walked out of her room, I came back and told her, "I think I found a way to end my story."

My Fabulous Sister ... Yada Yada Yada

Amanda Angus aka Mosquito, 16,
Eastern/Central

Almost all my life, my sister has been better than me. She's always been prettier, smarter, more popular, and more motivated than I have. There has never been a moment of my life that I haven't been jealous of her. To me, Jessica is up on this level of greatness that I can never hope to reach. With her being seven years older than I am, I admire her more than I can express. Yet at the same time I wonder how much of a disappointment I am to my parents when compared to her, because I know I disappoint myself.

Jess was valedictorian of her elementary school. It doesn't seem like much, but the night she graduated, when I was only seven years old, I knew that I wanted to keep up with her and be valedictorian when I graduated from elementary school. Time passed, and my schoolwork wasn't great and I wasn't athletic and I wasn't a leader in my school, so valedictorian was out of the question for me.

She was a great leader in high school. She was vice-president, and then president of the student council. Jess co-founded ESCAP, and had student councils in Ajax and Pickering communicating like never before. She was the conference chair of the Central East OSSSA. She brought school spirit back to her high school when everyone thought it was dead. Jess is still the only person to complete both the Gifted and the French Immersion programs. All of this in her OAC year, when she was busy applying to universities. For the record, she got into the university of her choice with several scholarships. I, on the other hand, was "Jessica's sister" who was just *there*.

Now Jess is in university. She's not on the Dean's list, that's true. However, she has lived in France for a year, taking engineering courses in French. While she was there, she ran for vice-president of the McMaster Engineering Society. She won, and *she wasn't even in the same continent.* She's now president of the McMaster Engineering Society, and being a bilingual female engineer, she has so many opportunities ahead of her. She is in a great relationship, and has amazing friends. Meanwhile, I am in her high school. I don't have amazing grades, and I haven't made any significant changes to how our school functions. I am the girl with the loud laugh who is on anti-depressants. People try to comfort me with, "Well, Jessica is amazing, *you* could never live up to *that*."

Well, I *want* to live up to that. I want the good grades, and the pivotal role on the SAC and the popularity and the scholarships from universities. And try as I might, I just can't do it. I just keep on disappointing myself and imagining what my parents actually think of me.

I know that living up to my sister is next to impossible; that I shouldn't compare myself to her; that my parents aren't really disappointed. But I've been hard on myself ever since she gave her speech at her Grade 8 graduation, and it is incredibly difficult to stop that kind of habit after ten years.

I love my sister with all my heart and soul; I do. I'm proud of her, and I'm happy that her life is going so well. I just wish I didn't feel like such a failure in comparison.

My Mother's Love Life & How I Survived It

Anna Humphrey, 20,
Eastern/Central

I remember the night Jon broke my mom's heart. I was eleven, and I snuck out of bed and sat at the top of the stairs listening in on the phone call. First she was yelling into the receiver, which was what woke me up in the first place ... but before long the yelling dissolved into sobs, and that was what kept me there listening. From her end of the call it wasn't hard to figure out what had happened. He was sleeping with another woman. It was the night of her fortieth birthday, and he hadn't shown up. She'd opened her presents and smiled through the party anyway, but you could tell that something was wrong.

I guess I remember that particular night, and those particular tears, because Jon was her first real boyfriend since the divorce. Until then, it never occurred to me not to like the men my mother dated. They came and went, but while they lasted, they were usually fun. There was Mohammed, who could ride a bicycle backwards; Dean, who had a Dalmation I could play with; Anthony, whose car could talk (it told you if you forgot to put your seat belt on); Mark, the musician who played a synthesizer with a million buttons on it.

If she cried when those relationships ended, I never knew about it, but with Jon it was different. My mom and I spent a whole year with him and his daughter Sarah, and then in one sudden phone call, he was gone. I don't know if it was that night, sitting on the staircase, or if it happened later on—maybe the next time a man made her cry, or else the time after that—but somewhere along the line, I got cynical about my mother's love life. There was a pattern to it, and I got tired of watching it repeat.

My mom met Ron. She fell in love. He was the best thing that ever happened to her. She felt like she was eighteen again. She met Al. He wrote her a love poem and left it on the bumper of her car at work. She was walking on air. She met Scott. It was meant to be. Why on earth hadn't they found each other sooner?

The beginnings were always the best parts. I helped her coordinate her outfit. We'd pick out the best pair of earrings and make sure that her make-up was blended, then I'd go to see them off at the front door—partly to say good-bye, but mostly to check her date out. Later, when she got home, we could discuss whether or not he was "hot."

But then came the middle parts, which got more and more tedious. These were the times when they were as happy as could be. They had so much in common and so much to learn from each other, and every day was a beautiful discovery (oh puke!). Before long, he'd be over two nights a week—then three or four. He'd be sitting in the kitchen when I got home from school. He'd be slouched on the sofa watching football, or nature shows, or sitcoms, or whatever it was this one liked to watch. And then by ten, he'd be in my mother's bedroom, and the door would be closed against me.

I admit (and not with too much pride), that I was much less than friendly towards these men. I snubbed them. Rolled my eyes at them. Ignored them and wrote mean things about them in my diary.

I remember once, when I was fourteen, Al (the current "loser-boyfriend," as I used to call them) wanted us to do something as "a family." He decided we should all go up to his cottage, and since I'd been wanting to dye my hair red, we should all dye our hair in the lake together. I can't deny that I considered it a personal victory when the permanent red dye turned his grey hair pink.

To Al's credit, though, and to the credit of all the men who came and went from my mother's life, every single one of them tried to reach out to me. They bought me gifts, learned my interests, and continued to say "good morning," even when I grumbled at them and looked off in the other direction. They all wanted to build a relationship with my mother, and as a result, wanted to (or else felt they had to) build one with me, but I pushed them away. Don't get me wrong ... I wanted my mom to be happy. I didn't purposely try to stand in the way of her relationships. I just did my best to ignore them. What was the point after all, in giving them a chance, when they'd be gone in a month or two, or a year at the absolute longest? Why would I bother learning to like them, when I knew all along that they'd break my mom's heart?

And that's where the end part comes in: Maybe he'd just get bored. Or maybe she would. Or maybe there'd be another woman again. He was just too cautious; too predictable. She was too head-strong; too independent. He was going back to his ex-wife. She couldn't stand his neediness. He wanted a baby. She didn't. The little disagreements and tensions would start to pile up. She said he didn't know how to communicate effectively. He said that she made an issue of everything. No matter how it ended, there were tears, and resentment. The telephone receiver was slammed down, sobs came from behind her bedroom door, and she told me she was never going to date again. It was just going to be the two of us and our cat, and we'd be okay, and we'd be happy ... but then the next one would come along.

So in the end, what did I gain from having a mother who dated a lot? I guess I'd have to say that above all I learned that love is work. It starts out full of roses, clichés, and blissful, googly-eyed gazes ... but eventually, whenever two people come together there's going to be tension and disagreement ... and sometimes you can work it out, and sometimes you can't. Maybe to some people that sounds cynical, but to me it just sounds realistic.

I've also learned that it's important to "shop around" when it comes to love, and try to figure out what you want from a relationship. If my mother had wanted to, she could have stayed with the man who cheated on her, or the one who lied, or the one who yelled at us ... or one of the ones who bored her ... but she didn't, and in part, I have to admire her for moving on, even when it was painful.

Mostly, though, I think that I admire her for refusing to give up. Time and time and time and time again, she took a leap of faith and let herself love somebody new, even if she'd just had her heart broken, even though she'd had her heart broken a dozen times before, even if chances were it was going to happen again, even if I was there snubbing the current "man of her dreams," and making things that much more difficult. The ups and the downs of it all weren't easy for me, and they certainly weren't easy for her, but I think that she always knew, even through her tears, just as much as I did, that she didn't mean a word of it all those times she said she'd never date again.

Chapter 4

Dating

Love Is in the Air / Breaking Up is Hard to Do

I'm a coward when it comes to breakups. Normally, I love confrontation, but when I know the relationship is past saving, I'd rather not have to talk about all of the problems, and what we could have done differently, for hours on end. Besides, there's nothing to be gained from telling someone the reasons why I don't think we're compatible. It would just be putting off the inevitable, until it became painfully obvious to both of us that this is a relationship that fun forgot.

Breaking up with someone for a "soft" reason—like you're bored, or you're bored, or you're bored—is never easy. By "soft" I'm not implying that these aren't legitimate reasons, I'm just trying to make a distinction between incompatibility because you don't share the same interests versus a much more serious issue, like verbal or physical abuse, which you shouldn't put up with for any reason.

Though it might seem like a no-brainer to end a relationship that makes you feel bad or that is demeaning, it can be hard to leave someone who is abusive or controlling. I think this is, in part, because relationships function like cocoons in that they create privacy and exclusivity, which can also make it easy to lose perspective.

If your relationship is like a cocoon and you are not careful about striking a balance between seeing your love, seeing your friends, and pursuing your own separate interests, you might inadvertently end up being more forgiving than you should be about your partner's inappropriate behaviour.

Spending all of your free time together can mean the development of a kind of emotional co-dependency as well, which can make it harder to be apart from someone, even when they are mean or cruel to you, just because you're used to being with that person.

Self-esteem plays a large part in all aspects of relationships. How you feel about your own self-worth can have an impact on your decision to walk away from any relationship, including friendship. Sometimes, it's clear to us that the person we're dating doesn't offer us enough affection, intellectual stimulation, or care and attention, but we still have trouble saying goodbye. You might want to ask yourself a couple of questions to determine why you either stay in the relationship or return to it when you know it isn't enough. Start by asking yourself, "Is it good for me to ______?" It's important not to say "Do I want to ______?" Asking yourself if it's good for you to stay, or to pursue it, or to leave will help you identify the reasons why you are having trouble moving on. You should also ask yourself what the person offers you in the relationship. By figuring out what they offer you, you're determining what you think you're worth.

If you're having trouble breaking up a relationship for a "soft" reason—you're used to hanging out, even though it's no longer a blast; or he's really nice, even though he's equally boring; or the affection is something you're not ready to do without just yet—that doesn't make you a weak person. If you find you've fallen back into something that was a mistake, the problems in the relationship probably haven't been resolved, which means you'll be in "breakup mode" sooner than you realize, and this time you'll be able to do it properly.

While breaking up is hard to do, what if you're done with the relationship but your ex won't let go? Now what?

One of the hardest things about getting rid of someone is reasoning with them. They will try to engage you in all sorts of conversations about fixing problems, your flaws, the relationship's potential, your inability to stick with things, their desire to make you happy. There will be lots of words and sentiments that will make you want to try again. Not a bad thing, if you genuinely believe the relationship has a future. If, however, your instincts are screaming "No, go away!" but you find yourself being the good girl, the compliant girl, the girl who can't say no, you might need a breakup strategy.

A friend of mine told me about a method she used to get rid of a man in her life who wouldn't stop calling, even after they had decided to end it. Every time he would call and try to persuade her to come back, she would refuse to get into details or discuss the past. She basically declined to engage in a conversation about it. Instead she would tell him, "I'm happy with my life the way it is." She repeated this phrase enough times for him to eventually get the picture.

At the end of a relationship there can be lots of sadness, and those feelings aren't necessarily exclusive to the person who has been dumped. I tend to hibernate when sad things happen to me, but I like to have lots of goodies and treats around to soothe and comfort myself. When I broke up with one boyfriend, Saturday mornings became the worst day of the week because I didn't know what to do with myself any longer. We had a routine: coffee, the market, squash in the afternoon. Without him, I didn't want to go to the market. I didn't want to explain where my friend was to the fruit-and-vegetable guy or to the cheese lady with the big breasts. Plus, the market held all sorts of cooking and togetherness memories. I didn't have a squash partner any longer. Fortunately, I still had coffee. Saturdays became easier, but I had to make a conscious attempt to be sure there was something I had planned and looked forward to doing on the weekends, now that I was doing it alone.

Though all I ever wanted to do was lie in bed and read on Saturday mornings, my boyfriend would ring me before 7:30 because we had to go for a run before the market. Now that he was gone and my mornings were my own, I bought all sorts of magazines and books and breakfast treats and spent my Saturday mornings lying about, reading, and eating.

I'm a bit of an introvert, at the best of times. I like hanging out in my home doing nothing in *par-tic-u-lar*, but I would try to make plans to see a friend on the weekend, just so that I had some contact with other people, and I almost always enjoyed it.

I think breaking up is hard to do because we fear feeling sad. My brother told me something a long time ago that helped me after a particularly difficult breakup. He said that he thought he was lucky to be able to experience the spectrum of feelings, including the terrible blues. Hearing that it was both okay to be so sad and good to be able to be that miserable made me feel a little better. The wondrous highs do mirror themselves in awful lows, but things change, and eventually you wake up and recognize your fabulous self again.

Myth:

Relationships are *hard* work

I've often wondered why the end of some affairs are so painful and bruising. After all, the breakup usually comes about naturally, generally when all of the love and fun has run its course and then run out. I've come to believe that the unwarranted pain comes because of the expectation that every relationship will be *the one*.

Maybe it's because we are idealistic and we want every relationship we embark on to hold the promise of everlasting happiness; unbridled optimism is a wonderful thing, don't you think?

Perhaps we begin relationships not knowing what the outcome might be, but once we become intimately involved we feel that it should be *significant* and *meaningful*. When they're problem-filled, we assume that we just need to work harder. Relationships do require care and attention, but they should never leave you feeling drained or exhausted or on eggshells.

Like a lot of people, I don't believe in coincidences. One night when I was sort of fretting about some of the non-starter relationships I've been in, a friend of mine reminded me that the people I choose to date or to be with are all a reflection of who I am. His words helped me understand that I sometimes choose partners who I know will be in my life for only a short time because they fulfill a particular need or desire, and as much as I might want to believe that these relationships will work and turn into something special and lasting, they can't.

It's actually kind of a relief to accept the fact that not all relationships are meant to last forever. It makes me look more closely at the reasons why I become involved, and it prevents me from deceiving myself about the place and importance of each relationship.

Addicted to Love

Anna Humphrey, 21,
Eastern/Central

I'm only twenty-one, but I've been in love (or thought I was) more than a dozen times. I'm pretty sure that lyric "Might as Well Face It, You're Addicted to Love" was written specifically for me. I was in sixth grade the first time I got all starry-eyed over a boy, and I haven't stopped since. His name was Jeremie. He told me that he was going to run my cat over with his bicycle, and I told him that he smelled bad. We used to walk home together after school to watch basketball at my place, even though I hated basketball. I was going to marry him. Of course, I never did, but that relationship (if you could even really call it a relationship) began the trend of me deciding that every single boy I had a crush on, or a relationship with, was going to be "the one." The man of my dreams, the father of my children, the love of my life.

Sean, when I was fourteen, who told me I should pull my shoulders back to make my boobs look bigger. John, when I was sixteen, whose breath smelled like hot dog relish. Aaron, when I was seventeen, who nearly flunked out of high school and couldn't spell. (I still have the poem he wrote me ... The first line goes "You smell so sweat" ... but I'm pretty sure he meant to say "sweet.") Chris, when I was eighteen. When we had sex for the first time, he got so excited that he banged his head on the wall above the bed and made his forehead bleed. Kyle, who never loved me back. Kevin, who was so religious he couldn't tell his parents that he had a girlfriend. Jason, who talked about himself so much he never bothered to figure out who I was ... and the list goes on, but you get the point.

I was going to marry them all. I was so sure that our love was the kind of love you hear about in pop songs ... the kind that is supposed to conquer all and endure forever and move mountains. I leafed through bridal magazines and picked out my favourite dresses. I decided how many kids, and whether or not we'd have a dog. I tried on their last names and considered hyphenation (I'm a feminist after all).

And I guess there's nothing really wrong (or uncommon) about having had a string of unsuccessful relationships. I guess it's also not uncommon to believe that every single one is "the one." I mean, otherwise getting involved and letting yourself fall in love wouldn't make so much sense ... But what is uncommon is the speed with which I seem to go through boyfriends. I'm never single, which is why I say I'm an addict. I love love. I can't get enough of it.

I'm addicted to the companionship part of it. The idea that since this is definitely going to work out, I will never have to be alone again. I love having somebody to call every night before going to bed. Somebody who cares how my day went, who listens to me whine about the fight I had with my best friend, and who comes right over if I'm upset and crying. I'm addicted to the physical part of it, especially that feeling of starting something new. Those times in the movie theatre when our arms are just barely touching, and we're both trying to work up the courage to reach for each other's hands. That first kiss that gives me the shivers, even if first we bump noses, and then he opens his mouth but I don't open mine, and the whole thing turns into a big slobbery mess. I'm addicted to the emotional part, that feeling of having somebody think I'm incredible, and beautiful. I love waking up beside the boy I currently think I love, and seeing that he's been propped up on one elbow, watching me sleep. It's that feeling of being admired, and the feeling of admiring, even adoring somebody in return.

And then of course, I'm addicted to the drama of it all: the thrill of the first time we say we love each other, and the tension every time we have a fight ... even the feeling of total despair when the breakup finally comes. How I call all my friends and they tell me they never liked him anyway. How I feel like I'll never get over it, but then of course I always do, and the drama starts all over again.

My friends, who are less addicted to love than I am, tell me, every single time I call in tears, to take some time to be by myself. You can't love others until you love yourself first. I've heard that line more than once or twice or ten times! But really, I don't think that not loving myself is the problem. I do love myself. I love myself a lot ... but I also love being with another person. I love the thrills, and also the sense of security that comes with a committed relationship. I think that as long as you have other friends, and other interests, and you don't let your relationships become the centre of your universe, being addicted to love really isn't the worst fate a person can suffer. It's healthier than being addicted to drugs, or alcohol, or even caffeine.

Falling in love (or even thinking that you're falling in love) is a completely natural high. It doesn't cost anything, and getting to know new people is a great way to pass the time. And who knows ... I bet that by the time I'm finished with all the dating I will do (and have already done in my life), I'll have a pretty good idea of who "Mr. Perfect" isn't ... which, ideally, should help me to recognize him when I actually do find him.

The Ongoing Quest for a Boyfriend

Catriona McEwan, 16,
Eastern/Central

I must admit that as much as I tease those teen magazines and their articles entitled "How to snag the boy of your dreams!" and "How to make him take notice!" I usually consider the pros of having my very own boyfriend. Someone to go to movies with and gush to all my girlfriends about on the phone after each precious and magical date. I quickly snap out of it and remind myself that boys are just way more trouble than they're worth. At least for now, at this point in my life. But my fantasy remains. It lingers and pulls at me. Every time my friend mentions a boy she has her eye on, or we get into the whole dating discussion over fries and a Coke, it usually turns into this heated debate about my feelings on the subject. How we're all programmed to "need" a boyfriend and how most of us girls are rushed into serial dating just to please our parents or peers. Sometimes it's not even that simple. Most of the girls I know feel that I'm overreacting and that dating boys, even if they're hardly interested in them, is necessary to practise for future relationships. Although I'm sixteen, I still don't feel quite ready to date anyone—seriously or even just for the fun of it. And

I know I'm not alone, but most of my friends rarely admit to sharing these concerns. They're busy daydreaming those Cinderella fantasies where a beautiful man arrives out of nowhere and rescues them from their lives of homework, minimum-wage jobs, and increasing boredom.

We all want to fall in love, and I'm no exception, but I can't surrender this—however naive—belief that most of these girls aren't ready for the reality of their fantasies, reality that will hit them when they realize they don't need a boy to make them completely happy or fulfilled. That it's not their life ambition to find "the perfect boyfriend." Or at least, that it shouldn't be. A lot of the girls my age are practically force-fed the message that their worth is based on the boys they're able to attract and hold onto through meaningless relationships. Once adolescence arrives, it's every girl for herself! She must find the most desirable, available boy and make him hers or face the guilt and loneliness that comes with being a single teenage girl. She has to face the questions her relatives and family friends direct her way at every social event and gathering: "So, you have a boyfriend yet?" "Have your eyes on anyone special?" or my personal favourite, "What's a pretty young lady like yourself still doing single?" It's all a young lady can do to keep her unpleasant thoughts to herself and a polite smile on her face.

Although I don't like that most girls my age are involved in relationships they hardly care about or need, it's not my biggest concern. I worry most about the girls who aren't able to start a budding romance with a boy and eventually begin to doubt their own worth. A lot of young women buy into the myth that having a boy on their arm will somehow complete them or make up for other things they're missing. Maybe they aren't supported or loved enough at home and they find some of that nourishment in relationships with boys. Or maybe they just really want to feel desired and can only prove that significance to the world by being involved in a relationship. Or probably we girls just want to be recognized as whole persons and can only partly achieve that by being part of a couple. Either way, this constant fear is always hanging over girls' heads, whispering doubts and insults every time they refuse to flirt back or ignore boys' advances.

What if I never have a boyfriend? Won't I be miserable and

unhappy watching all of my friends date? Wouldn't I be happier in a relationship?

No. You should be happy now.

The Science of Love

Maria Zlotorzynska, 16,
Eastern/Central

St. Valentine's Day comes and goes, and with it Cupid sends out his usual myriad of arrows. Love is everywhere: in TV, movies, on billboards, and in trashy novels. This overwhelming human emotion is one of the most complex mysteries of humankind. Or is it? Apparently, according to research, love is just a matter of chemistry.

According to scientific evidence, Cupid does not use arrows but rather pheromones. Pheromones are hormone substances released by an organism that get a response from another, most often of the opposite sex. Therefore, we use pheromones to attract a mate. Pheromones work mostly on the olfactory system; however, we cannot consciously perceive them. This is why some people can draw you with an inexplicable charm, while others repel you for no reason.

Another important role in the chemistry of love is played by neurotransmitters. One of the most important mood-controlling neurotransmitters is serotonin. Recently, a team of Italian scientists found that people in love had very low serotonin levels. Even more interesting is the fact that serotonin levels in people suffering from Obsessive Compulsive Disorder (OCD), a disorder that causes people to feel compelled to repeat single actions, were just as low. It was observed that the thoughts of the lovesick study group followed the same obsessive pattern as the OCD group. However, after a year, as passion subsided, the serotonin levels in the lovesick returned to normal.

Another neurotransmitter that plays an important part in relationships is dopamine. Studies have found that people with higher levels of dopamine are more faithful and are more likely to stay in monogamous relationships. People with low dopamine levels, on the other hand, have a tendency to be more promiscuous. However, dopamine levels are also high in drug addicts. Cocaine and amphetamines produce similar effects on heart functions and behaviour—further proof that people in love are just a little nuttier than the rest of us.

Since the dawn of humanity, we have sought to explain the great mysteries of our emotions. Although it might seem that we can now rationally explain the phenomenon of love, anyone suffering from low serotonin levels will attest that this miracle that makes the world go 'round is utterly enigmatic. No matter how long and intensely we muse over this puzzle, we will never fully understand the rationality of love. Yet is the quest not at least half the fun?

Remembering Me

Maya Krishnaratne, 17,
Eastern/Central

From the moment I first laid my eyes on him, the most heavenly creature I had ever seen, I knew I was in love. He was perfect and polished in every way. I don't know if it was his hypnotic eyes that seemed to capture my every thought, or if it was the smooth hum of his angelic voice. I think it was his smile. Oh, his smile. It blew me a thousand sweet kisses without him even knowing. It sent me soaring above the skies and into the deepest heavens. One thing I knew for sure was I was his. He had me.

From the day I heard him say he liked my name, to the last time I saw him, I was wrapped in a magical dream world, which was powerful and real to me in every way imaginable. We would talk about the things I had always longed to talk about, and he actually seemed to understand what I had to say. If he was ever unhappy during the short time I knew him, I never saw it. This guy was all smiles.

He was everything I had ever dreamed of having in a boyfriend, and he wanted me. I felt as though nothing in the whole world could go wrong. He was it, and it wasn't even important that I couldn't concentrate on anything else. What I felt for him was more than any other feeling I had ever known, and that in itself made the whole thing worthwhile. It might have been the way he kissed me, or the way he held me. I'm still not sure. However, it was definitely the way he looked at me that made me feel like the queen he had built me up to be.

Then one day, that all changed. He said he didn't love me. He said he never had. He said I was just a vulnerable object in a well thought-out plan. The fact that I went from everything to nothing in what seemed like no time at all ripped me into a thousand pieces of loneliness. I suddenly wasn't sure where I fit into the world around me and when no one could understand that, I was thrust further into melancholy. My days became painful, and my nights dark and empty pits of nothingness without him.

Then one day I looked at myself in the mirror and asked, "What was the point of all this nonsensical crying and all this misery?" I was putting myself to a test without realizing it. It was a test I seemed to be failing miserably. It was the test of time. I simply wasn't giving myself the time to heal. I was prodding myself on to stay unhappy, because I thought it was the only feeling I was allowed to have. I seemed to have forgotten that things happen in life, not necessarily for a reason, and not because we want them to, but that they just happen. The best we can do is learn from them. There comes a point where we have to stop berating ourselves for the things we don't have control over, and let time heal us. When I finally began to recognize this, I found a truth in myself that allowed me to look for love somewhere else. When I opened my eyes, I came to see that it was everywhere. It was in the air. It was in the laughter around me. It was surrounding me. Most importantly, it was within me.

Of course, I did learn to love again. I found someone else, someone who captured my heart in ways I had never before dreamed possible. But you know what I realized? One day I may turn around and find that he's gone too. I may hurt. I may feel every bit as lonely and upset as I did before. I may not even remember that I'd ever learned to love again. I will remind myself to question why I'm allowing this pain to control me. I'll question exactly what I'm getting

out of it. And like the first time, I'll open up to what's around me, instead of letting anger and confusion boil up inside me. There will be a day when, like someone said, "I'll know it's love when I can't fall asleep because reality is better than my dreams." And it is. I just have to find it in myself first.

Oh Honey, Things to Do When You Break Up ...

Kate McGee, 17,
Eastern/Central

1 Return to yourself. (Convince yourself this is the fun part.) A good first step—please don't be too drastic—is some superficial change to your appearance that announces your rejuvenation-in-the-works. When you look in the mirror, you'll be pleasantly surprised for the first few seconds—"Oh, hey, someone else! Oh no, wait, me." Personally, instead of shaving it all off, I dyed my hair from blond to a colour that actually matches my eyebrows!

2 Listen to your favourite songs, but don't wallow in the songs you listened to as a couple. Problem is, it rules out so much damn good music. Bouncy '80s stuff rocks—how about "Girls Just Wanna Have Fun"? This was so bad—the day after the brutal breakup with Angel Boy, I was lying in my bed halfway between catatonic and the depths of utter despair, and my sister's radio started blaring "Breaking Up Is Hard to Do." I managed a wry smile, an anguished moan, and a "You don't even know the miserable half of it, baby!"

3 Cry, sure. Cry loud when you can. Wrench those sobs out. If you've been holding back the sobs while on the phone to one of the five best girlfriends, filling her in on every detail, take a break to really release. *Aaaaaaaaaah!*

4 Go out with your girlfriend who loves you and makes you laugh so hard you pee in your pants. Maybe you should bring a fresh

pair of underwear because, honey, the last thing you need right now is some kinda infection.

5 Don't ask for your poems back. Assume he needs them for fuel now that he has no one to keep him warm. Ha ha on him. Anyway, you wrote them for him, so they really are his in some strange way. Hope he'll run across them cleaning his room and suddenly realize what a wonderful, rich, deep person you are and come crawling back. God, how I wish that happened. Oh, please, don't let me even hope it.

6 By the way, this worketh not both ways. Keep his comfiest clothes and simply detach them from his woeful memory. If that doesn't work—toss them out! The last thing you need is a painful reminder. This breakup stuff is fun! Whee!

7 Work hard at your job, or that big essay, or even exercise. Your body is amazing, so jump it around a bit. You love living in here! A brisk walk will do.

8 Be alone when you have to, and avoid the wrong people if you can, for example, his deadly cute and vastly more mature elder brother (bad idea), or the sleazy boy who's going to try to take advantage of your state of physical withdrawal, or simpering people who say "Poor you." When my mom asked me (I grant sweetly) for the ninth time if there was anything she could do, I finally said, "Buy me clothing with your money, of which I have no finite concept!" Instead, she mended my cardigan. If your mom buys you stuff, then please send her to me in the mail.

9 Do hang around, in addition to your confidence-boosting girlfriend who made you pee in your pants (by the way, do some Kegel exercises for that incontinence), with your sweet homeboy who knows you far too well ... and restores your faith in boydom. This is crucial, especially when you feel that the amputation of boyfriend really equals the amputation of "r" from the word, and its application to the general male population.

Chapter 5

Sex & Sexuality

Dorothy, You're Not in Kansas Anymore

When I was nineteen, every girl I knew seemed to be toying with the idea of bisexuality. We all wanted boyfriends *and* girlfriends—or at least we thought the idea of being free enough to have both, to experiment, to let our fantasies spill over and sweep us off our feet was too thrilling to ignore.

There was something terrifically glamorous about the idea of having a "lipstick lover." In our minds, being bisexual was all about dressing up in strappy, slinky dresses, holding hands in public (which of course would stop traffic), being playful and flirtatious with each other, and being admired and desired because we were oh so provocative. We didn't stop to consider the reality of loving a girl or her body. And there is a distance to bridge between fantasy and fact that kept many of us from taking the plunge, so to speak.

Yet, if the attraction is real, if the desire is honestly expressed and shared with another person ... what then? Sexual orientation is, I think, something that reveals itself to you. I don't think you pick it.

Figuring out what your crushes mean, making decisions around what and whom you like—it all takes time. You don't need to make any hard and fast decisions by the time you're fifteen. As a human being, you're also a sexual being, which means that as you learn more about yourself, your ideas about sex and love, and who you can love, might change.

Sometimes though, very early on, people have a strong and clear sense about it, and they know that they have physical and romantic desires for people of their own sex. When you know that, you might decide that its time to let others in on the news. It's important then to think about the notion of "coming out," and why you think you should. What will it mean to you and to the people you are coming out to? Will letting other people know make you feel freer and more honest about who you are? Will it mean you're able to talk openly about your experiences with people you trust? Or are you disclosing your sexual preference to draw attention to yourself? Are you doing it to test the notion of unconditional parental love?

It's necessary to understand your motivation before taking action on any big decision in your life. A friend of mine taught me that it is important to include a certain amount of abandon when making decisions, because people will not always like the things you tell them and you have to be prepared to be met with resistance or disapproval. Let's face it, coming out isn't easy—we're not yet at the point as a free society where we can all accept each other's choices and lifestyles. But if you are motivated by goals that you can identify as positive and not vindictive or attention-seeking—forging a more honest relationship with the people you care about, sharing your good feelings about your loves with others—you will at least be happy with your decision to reveal something as potentially explosive as a sexual orientation.

When you do decide to disclose your sexual orientation to your family and friends, the best "scene" is no scene at all. Hopefully your parents will surprise you with their love and support for all of the big decisions you make.

What if they flip, though? Parents are often much more open-minded and rational about issues when their kids are *not* involved in the equation. Why else would your friends like your parents so much?

If your parents are upset, recognize that they're probably afraid of all the things they can imagine happening to you. They fear for your health. They are afraid for your safety.

Your revelation might also force them to examine their own beliefs and prejudices. And maybe they won't want to adjust, review, or acknowledge their views on homosexuality or bisexuality. Even the most progressive of people can have very old-fashioned ideas about relationships and what is "normal."

If your parents do come down hard on you, you might have to give them more space to come to terms with what you've told them. Maybe, as time goes by and they see that you haven't really changed, and that you're not a radically different person from the one they had breakfast with last week, they'll be able to relax a little. Maybe they'll open up a bit more to talk about it. Or maybe they could benefit from a bit more information, or from hooking up with a support group for parents of gays and lesbians (PFLAG—Parents and Friends of Lesbians and Gays—is one). Probably the worst thing you can do is throw it in their face and try to shock them—that will only confirm their worst fears and prejudices.

You have the right to make honest decisions for yourself. You have the obligation to be true to yourself and to respect the truth of who you are. Respecting that means not letting other people impose their views or feelings on you, or persuade you to conform to their way of being if it's not who you are. At the same time, it doesn't mean that you shouldn't listen to the way they feel and help them understand how you came to your decision. If you're involving people you care about, you need to consider their feelings and thoughts. This isn't entirely about you.

If you are having difficulty understanding your own rush and excitement, you should talk to someone trustworthy who can put you in touch with groups, materials, and the kind of guidance you might need to better explore the way you feel. Taking steps towards learning about your sexual yearnings will help you feel more secure in your body and with yourself. There are lots of books, resource centres, and groups to help you learn more about being lesbian or bisexual.

One of the better books I've read on the topic, for both you and your parents, is *So Your Child Is Gay* by Dr. Jerald Bain. He lists plenty of resources in cities across the country. He also suggests the library as a way of finding gay and lesbian bookstores, newspapers, and periodicals. There are also a number of websites that talk about figuring out how to come out to your friends and family and exploring your sexuality.

The important thing in exploring your sexuality is finding out who you are and being true to yourself, even though the trip might take you down a few rocky roads.

Myth:

Sexuality is carved in stone

My pal Joseph made an announcement at dinner a few nights ago. He told a bunch of us that he had fallen in love with a woman he met at the gym. We were stunned and speechless for the most part. Joseph is a gay man. Up until a year ago, he had been in a long and monogamous relationship with a man he met while in his first year of university. We all liked his partner and were sad when they split up. Ten years ago, when Joseph first came out, many of us spent a lot of time reassuring him that his sexual preferences were his business and didn't make any difference to us. A decade ago, we knew less and we were just beginning to learn about gay sex, the transmission of HIV, being bisexual. Still, since we thought of ourselves as sophisticated and liberal, we wanted Joseph to know we valued him as a friend and loved him unconditionally. Over the years, Joseph's flamboyant nature, his meticulous habits, even how smart he is helped us put him in a neat little box marked: gay man. Now what?

The arguments around the table were, in retrospect, a little embarrassing. Some of his friends thought he must just be confused because sexual orientation is genetic and you can't just change your mind, right? Others thought it was understandable and reasonable to go from being straight to gay, but not the other way around. Presumably family pressure, expectations, friends, and even faith can prevent you from exploring the possibility of anything other than heterosexual sex. Somewhere in all the arguing, we forgot that we were talking about a friend who had made a very important decision and that regardless of what this meant for us, the important thing was to support him. Joseph explained his decision by saying that over the past few years he found his attraction to men diminishing, while his desire to be with women had increased to the point where he could no longer deny his feelings. The ensuring conversation about sexual orientation brought up a lot questions. How much of a person's orientation is based on environment? Can you change your mind simply based on being open to your feelings?

A few of us agreed to having been attracted to members of the same sex and having repressed those feelings because that was easier than exploring them. Joseph actually got us to examine our beliefs and to recognize that ideas about yourself can and do change, even with things that you've always taken for granted.

What Does Queer Mean?

Angela Kostenko, 19,
Eastern/Central

What does it mean to be queer? And who are the real queers? I'm a pan/bisexual dyke. That means I'm queer. I like girls, mostly. But I like boys too. One day I might even have sex with a boy (imagine that!). One day I might have sex with a girl (the horror!). One day I might have a boyfriend or a girlfriend. But likely I'll just be terminally single, crushing out on unattainable dykes and femme boys.

According to some girls at "the club" (and some queer people in general), I'm not a real "lesbian." I never claimed to be a "lesbian." And I don't know what would make me a "real" one, as opposed to the fake one they apparently think I am. What makes me queer? What makes them more queer than I am? Is that even possible? Is it because they fuck only girls, and I might not one day? Is it because they've fucked a girl and I haven't (yet)? Is it because I'm occasionally attracted to boys? Is it because I'm attracted to trannies? Is it because I don't dress like them? Is it because I'm not attracted to them? Does this have anything to do with me at all? Your opinion is what makes me more or less queer. I don't think there's a standard that you can measure me against.

I didn't come into "your club" to be cut down. I didn't come here to be told that I'm not queer, or not queer "enough." I'm out there being visible. I'm working in the community, trying to make a difference—a community that seems to be hostile to me a lot of the time. No doubt, you're visible too, but what makes your visibility so much more important?

Sometimes I don't know why I bother trying to help "the community"—the community that doesn't want me because I don't look like them, because I don't fuck like them, because I'm not like them. I'll tell you what. Ignore me, call me names, and tell me what you think I am, and what I'm not (you're probably wrong). But let me ask you: Does my sexuality intimidate you? Does it bother you that much? I'm not asking you to fuck me, or love me, or be my friend. I'm asking you not to judge me. To accept me.

You cannot measure how queer I am. You can't hold up a ruler, or put me on a scale, or pour my blood into a cup and come away with any number that might indicate my level (or lack) of queerness. You can't scare me away. I don't care if you don't like me, and I don't care if you tell all your friends that I'm some sort of fake. The right girl will find out exactly how queer I am.

The rest of the world doesn't see me as "not queer enough"—they only see "queer." When I deal with crank callers, when I solicit donations, when I speak to straight people "as a queer," when they see me on a date with a girl, no one cares to hear about that one boy I'm currently attracted to. You've seen me on dates, you've seen me making out with girls on the dance floor, you've seen me putting it all on the line and getting abused and queer-bashed. What do I have to do to be queer enough? What does "queer enough" mean, anyways?

O.R.

Playgirl

Giselle DeGrandis, 16,
Eastern/Central

Rebel, Rogue, Mischievous Babe

A few weeks ago I bought a *Playgirl* magazine. You know, the magazine that's full of naked men. Not partially clothed ones, like those sexy CK underwear ads—100 percent merchandise-on-display, just-let-it-all-hang-out, buck-naked boys. So I looked. And I looked a little closer. You could even say I leered. Why the hell not? Men leer. Men buy *Playboy* and *Penthouse* and any of the large assortment of dirty magazines on the "top shelf" at the convenience store that cater to their sexual fantasies.

Yesterday, while buying a Freezie at the convenience store (not the same one where I got the *Playgirl*!) a grisly old man was thumbing through the pages of a *Live Young Girls* magazine, which featured a girl who looked about twelve on the front cover. Somehow, nothing seems more obscene than that. Yet even this segment of the population is catered to. How many magazines featuring scantily clad boys do I have to choose from? Very, very few. And even those in existence target, again, the male population—the gay male population, that is.

Playgirl is read by a largely homosexual male audience—despite the caption "Entertainment For Women" on the front cover. Shall we reclaim *Playgirl*, ladies? Or is it even worth it? Likely there is some guy in a suit on the receiving end of all the money made off the magazine.

If gender equality can be measured by the number of adult magazines catering to each sex, we definitely have a long way to go, baby! As a "raging feminist," I won't be happy until there is some woman somewhere in a housecoat and slippers surrounded by completely subservient gorgeous men at a Playgirl mansion—Hefner's daughter, maybe?

As a result of having a number of *Playboy*-subscribing male friends, I decided on a whim to buy the female equivalent, just to wave it around in their faces (and hopefully make them feel the weensiest bit inadequate for once). It wasn't just any old issue, either—it was the "Twins: Too Hot, Too Sexy, Too Hard" issue. The man at the cash didn't say anything (I was worried about getting busted for being only sixteen), but he kind of did a double-take when ringing the sale up, as if he were thinking: "What's the price of this thing? ... Whoa, dirty magazine. Whoa, young girl buying dirty magazine! ... Okay just don't say anything, you don't want to lose the sale!" So he kind of winked at me and asked me if I wanted a bag for it. I said sure, and he slipped it into a silly little see-through thing.

I bought the *Playgirl*, in part, because there is almost nothing online for the young, curious, and female, like myself, to look at. I've accidentally stumbled across enough tasteless photos of naked women to know that there is plenty of that on the Internet. So much that one can't type in the word "girl" in a search engine without hundreds of pornographic sites being listed—a real shock for my little sister who was naively looking for an online pen pal, not exploitative pictures of adolescent girls sexualized before their time. And that's generally the extent of females on the web—they are seen and not heard.

So, why do I have such a double standard? It's okay to exploit the male body but not the female? It's the simple difference between not enough of one thing, and too much of the other. Pornography, as an institution, appears to be a means of oppressing the female and placing further emphasis on our looks, bodies, and physical attributes. It would be nice if the porn industry collapsed entirely and males and females learned to respect one another solely for their personalities, intellectual merit, etc. But that won't happen. If anything, sexual liberation is what we are all still striving for, even years after the sexual revolution—not a reversion to modesty. As the old adage goes, "If we can't lick 'em, we might as well join 'em," and based on this premise, we should be able to "enjoy" men in the same fashion that they "enjoy" women.

Fortunately, there is a growing sector in the sex industry targeting heterosexual women as a market. Something like 30 percent of all adult movies are rented by females. Recently, a Toronto woman tapped into this idea when she started making porno videos for women—ones that actually specialize in what women want to see: a good plot and some foreplay action (as opposed to the "I'm the plumber, let's do it"-type storyline that men seem to enjoy). Stores specializing in sex toys, books, and movies for women are also popping up; women are behaving as sexual counterparts to men. However, I'm still looking forward to the day when my *Playgirl*, carefully hidden under a pile of university brochures in my closet, will once again see the light of day. I'm too embarrassed to overtly possess it. It will be a glorious day when women can use their vibrators at the loudest speed, leave their *Playgirl*s on the coffee table, bookmark eroticaforwomen.com on their computers—and not give a damn about what anyone else thinks of it.

I Am Gay

Alex Ribera, 15,
Eastern/Central

As I flipped through the winter issue of *Reluctant Hero*, an issue dominated primarily by articles addressing girls' sex, sexuality, and sex education, I searched to see if anyone had tackled the ever-avoided issue of girls who like other girls, and I don't mean in a friendly way.

I am familiar with a lot of the girls who write for RH, and I have found them very liberal or "open-minded" people. Why, then, did many of the writers only refer to boys when talking about girls' first experiences with sex, dating, and emotional and physical boundaries? Why, when discussing being so-called sexually liberated individuals, did no one address the fact that there are lots of us who simply don't fit into the heterosexual mould waiting for us on the assembly line of female adolescence? Is it because no one who reads or writes for this magazine is gay or bisexual?

Contemplating this, I began to feel that all-too-familiar sense of isolation as a result of my sexual orientation. Flashbacks of junior high, coming out to myself and my mom while staying closeted at school and to all my close friends, made me think. Chances are that some girl is going through what I went through in junior high right now, probably feeling that she is the only thirteen-year-old lesbian on the planet.

Here's my story. It was my first time going out with someone and her first time seeing a girl, so I think it's fair to say we were both a little insecure, but for different reasons. We had been friends for a while, and as our friendship evolved, I developed a crush on her—and, knowing she was bisexual and really open-minded, I told her. I was secretly worried she'd be really mad and not ever want to see me again, but instead she said something that shocked me. She told me she had "sort of" had a crush on me since she had met me a couple of months before.

Maybe my first clue should have been in the way she told me. It was sort of muffled and embarrassed—dare I say a little shameful. I didn't see her that much afterwards, and when I did, it was kind of tense because I realized she wasn't entirely comfortable with having a crush on me, a girl. There seemed to be a lot of unspoken fear. What would people do if we held hands? What if we ran into my mother?

I was really angry that all these homophobic messages we receive both directly and indirectly from the media, our parents, and school had finally weaseled their way into my first dating experience. I felt cheated and confused.

Coming out was a weird experience. My mom was quite supportive and even drove me to a local lesbian/gay/bisexual youth group in the hopes that by speaking to other gay youth, I would feel less isolated. Of course, I wasn't quite thirteen years old and everyone there seemed about seventeen or older. For a while it seemed okay, but now I realize that she didn't have much space or time to come to terms with it on her own level. Instead, she focused her energy on making me comfortable with it. And so now there is conflict between us because I feel as though she disapproves and resents this part of me. I value the relationship we have, and I know that it's going to take time to work through.

Roundtable

Bisexuality, Masturbation, Need We Say More?

Oh, yesssssss!

Have you heard? Everyone's bisexual these days. Is it true? Is it a trend? We decided to ask a bunch of girls what they think. Irene and Sharda are sixteen; Javiera, Kathleen, and Sonia are fifteen; Kate and Temwachi and Gill are eighteen; while Nicola and Julia are seventeen.

Is it trendy to be bisexual?

Pam: Yes, it is trendy.

What makes it trendy?

Gill: I think it's trendy because people are just more aware of it.

Pam: No, I think it's trendy because sex is always trendy. Now people are jumping on to the latest bandwagon, which is the whole gay movement.

Kate: There was an article in the paper recently about it. Basically, we talk more about sex than any other generation. They're just more comfortable with their bodies now that they experiment sexually ...

Irene: Half the people I know go on about how they're so bisexual, how they're so free with their love and on and on and on. I think it's just a fashion statement because the minute they're put in a situation where they're actually being brutally honest about it, and like, say they found out that one of their friends truly is bisexual and went off with another friend and had a sexual experience, all of a sudden, it's really hush.

Kate: I found that out too in my high school. This happened a lot among the super well-read, super trendy. I'm in the drama club, girls. But when we worked with a feminist group and did outreach stuff with them, and when the gay rights group actually sprung up in my school, there was a major public outcry among people who were not from that socio-economic bracket or people who were not raised on Madonna.

Nicole: I've never met any bisexual guys.

Pam: My friend is gay. He's a guy.

Nicole: I've met guys that are gay, I've met girls that are bisexual, and I've met girls that are lesbians, but I don't think that I've ever met someone who is male and bisexual.

So what is it about being bisexual that appeals so much to girls?

Javiera: I have a couple of friends who actually decided that they should become bisexual. It's a completely trendy thing to do. It was because at that time they were without boyfriends.

Pam: Oh my gosh!

Gill: Well, you need to get your action somehow.

(Laughter)

Javiera: They were like, well, if we can't get guys, then we have to think of something else we can do, right? It wasn't really because they would have more options, it was so that they would be more attractive to guys, because guys have that lesbian thing.

Everyone: Oh, that fetish thing!

Pam: What whole thing?

Javiera: That lesbian thing. Guys love lesbians.

Pam: You mean watching two women together?

Everyone: Yeah!

Javiera: Yeah, they just freak out. So that bisexual thing would be like, well, if I'm bisexual, and I like this guy, and my friend is also bisexual, and maybe she likes this guy, it would attract the guy more to the girls because there's the possibility of the girls doing something together in front of him. That would freak them out completely.

Gill: I was talking with a boy and how it seems like the majority of people that are homophobic happen to be males. He actually said that it's okay for girls to be gay, but not for guys. I thought that was an interesting viewpoint. His take on it was that the female body is much more attractive than the male body ...

Kate: That's how I feel.

Gill: ... and he was asking, which is more attractive for a woman to look at, a naked woman's body, or a naked man's body? I was thinking, probably the woman's body because we can identify with it, and I kind of agree with him that women's bodies do look nicer than men's. That was his reasoning behind his position.

Nicole: I don't really agree. I like looking at guys' bodies. I've never seen a naked guy and a naked girl and compared, but I like looking at guys' bodies, more so because with women's bodies it's like, whatever. With guys, it's ... *I like it.*

Kate: The points that the guy brought were accurate, at least for me. I live with a really misogynist, stupid man among sixteen other students, but he is particularly bad. He said the same thing: he could see girls being bisexual more than guys, because women are naturally more attractive. When I did have a sexual experience with a girl, it was like having another me in bed. This might sound terrible to any person who is politically gay, but it felt like extended masturbation. It was like there were two mes and, plus, I already had the same body shape as the girl anyway. The same brain. That's how we ended up there.

Irene: When I had my first experience with a woman, I thought it was a lot different from being with a guy, but that could be because my first experience with a guy was so scary.

Kate: I felt the same way.

Irene: I thought it was a lot more sensual being with another girl and a lot more ... I don't even know how to describe it. It was different, but not in the same way that I felt with myself.

Kate: For me it was almost the same. It was just so comfortable, partly because our bodies were the same, but also because there was a complete absence of fear. When I'm with a guy, I'm always super nervous. I can be really excited to be there, doing stuff, and then just ... shut down and want to stop.

Irene: I guess a lot of women feel that way, and that's why as long as they're in control, as long as they feel they can direct where things are going, it's very reassuring.

Kate: That was another thing. The communicative difference. My relationships in general with women are so much more sensual and body-based because we are so comfortable with that. We talk about it beforehand, and during, and afterwards. We're more open. Whereas experiences with guys, the next morning they're like, "Ugh, that's never happening again because it'll ruin our friendship and I'm insecure." And that's the end of that.

Javiera: I didn't have that kind of experience. For me, it's been the next day, or five minutes later, we completely talk about it. We can dissect the experience for, like, three hours and go through the whole thing. "I liked that part, but not that part." Big-time communication.

Pam: That's really good. That's lucky that you ...

Kate: It really depends on the guy.

Gill: Where did you get him?

Javiera: Some guys think they know exactly what they're doing, so they just go ahead and do it, they don't even ask. But that's not how it should be.

Kate: Honey, if you're not going to ask for directions, how'm I going to know your needs—a guided tour?

So what did they teach you in school about bisexuality and masturbation?

Everyone: Nothing! Nothing!

Kate: I had a conversation about masturbation with a guy friend. We told each other how we stumbled upon it, and he said that he thought it should be taught in schools because he had no idea what he was doing, and neither did I. It was pretty funny.

Kathleen: Well, I go to a public school where we don't get sexual education. I don't even remember people bringing it up.

Kate: The other thing I notice about masturbation is that guys can make endless jokes about it. They even have a hand motion for it! How hard would it be for a guy to figure out how to masturbate?

Whereas girls aren't really allowed to talk about it, and we don't know about the Great Showerhead Mystery of the Universe. We have to find out on our own.

Pam: I had no idea what a clitoris was, or where it was.

Kate: Me either, until I found it with my showerhead!

Pam: It's definitely the bathroom. The bathroom is the place.

Kate: A place of wonders.

Pam: It's your secret garden.

Temwachi: It starts when you're little, because if your mother won't even say "vagina" around you ... When I started taking showers by yourself, mine would ask me, "Did you wash down there?" Already, you get this feeling that you are supposed to leave it alone from a young age.

Pam: It's like, "Let's not talk about it."

Kate: Or it's "Don't do that," although kids naturally touch themselves. Ever tried to change a baby's diaper? You feel like saying, "Don't touch that, I'm trying to change this, there's shit there, could you please not touch that?"

How easy or hard is it to talk about masturbation with your girlfriends?

Temwachi: I've talked about it with mine.

Pam: I've done it, but it depends on how close you are.

Gill: It's not difficult, but I don't.

Temwachi: I'm very close to my girlfriends. It usually comes up after the topic of guys jerking off comes up. It could be that someone made a joke about it, but after a while, someone always wants to know whether you've done it. No one is willing to answer the question right away.

So why is it so hard?

Temwachi: Because we don't really get to talk about it as freely as guys do.

Pam: Guys are more proud of it.

Sonia: It's almost like it's shameful.

Gill: It's natural for boys but unnatural for girls.

Irene: I read this article that said that 60 percent of women don't even do it. Maybe they've tried it once, but they don't feel comfortable enough with themselves to actually do it.

Gill: Well, I can agree with that because I don't.

Irene: That's exactly my problem.

Well, do you ever use visual aids? Or a Harlequin? Is that when girls start?

Gill: I never read Harlequins.

Pam: I've read a vast numbers of Harlequins and I'm proud of it, thank you very much.

Sharda: What's Harlequin?

They're romance novels.

Pam: Here are the stats on Harlequins. Women who read them have sex about three to four times a week, as opposed to those who don't, who have sex about once to three times a week.

Gill: That's made up, I don't believe that. If they're so busy reading, they don't have time for sex.

Who here masturbates?

Pam: Do we have to say?

Is that question harder to answer than "Who has sex?"

Everyone: Yes.

Pam: It's like asking if you're gay.

Do you think it's a dirty thing to do? Where did that idea come from?

Sharda: Just the idea that ever since you're little, girls are cute, pretty, and clean. Boys are the dirty ones. So if a girl touches herself, she's nasty.

Irene: If a boy pulls himself, he's just a boy. If he hawks on the ground, that's another boy thing. I remember distinctly being told by my mother, don't do that, boys do that.

Even with scratching, boys can do it, girls can't.

Temwachi: You have to go to the bathroom if you want to do that.

Pam: Guys shouldn't scratch in public. They shouldn't hawk on the ground, either. I think all that's dirty.

Everyone: But it's accepted.

Javiera: The guys themselves feel more comfortable doing it.

Pam: Personally, I have no hang-ups talking about masturbation. I masturbate, okay? There you go. I don't have a problem talking about it with my friends, but I wouldn't talk to my parents about it. I wouldn't talk about sex at all with my parents, and that's just the way it is.

Irene: Yeah! That's a non-comfortable thing in the house. I remember once when my boyfriend came over, my mother turned to him at the dinner table and told him that she didn't approve of him fucking her daughter. I ingested my tongue! He said, "I'm sorry that you feel that way because I'm really in love with your daughter."

Were you having sex in your bedroom?

Irene: Yes. I wasn't going to do it in a back alley.

Are you allowed to have sex in the bedroom?

Irene: It's not discussed. My parents said that they didn't feel comfortable with the idea of us screwing in the bedroom.

What time of the day does this happen? Is it an evening thing?

Irene: It's not like we have a schedule we follow.

Do you do it when your parents are home?

Irene: Yes.

Pam: I think that's wrong. Even if I had a boyfriend, I wouldn't have sex with him while my parents were home.

Gill: Your parents have sex while you're there.

Pam: That's different. That's their right, they live in that house. For me it would seem disrespectful.

Irene: I asked my mom if she would rather pretend that I don't have sex when she knows that I do. She seems pretty free to talk about birth control, but when it comes to actually doing the deed, she would rather that I did it hush in some back alley. If she's comfortable enough to tell me that I need to use a condom, why can't she be comfortable enough to accept the fact that I'm actually going to use it?

Temwachi: No, I think it's about respect. If your parents told you not to have sex in their house, you should respect that.

I guess all parents want their kids to be safe. So I suppose if there's nowhere else to go with your boyfriend, your parents might let you, but ...

Pam: ... they don't want to condone it by saying, yes, have sex in my house.

Irene: I've noticed certain little things that led me to believe that they are presently aware of me having sex and that they are okay with it. The other day my boyfriend came over, and we eventually had sex in my room. Later, I learned that I had had seven phone calls, but my dad never came up to tell me.

Pam: Your parents are soooo open-minded.

Sharda: My mom won't let me sleep over at my friend's house, girl or guy. They have this freaky idea that I'm going to a friend's house to have sex all night long. It's something that I don't understand. I'm a teen. I want to spend some time with my friends and eat cookie dough, or have pillow fights, and that stuff can only be done at a sleepover. You can't!

Pam: The same with my parents. I've never slept over at anyone's house ever.

Javiera: I sleep over at my friend's house and his mother is convinced that we're having sex. They can't accept us being just friends. When I sleep over, I get his room and he has to sleep downstairs on the couch.

Sonia: I think my parents would be comfortable talking to me about sex, but I wouldn't feel comfortable talking about masturbation with them.

Pam: Exactly, what would you say? "Dad, by the way, don't come into my room tonight, I'll be masturbating."

Javiera: I think it would be awkward to talk to your parents about what an orgasm feels like.

Nicole: My parents gave me books to read.

Javiera: It's hard to get information, though.

Pam: I think the issue is being comfortable with your own body. If you do it, and it's good for you, fine. That's what I want to tell people. It's okay to talk about it. It's not wrong, and you're not going to grow hair on your palms. And if you don't do it, that's okay, but make sure you're not doing it for the right reasons. Make sure it's not because you can't touch down there because it's a forbidden place, because that's called repression.

Temwachi: There's a test in a book I read once. It tells you to go get a mirror, take off your panties, and look. Some people have never done that. They don't know how their genitals look. I think you can use the masturbation thing as part of finding out about yourself. Go get a mirror and look anyway.

Javiera: If a guy knows that a girl masturbates, he finds it attractive. Part of the reason being that the girl then knows what makes her feel good, so she can tell the guy, too. That's important.

Sonia: We should be comfortable with the idea of masturbation, whether we do it or not. It's also good to know your body, to be comfortable with it psychologically, as well as for health reasons. You have to know if your body changes or look for signs indicating that something is wrong.

Playing It Safe

Deciding whether or not you are ready to have sex can be difficult. It's something you have to be really certain about, and also something you should spend some time discussing with your partner. If it's not a subject the two of you can talk about comfortably, you might want to wait. Hey, if you're not ready to talk about it, you might not be ready to do it, either. Once you have sex, everything changes. It's a weird thing, but once you've done it, it's hard not to want to do it again. Your body kind of craves it. You also need to think carefully about whether or not you're ready for changes in the way you feel that come with having sex. Many young women who have become sexually active say that they wish they had waited a little longer because the focus in their lives changed as a result. "I went from hanging out with my friends, doing stuff by myself, to totally focusing on how to be pretty for him," one young woman says.

Sex is something we all wonder about, and whisper about—so why is it so difficult for our parents and teachers us to talk to us about it openly? The mere mention of the topic is enough to turn parents into frightened rabbits, scurrying off for a copy of *Sex, and How to Live Without It*, or one of those frightening medical school anatomy texts with pop-up pictures of the reproductive system. And the attitude in schools seems to be "Please don't ask, so we don't have to tell you, because quite frankly we haven't figured it out yet ourselves."

"Most sex education in schools is about avoidance," says Kim Martyn. Martyn is a sex educator, and I called her to find out what she thinks of the new standardized curriculum recently introduced in Ontario schools and its approach to sex-ed. "The curriculum has only the very minimum of what kids need to know. It can be taught in an hour. There's nothing in the curriculum that imparts knowledge, or opens discussion regarding sexual exploration, orientation, or pleasure."

One young woman I spoke to believes that the issue of feelings is never addressed because "teachers are afraid that it's going to make girls promiscuous and turn into vixens just because we're coming to terms with our sexuality. They talk about girls as sexual predators. And we're told that 'boys will be boys' and they can't control themselves. They should give everyone some credit."

To improve the curriculum, "kids should be taught to talk about their emotional needs, and about everything in the context of a relationship, and in the context of respecting your body and yourself," one high school student suggests. "They should also talk about alcohol and how you should avoid it because it becomes an excuse for not saying, like, 'Okay that's enough,'" she adds. Another young woman believes that at least parts of sex education should be taught in co-ed classes so that the genders can talk to each other. She says, "I think boys need some direction, because when they get into some situations where they're with a girl, they have no clue, so they're really aggressive. If they were in class with girls, the girls would be able to tell them, 'This is how we want to be treated.'"

If you've decided that you are ready to have sex, you should talk with your partner about birth control and protection from sexually transmitted diseases (STDs). You can actually die from have unprotected sex. And while you might not know anyone who has AIDS or HIV, that doesn't mean you are safe. You can't really rely on someone telling you about their sexual history and any STDs they might have had along the way. People do forget. And sometimes they lie.

Having sex for the first time is a huge step. If you're ready to have sex, you are ready to set boundaries and rules for yourself concerning safer sex. If you decide that you will never have sex without a condom, and that you will stop if you don't have a condom handy, even when things get passionate, you will almost always be safe. But the decision to protect yourself must be made *before* you ever begin. It's not something you can easily decide at the time, because all that desire gets in the way.

In terms of contraception there are lots of choices. There is, of course, the pill, at least to prevent pregnancy. If you can handle the hormone hell (severe mood swings) it can sometimes put some bodies through, especially during the first few months, it's an effective choice when taken consistently. Take it consistently and couple it with a condom against STDs, and your bases are covered. By the way, in order for the pill to be effective, it needs to be taken for a complete month before you can have sex safely. Think of that time as a kind of grace period, a chance to think things through again and be sure that you are really comfortable with your decision.

Another option is the female condom, which is actually pretty good. It really doesn't look or feel like you're wearing a great big garbage bag, contrary to popular misconception. It is a little pricey at $12 for three. And it takes a little getting used to, so you'll want to experiment, the same way guys are told to practise using a condom in private before whipping one out for the big moment.

There are at least seventeen different methods of birth control available. You might need to make a few visits to your doctor to find one that is right for you. If you are not comfortable talking to your family doctor, look in the Yellow Pages for a walk-in clinic. If you are unclear on how to use the contraceptive method you've chosen, insist on being shown and told again—it's too important to leave to chance. A twenty-minute visit to your doctor isn't really enough time to know that you're ready to have sex, or that you've selected and understood how to use a method of protection that's right for you. Once you become sexually active, you'll need to visit your doctor annually for a Pap smear and a gynecological exam. Annual Pap smears are necessary to detect ovarian cervical cancer.

Once you're sure you're happy with your decision, and you and your partner have figured out what to do about protection, it's time to think about setting the scene for that first time. Too many first experiences are lousy. They happen in the back seat of cars, at parties, in ways that are not special and memorable. If you find the opportunity presents itself, but the setting isn't right, or you don't feel good about it and you've changed your mind, stop. Ask your partner to stop, and tell him very clearly that it doesn't feel right. If your spidey-sense is tingling and you are feeling weirded out from the beginning, DON'T LET IT GO TOO FAR. It's not fair to be too easygoing about your responsibility. Besides, you don't want to take the chance that your partner will not hear you or heed you. If you've decided to take this step, make sure it's fabulous and not traumatic.

Hopefully, you will have plenty of time and a comfortable setting and lots of condoms handy, just in case the first one doesn't quite work, or stay on, or whatever.

Now, what happens if your birth control method fails? Remember, if you are going to be sexually active, no birth control method is foolproof. Are you ready to handle the consequences of becoming pregnant?

If your period is late and you suspect you might be pregnant, you should speak to your doctor. You might want to buy a home pregnancy kit to test first. They're about $12 to $15 and easy to use. If it turns out that you are pregnant, see your doctor as soon as possible.

Your faith or upbringing will probably play a role in determining whether or not you can terminate the pregnancy, put the baby up for adoption, or find the support you need to raise your little one. Although only you should decide what happens to your body, maybe the first step is to talk to your doctor, who can advise you on how to tell your parents and the baby's father. In Ontario and B.C., teenagers are considered able to consent to an abortion. In other provinces, the age when hospitals require a parent's consent varies. If you keep your baby, raising a child is not easy. You will need lots of emotional and financial support. Will the baby's father help you? He does have a financial obligation towards the baby, which is enforceable by law. Will your parents help you? Will you be able to continue your education? Are you prepared to be a parent? These are good questions to ask yourself before you have sex. Although the final decision about carrying the pregnancy to term or having an abortion should be made by you alone, you don't need to weigh all of the factors by yourself. Talk to trustworthy adults, including your parents and your partner's parents and your doctor.

Many times, however, talking to your parents and your partner's parents can seem absolutely impossible. There are counselling services available through Planned Parenthood, various youth hotlines, and women's health centres at hospitals, which a doctor could probably steer you towards.

If you determine that you're not ready to bring up your baby, you might want to consider giving the child up for adoption. Abortion is not your only option. Whatever decision you make, it will change your life. You need to be able to accept that change and be ready to deal with it.

Deciding to have sex, choosing the right birth control, and protecting yourself from STDs can be very complicated, but it needs to be done. If all of this feels like it's too much, you might be better off just fooling around. Spending hours kissing and touching and even giving and receiving oral sex might be an appropriate alternative to going all the way.

It is possible to contract an STD through oral sex, so health practitioners recommend using condoms or a dental dam. A dental dam is basically plastic wrap that covers the vagina, so that mouth and vagina never come into contact. And fingers work really well, if you're not interested in putting your mouth on a penis or vagina.

Learning how to make your partner feel good, and also being able to tell him or her what feels good, is a skill. Before taking the leap to the big stuff, figure out if your partner can please you and take direction. Get used to letting your partner know what you like. Being able to do that will lead to more satisfying sex later.

Though sex comes into your life all wrapped up in out-of-control feelings and difficult decisions, it can also be one of the most amazing and important things that will happen to you on the way to being an adult. Enjoy it. If you're online, caral.ca is a good resource.

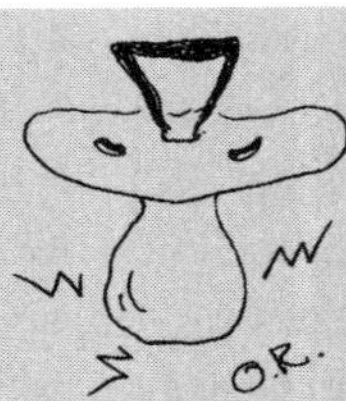

Myth:

Having a baby will make everything alright

Sometimes I have this crazy feeling that my biological clock is ticking and I want to have a baby. Normally, I don't even notice babies. I think they're okay, but I'm not really driven to *ooh* and *ahh* and coo at them. Sometimes, though, I still get the urge to have one ... and then I get over it and wish for a puppy to wrestle with instead.

A girlfriend of mine pointed out that often girls and women desire to have a baby when they feel insecure or unloved in a relationship. I thought her observation was pretty astute. I began to talk to other women—some with children, and some who have been in long-term relationships—to see how they felt.

I know that it might seem as though most teenage pregnancies occur because adequate contraception is not used. But actually, for many of the young women who had a child while they were in their teens, the desire to have a baby was related to the expectation that a baby would provide them with the love they were missing.

I don't think that expectation is very different from the hope, expressed by some of the adult women I spoke to, that having a baby would "fix" the relationship. They imagined that the baby, acting as a symbol of all the love between them, would be a reminder to both people of their reasons for getting together in the first place.

Having a baby as a single mother can be the toughest, most exhausting, most isolating experience there is. It might be a long time before you really feel any of all that love that you bestow on a demanding infant coming back to you—it's a pretty one-sided relationship. And even a secure, happy marriage can be put to the test when a baby shows up.

If you have the urge to procreate, try to identify the reasons for your feelings. Are you in a relationship that is loving and strong? Is that relationship secure enough to bring a child into?

So You're Ready to Have Sex

Amanda Angus a.k.a. Mosquito, 16, Eastern/Central

"You want to know why teenagers have sex? It's wonderful, it's fantastic, it's sensual, it's unbelievable, it's orgasmic, it's erotic—and sometimes, just sometimes, skateboarding can't do that for you."

—Unknown

So you've decided that you're ready for sex. Maybe you just want to get the whole first time over with. Or maybe you're sure that casual sex is your thing. Or maybe you're even head over heels in love, and you've decided that this person is who you want to share your first sexual experience with. Whatever your reason for deciding to do the deed, there are some things you should make sure of first.

You are comfortable with nakedness. When I decided that I wanted to have sex, I was ready for the actual sex part. I was not, however, actually ready to be *naked*. I hated my body for various reasons and I was worried that my boyfriend would think that I was ugly. Of course, I wasn't aware of all this until the time came to have sex, so I freaked out a little. I'm still glad I did it, but I wasn't as prepared for nakedness as I could have been.

You're not being stupid about protection. Duh. Have, at the very *least*, one of these: condoms, spermicide, birth control pills, diaphragm. Pregnancy when you're young sucks major ass, whether you decide to abort or keep the baby. Keep in mind, though, that condoms are the only ones that'll protect you from STDs, which also suck. Which brings me to my next point ...

You want to have sex with your partner. That means that you know they don't have any diseases. It also means that you are both aware of what you're expecting. Are you just in it for casual sex, but your partner wants a meaningful relationship, or vice-versa? Make sure this is clear. Also, if you just want a fling with someone you don't really know (which isn't a good idea, but still), try to make sure they won't become a clingy annoyance afterwards. (This goes for just making out with someone too.) I once kissed a guy I didn't really know simply because he seemed nice and I figured I'd never see him again after the weekend, only to have him think that we were in a serious relationship and tell me he was in love with me after a day. Eek.

You know how you're parents would react. I'm not saying that you shouldn't have sex because your parents would disapprove. I just mean that some parents are okay with it, and might actually help you get birth control or other forms of protection. My parents always made a point of saying that I could go to them for anything, so I asked my mom if I could go on birth control. She said yes, and made an appointment for me. If you know your parents would freak out and whatnot, or if you're not sure how they would react, don't tell them. Obviously.

You're not expecting some immensely orgasmic experience. If you're a girl, chances are that your first time is going to *hurt* like *hell*. I'm serious, it hurts. The hurt is over fairly quickly, but while it's there, ouch. And even after the pain goes away, your first time probably isn't going to be *amazing*. Don't worry, sex gets better, but don't set your hopes too high the first time, unless your partner is a wildly experienced super sex-machine.

Have all of the above figured out, and your debut sexual experience will probably be a lot better than if you ignore it all. If you choose to ignore it, well, fine, but don't blame me when you freak out about being naked, the sex isn't as good as you thought it should be at *all*, you get pregnant and get genital herpes, your partner decides you should get married when you just want him to go away, and your parents tell you that when you do decide to have sex, you can come to them if you want to go on birth control.

Giddy-up.

Sexual Myths and Misnomers

Corinne Alstrom a.k.a. Mophead, 15, Eastern/Central

Virginity and the Hymen

So when I have intercourse for the first time, will I bleed because my hymen broke?

This is wrong on so many levels, I'll answer it a bit at a time.

A woman who has not had sexual intercourse before (a.k.a. a "virgin") does not always bleed during her first time, and it is not always painful. If her partner is patient, both she and her partner are prepared for the task, and the vagina is lubricated either naturally or with an artificial lubricant, first intercourse can be quite comfortable, and doesn't have to hurt. (By the way, you can get pregnant during your first time, but you knew that, right?)

A hymen is a piece of tissue that covers the vaginal opening, and it does not "break." Usually, the hymen has small holes (or one big hole), and those holes erode and get bigger during a woman's life. When she is first penetrated, there is no popping sound, because the hymen does not and cannot pop. On very rare occasions, a woman's hymen is completely intact. In this case, it needs to be operated on by a gynecologist, who makes a small incision in the hymen, to allow menstrual blood and vaginal fluids to come out. The hymen is not way up in the vagina. If you've felt sort of a "plug," it was probably your cervix way up there. That would feel like the end of your nose, with a little dimple in the middle.

Many women are born without hymens, and those who are usually rupture it pretty early in their lives. When a hymen erodes, or gets small tears during sex, tampon use, or hard sports, there is often a small amount of blood. But these activities don't always tear the hymen, and it doesn't always bleed.

By the way, being penetrated with a larger object or penis will not widen or "loosen" a vagina any more than those giant Gobstoppers loosen your mouth.

If I have manual/oral/anal sex, am I still a "virgin"?

Actually, here's the deal on "virginity." Only you define what it is to you. Some people think that only vaginal sex determines whether someone is a virgin or not. But by this definition, lesbians and gay men remain virgins for their entire lives, no matter how much sex they've had. Also, rape and abuse victims usually don't consider themselves "de-virginized" by the attacker, even if it was vaginal sex. And as you already know, the hymen has nothing to do with virginity. Does it empower you to base your entire sexual identity on a piece of tissue?

So basically, if you think you're a virgin, you are. If you think you aren't a virgin, then you really aren't. Personally, I prefer not to use the word at all, but instead I say "a person who has not had sex yet." At any rate, there isn't any way for a person to know whether or not you've had certain kinds of sex, unless you're wearing a sign. Or, of course, you tell them.

The Elusive Orgasm

How do you know if you've had an orgasm? Is it like on those Herbal Essences commercials?

Well, let's start off by defining what the orgasm is. In simple terms, an orgasm (coming, cumming) is the peak of sexual excitement.

Before the orgasm come several stages. The first is the stage of sexual desire. This is basically "wanting sex," or "being horny." This stage is completely in the mind. The next stage is sexual arousal. That's when your body joins your mind in wanting sex. Blood starts pumping toward the genital area. In men, this means getting an erection of the penis, or "getting hard." The blood fills up these sponge-type thingies called the corpus cavernosa, and when they're full, the penis is hard. Isn't that neat? In women, the blood collection means that the clitoris and inner labia get firmer and a bit larger, almost like a man's erection. The clitoris peeks out of its hood (although some clitorises are so small that they don't, and some are so large that they're already out of the hood). The vagina also produces lubrication. The plateau phase comes next. This is a stage of intense excitement. Often men produce Cowper's gland secretion, or pre-cum, at this point. Yes, it does have sperm in it, and yes, it can certainly get someone pregnant.

The orgasm (yay!) finally comes after this. Different things bring different people to orgasm, which is why those "secret sex tips" in magazines are usually just tactics to get people to buy them. Some people can be brought to orgasm by having their elbows massaged, and some people can even have orgasms without ever being touched. In women, this may or may not involve the ejaculation of a clear fluid. Surprised? It happens. In men, the orgasm may or may not include ejaculation of semen (cum). This is also called "shooting the load." That's kind of a misnomer because it doesn't always shoot across the room. And that's okay.

The blood that's been pooling in the genitals is expelled by a series of muscular contractions. Sometimes people make sounds during different stages, and sometimes people are silent. It really depends on the person. Orgasms come in all different forms. Sometimes they're just like a tickle, sometimes they're like an atom bomb.

Most people get their first orgasms from masturbation. Most people do masturbate, and no, it doesn't cause blindness, back problems, or hairy palms, whatever that is. Have you ever seen someone with hairy palms? No, it's not "gross," and no, it doesn't make you "lose your virginity."

After the orgasm comes the resolution stage. This is just a relaxation of the entire body. Sometimes people fall asleep during this stage because the body is so relaxed. In the mind, there is often a feeling of well-being. You don't need to have an orgasm to reach the resolution stage. Lots of people don't know that. For example, some people complain about vasocongestion (blue balls), and say that they "need sex," or they'll be hurt somehow. They won't. They can just let it go away. Extra blood drains out of the genitals, and the heartbeat slows back to normal. Erections go away, clitorises retract.

Phew! Yes, it is a lot, but it's darn complicated science. And you thought you just had to use organic shampoo.

My Experience with Jesus H.

Leta Malcolm a.k.a. Super Banana, 16, Eastern/Central

Note to readers: Just so you all know, Jesus H. is the "Baby Think It Over" that I was required to care for one weekend for my parenting class. He is Satan spawned.

When I first received Jesus H., I expected pretty much what I got. He cried *constantly*, and would never let me have a moment's peace. I did, however, expect a pattern of some sort, like you would get with a real child (e.g.: feed, then burp, then change). Unfortunately, this did not happen according to my plans. Jesus H. apparently found it "funny" and "cute" to need to be fed every fifteen minutes. He ate more than anything I've ever seen in my entire life, and did a fine job of eating just as much at night. Jesus H. loves attention.

By having basically raised my friend's child, there was not too much about the experience that caught me off guard. I think the biggest thing I had to deal with was my ID. (My ID was an electronic tag that I had to place on his back before he could receive care.) It took me some time before I would remember to put in my ID before trying to feed Jesus H. Being a parent is not my idea of a great eighteen years, but I knew this before.

People are a lot more gullible than I previously thought. I took Jesus H. along with me to the movies and prayed he wouldn't cry. Fortunately, he chose that time to stay quiet. I had a lot of people walk up to me and start saying things like "Oh, is he yours?" "How precious" "Can I hold him?" "How old is he?" and "Ooh! What's his name?" I would usually respond by showing them his face so they realized he's not real, and explain the situation. A few times, I couldn't be bothered to explain anymore, so I claimed that he was two months old, named Jesus H., and yes he was mine, and no you can't hold him, he's sleeping. People actually believed Jesus H. was real. This astounds me. A very telling experience was when I got kicked out of Chapters when he got fussy and I couldn't quiet him. I was surprised, because if Jesus H. was real they wouldn't have kicked me out. But unfortunately the guard had seen me try to use the key, and realized he wasn't real. I got mad and took full opportunity to "express" myself to the guard. Friday night was odd, however. Jesus H. decided to play dead, and didn't make a *single noise* for five hours. I thought I had killed him and was duly upset. Just as I fell asleep at 2:30 a.m., Jesus H. started to cry. I was very relieved. IT'S ALIIIIIIIIVE!

My family's reactions were quite varied. Everyone was annoyed when Jesus H. cried loud enough to wake us *all* up. During the day, however, everyone's reactions were different. My little brother hated him. He wouldn't even talk to me if Jesus H. was near me. My older brother was indifferent, as long as he didn't have to hold him. My mum wouldn't help me so that it would be more "real." My dad just didn't care. He dealt with it. My boyfriend's reaction was along the lines of "Please don't bring that near me, it smells like a kid. I hate kids." It was actually kind of funny.

Overall, I can't say that I actually learned much. Raising a baby is really nothing new to me, but that doesn't make it any less taxing. I must admit, by Monday morning I will be glad to give him back. This experience, if anything, reassured my already solid opinion about not wanting kids, especially not right now. Jesus H. really chapped my ass.

Teen Parent

Twyla McLachlan, 15,
West Coast

This year has been one of the hardest years of my life. I am a fifteen-year-old girl. I am different from the rest of my grade—I am a teen parent. I have a thirteen-month-old son.

I still remember the dreaded day when I had to tell my parents that I was about to have a child. My parents didn't know what to say, and they didn't talk to me for a couple of days. I was eight months along, and I was so unprepared for what the future was holding for me. My parents and I had to go to a bigger city three weeks before I was due. While I was down in Nanaimo, I had a chance to talk to some adoption agencies and the doctors, but I was not satisfied with what they were telling me. I would only get pictures of my son and I would only get to see him a couple times a year. That just didn't work for me. On September 28, 1998, at 6:00 a.m., we went to the hospital so that the doctors could induce labour. That night at 10:43 p.m., my son arrived weighing in at 9 pounds and 1.5 ounces. My life had just started.

There are some times that I wish it never had happened, like when my son is sick and cranky. I don't know what is wrong with him, he is crying, I am getting frustrated, and all I want to do is cry with him. Teen parenting definitely has its disadvantages over being a regular teenager. When I want to go out to a big party and I can't find a sitter, it is frustrating to know how much fun all of my friends are having while I am at home with my son. One thing that happens to all parents is their children get up during the night, sometimes at 2 a.m. and again at 4 a.m. Sometimes they don't go back to sleep, and all they want to do is play. My son started to sleep through the night when he was 12 months, but he still gets up once in a while.

Some teens receive an allowance and they can spend it on anything that they wish. I don't get an allowance. I get money from the government and my day care is provided. Any money that I do receive I spend on diapers, milk, lunch stuff, clothes for when Logan gets too big, and medicine. At the end of the month, I don't even have enough money to get myself anything, like a new pair of jeans or a new shirt or a pair of shoes. Everyone tells me that my life is so easy. It's not that I don't have any spare time. Some of my spare time is spent on the ice. I play hockey for the Women's hockey team and the Bantam hockey team.

The good part about being a teen parent is the way you look at your child and the way they look back at you with their big loving eyes, showing just how much love they have for you. Also, when you go down to the park and push them on the swing they laugh because of all the fun they are having. When they say their first word, all you want to do is call everyone because it is so exciting. The most memorable moment that I have is the time that my son took his first step, and now we have to move everything up high and make everything so sturdy so he won't get hurt. I will never ever regret giving birth to the most important thing in my life: my baby.

Friday:

5:15 – get up and get ready for hockey
6:15 – on the ice
7:15 – off the ice
7:30 – go home and have a shower and get myself and my son ready for school
8:15 – leave to go to school
8:30 – start school
1:15 – finish school
2:00 – go downtown and go shopping
3:30 – start dinner
5:00 – eat
6:00 – clean up dinner mess
6:30 – put my son in the tub
7:00 – read book and put my son to bed

7:30 – do my homework
8:15 – leave for hockey
8:30 – on the ice
9:30 – off the ice
9:45 – go home and have a shower
10:00 – go to sleep
3:30 – up with my son for another bottle

Chapter 6

Boys

Bewitched, Bothered, and Bewildered

My younger brother and I are pretty tight. Maybe it's because our horoscopes complement each other, or maybe it's because of the seven-year age difference, or maybe we just got lucky. Whatever the reason, we somehow managed to avoid the usual sibling problems and instead became good friends. For a guy, he's an excellent listener, and he gives solid advice. He can almost always see both sides of an issue, but he invariably sides with me (so what's not to adore?).

Isn't that unusual? I mean, boys aren't supposed to be great talkers, and they're not supposed to be into anything but video games, cars, and girls. I'm willing to believe that he's unique, except that I have a few other guy friends who also talk, share their feelings, and act silly.

I thought maybe it was just my friends, but during one of my visits home, my brother and a bunch of his buddies were hanging out one evening in the living room. It was late, and after my parents disappeared for the night, somehow the conversation turned to sex. I was surprised to learn that most of my brother's male friends, except the two who had been in long-term relationships since high school, were still virgins. Isn't that unusual for nineteen-year-old guys?

It's not that they hadn't had ample opportunity—well, okay, maybe that was part of it. But they also said that they were waiting because they wanted it to be special. They even said that older male friends had told them that their first experience would affect the relationships they had later. "I know lots of guys who have had bad first experiences and feel that it had something to do with the series of one-night stands that followed," one of the guys revealed.

Who knew? Certainly, the desire for that very first experience to be special is something you hear from girls all the time. But guys? Not really. Or is it that we just assume things about all guys, like that they're only ever interested in one thing, or that they have trouble talking about their feelings?

Sometimes it is hard to know what guys are thinking or feeling. But in talking to young women about the men in their lives, it seems their experiences with boyfriends, brothers, and guys as best friends paint a picture that is quite different from the stereotype of a guy that we've been handed.

My brother's friends also talked about their fears of not being liked. I know guys have self-esteem issues, just like girls, but I was surprised at how comfortable they were talking about their insecurities concerning women and the expectations they have for themselves in terms of success. They also talked about how hard it is to figure out how to give a girl a compliment. "If you tell a girl she looks great," one of the guys said, "she'll immediately ask you if that means she didn't look great yesterday. What are you supposed to say to that?" And here I thought they just weren't paying attention!

Maybe some of the stereotypes about guys have developed because they don't speak up and refute them.

One of the most common ones is that girls develop eating disorders because guys want girls to be thin. But the guys I talked to actually said that they think girls who are athletic-looking are much more attractive than girls who look like beanpoles. The athletic figure can be just as challenging to have as the thin ideal, but I think when guys say "athletic," we interpret that to mean buff and toned, when really they're saying, "I want to hang out with a girl who likes to play, a girl who is comfortable in her body and doesn't look awkward with a ball, racquet, or club in her hand."

In a high school survey conducted several years ago, guys were asked to review four female body types that were sketched on a piece of paper, the images ranging from thin to fat, and to circle the one that most appealed. They almost all circled the figure with the average build—not too fat, not too thin. "Average" doesn't mean overly muscular or super-thin; it means in proportion. We've all seen girls who have "big head syndrome," where they've lost so much weight that their head looks too big for their tiny bodies, so they no longer look as though their parts are balanced.

Just as fast as the rules and roles for girls are changing, they are changing for guys, too. Maybe guys do have a harder time talking about their feelings because, in the past, they were given a more clear idea of what it meant to be a man. Men don't cry. Men aren't soft. Men are the providers. Now the message they're getting is: be soft and cry, if you want to. They might like that message, because it's healthier. But there are other messages that men find it harder to live with, like the ones that ask them to give up the responsibilities they once prided themselves on: the responsibility to protect a woman; the responsibility to provide for a family; the responsibility to represent the family out in the world. And then there is the backlash from men who hate the idea of ever having to look at the world realistically through a woman's eyes. I know lots of guys in their twenties and thirties who talk about how women are given more opportunities than men and that it's almost a liability to be a white male. They're wrong.

As it turns out, women still make seventy-one cents to every man's dollar for the same job performed at the same level. And men still hold most of the senior executive posts in most organizations, even in fields dominated by women. Take a look at the senior management at your local library and you'll see what I mean.

Understanding the myths and stereotypes about guys isn't easy. To figure out what they really think, we should probably take the lead and ask them. On the next few pages you will find the transcription of a roundtable discussion that features five guys. Instead of condensing everything they had to say about girls, including their ideas about what makes a girl seem sexy or attractive and what is a complete turnoff, I thought we'd let you read what they had to say verbatim.

Myth:

Guys have it easy

Growing up, my parents always seemed to be more lenient with my older brother. They bent the rules to accommodate his late nights, girlfriends, and occasional surliness—things I could never have gotten away with, even for a minute.

The double standard was just a fact, and no amount of quiet interrogation helped me understand why I was subject to a different set of rules. My parents didn't believe they had to explain. Fair enough. Those were the rules. I was simply supposed to understand that boys and girls are different and that the restrictions imposed on me were for my own good.

To be fair, I think I chafed against the "unfairness of it all" more out of principle than because it mattered terribly. It's not as though I was missing out on the parties or had tons of friends to hang out with; I was a bit of a nerd. I escaped peer pressure, but I was left with the niggling feeling that guys have it easy. They can do whatever they want without censure. They're confident. They don't worry about their weight. No one ever says "no" to them.

The truth is, my brother didn't really have it that easy. As the first of three children, he had to test, push, plead, and cajole my parents all of the time. He also often did things because he was rebelling against authority, rather than because they were the right things for him to do. As someone who was cool and tough, he had an image to preserve.

Guys might seem to have it easier than girls because they don't question their own ability to do things. The alchemy of courage and bravado many guys exhibit gives them and others the confidence to believe they can handle any challenge. Girls are sometimes saved from the scrapes and bruises of hands-on learning by fathers, brothers, even mothers who tell them what might happen based on previous experience. Confidence is born from engaging and doing, not simply reading or hearing about the experience.

The young men I've spoken to about "how easy guys have it" say that more and more, guys are asked to be sensitive new-age men, who can share their feelings, while also being "the man." If you look at current movies, a pretty good barometer of social attitudes, tough guys like Stallone, Schwarzenegger, and Van Damme are out. Actors who can play tough but sensitive are the flavour right now.

Some of the young men I spoke to also said that it's a myth that guys don't care about their weight or body image. "Would there be as many diet supplements, or muscle-building proteins, or steroids on the market if we didn't care?" one of them asked me.

So, guys don't necessarily have it easier than girls. Perhaps it seems that way because they're expected to get down and dirty and to learn by doing, whereas girls are not pushed as hard to get off the sidelines and into the game.

Backstreet Boys Mania

Charles Summers, 16,
Eastern/Central

Ohmigod, I feel sorry for all of you because you missed the, like, totally most amazing Backstreet Boys concert ever! Me and like all my superbest girlfriends went with Claire's Aunt Cheryl, who drove us in her van, to Ottawa. And, like, we actually got to see the Backstreet Boys in person!!!

Ohmigod, they were sooooooooo hot, I wanted to mate, like, with ALL OF THEM!!! Like when they sang "As Long As You Love Me," it was like they were singing to me!! Like, I couldn't believe it when Howie, you know, the funky jokester of the group, came up to near where I was sitting, I could like almost touch his hair!!!

Ohmigod, it was like, I couldn't stop crying, okay, these guys are so amazing! And they sing so good!!! Like, when I grow up, me and Nick are going to have a kid, right? And we're going to move to Orlando. Like, isn't Orlando like the number one place for musical talent right now??? Like, seriously.

Ohmigod. These guys are so romantic. Like when I was screaming, like, at the top of my lungs, you know, for no reason really, I think A.J. heard me when I said, "I want to have your baby!" And I think he made a peace sign with his fingers at me!!! Ohmigod, I really started to cry then.

Ohmigod. Like this big fat woman was blocking my way, so, like, I kicked her in the lower back, because I, like, couldn't see Kevin. Teach her to be fat. Like, why would the Backstreet Boys like her anyways? I bet if, like, Howie wasn't in the band, he'd be my boyfriend, you know? Cause like, they'd all have girlfriends, but they're too busy touring! Ohmigod, they just want a nice sweet girl, you know??? Like, think about it, they're so nice! Like, they aren't about getting pretty girls or anything, they're about love, and trust, and caring!!! Like, that's why even my mom likes them so much.

Ohmigod, once I get my braces off, I bet I would really be like what they want in a girlfriend. For sure! Ohmigod, why can't boys at school be like the Backstreet Boys?

Like, that would be doubleplusgood, so then, like, there would be just cute nice guys around. Boys are so immature. Like for sure.

Ohmigod, so many girls are jealous of me at school now, cause they didn't go!!! It was sooooo weird when I saw a Backstreet Boys video on TV the next day, it was like "I'VE SEEN THEM IN CONCERT!!!!!" Then I started to cry again!! Okay, so, like, if any of you want to go to the next Backstreet Boys concert, I'm organizing some car pools and stuff, so, like, get in touch with me, okay??? BSB 4 EVA!!!

Teen Love Flowers

Michael-Anthony Tamburro, 17,
Eastern/Central

Perhaps I'm not the best one to talk about teenage "love." I'm not even really sure that it exists. This Don Juan has had more start-and-stop, boom-and-bust failed relationships and crushes than my Scarborough high school computer lab has had fatal system viruses.

When in the presence of a pretty girl, I am capable only of stuttering and stammering like a confused caveman. When (and if) she decides to respond to my near-indecipherable "George of the Jungle" speak, I instantly turn to mush. Why? Because I have been cursed. From the age of twelve to twenty, love shall be a complete mystery to me, but I shall be compelled to search for it.

How can one escape the curse of teenage love? I don't think that you can. If you are young and around a lot of other young people day in and day out (as most are by law), then put on your safety restraint, cause you're in for some ride. I've taken the ride lots of times, along with all the other fools who hold a season's pass to the amusement park of the heart.

Everyone reacts differently to the curse. Those differences can be likened to the various ways teens act on a roller coaster: There's the Fat Kid, who originally wants to go on the ride, and even takes the first car, but starts screaming before it even starts. He wants off, but the conductor won't oblige; the ride begins. Then there's the Thrill Seeker, who puts his arms in the air and yells like a lunatic: "We're gonna die, this is great!" The Quiet Kid, who's silent the whole ride through because he's having a heart attack. And of course the Nervous Boy, who vomits all over everybody.

You can't escape love and you can't define it. I tried. Webster's English Dictionary defines love as: warm affection; benevolence; charity; sexual passion; sweetheart; to delight in; and, in tennis, as a score of nothing. Gee, that helps a lot. Game. Set. Match. And therein lies the very problem with love. When you try to define it, it becomes even more confusing than it already was. If love is confusing for Mr. Webster, what chance of understanding it does the average teen have?

I remember a girl in the ninth grade who really didn't understand love. She was more confused about the whole thing than me. To her, love was how long she could keep me on the phone against my will. She would constantly call and babble on incessantly about the earth-shattering life-and-death situations that confronted her in Urban Geography. My first year in high school was tough for me, too, but man, her story of having an HB2 pencil instead of the preferred HB3 on her multiple-choice local parkland scantron got a bit tired—the twenty-third time around.

Foolishly, I never suspected that the curse was at work on her, but I found out soon enough. It happened in an eerie incident that can only be described as ... The Call!

The following is an actual transcript of "The Call."

Her: Hi, Mike?
Me: Yes ...
Her: ...
Me: Hello?
Her: (she sighs) Well hello, Mr. Funny Man! Aren't you more than a little bit hard to get hold of?
Me: Gee, I am becau—
Her: Yes you are, because I just called everyone in the phone book with your last name.
Me: Oh, I see ...
Her: But I guess I've finally found you now, huh?

Me: Uh—huh?
Her: (she sighs)
Me: So?
Her: So? Tee hee tee hee tee hee!
(A long silence follows the schoolgirl laughter.)
Me: Did you want something?
Her: Okay, here it is ... Mike ... duh, ah, well, um, ah, are you like, dating anyone? You know, involved? 'Cause I was like thinking and stuff ... I like you and, um, I, er ... ah ... hope you like me.
Me: The thing is actually—
Her: So ... do you like me?
Me: Uh ...
Her: What, what, what, huh? I can't hear you, you sound like you're mumbling.
Me: ... Uh ... er ...
Her: Yeah, yeah, go on!
Me: Uh ... I ...
Her: I knew it! I love you too!
Me: Uh ... huh?

After the phone call from the Twilight Zone, we were "together." Whatever that means. I'm still trying to figure out who decided that and why I went along with it. I think it was her friends, 'cause that's who I first found out from that I had a girlfriend. I didn't really mind the idea of suddenly having a girlfriend, but I was nonetheless puzzled about how I had been left out of the decision-making process.

I admit I did like the idea of us going out, but I never thought that we were *going out*, rather that we were *going to be going out*. Like to the movies or bowling ... as in going out—eventually. So far we had only talked on the phone. Actually, she talked, I listened. I thought the term meant *going* as in *to be*, in the future, on one's way. It turns out the term is somewhat open to interpretation. The girl apparently didn't like that *I* was spreading rumours that we were "going out," so she "dumped" me. After telling me that we never "went out," she told me that it was my fault that I had "lost her." Wha? How one loses what they claim not to have, I don't know. This girl should have been writing speeches for politicians.

When I tried to approach her to see what had happened, she wouldn't even talk to me. Silence can be the loudest sound of all, sometimes. I had a right to know what had happened. What was she afraid of? I bet there's an X-File on this somewhere at the bottom of the pile of alien abduction stories.

The original title of this piece was "High School Love: Destroying More Young Lives than Alcohol and Algorithms." But on second thought, I didn't think that was fair. I don't even know what an algorithm is. Then I decided on "Teen Love Flowers" because teenage love is like a flower—the kind of flower that looks really nice but is actually a weed. Teenage love and weeds are constantly popping up, and when they do, they aren't wanted. A spray that kills either hasn't been found, and I doubt it ever will be. Then again, as I said before—what do I know about teenage love? After all, I'm writing this on a Friday night, by myself. But then, maybe that isn't such a bad thing.

Inside Eric's Brain

Eric Madison, 15,
Eastern/Central

Fetal pigs? Bloated frogs? While dissecting dead animal specimens may have been interesting for the other students in the science room, last year in biology class I had other, more important things on my mind; I decided to dissect my own head. Not physically. I mean, usually when you read about somebody doing that kind of thing they end up face down in a pool of their own caked blood, so I figured I'd settle for a detailed mental walk-through. Since the laws of paradoxical dynamics forbade me from being able to fit into my own head, I embodied myself in my frog. As the scalpels of my classmates eagerly sliced open the heads of their helpless reptiles, I looked up at my head through my cute froggy eyes, then leaped inside. When was the last time you did that?

Chances are that if you ever have a problem like the one I had (and I'm sure you will if you haven't already), you'll feel like you're stuck inside your head trying to figure out what's wrong with you every spare moment of your life. You need to break free. Get out of your head and float around for a while. Or just lie on the dissection table like a serene little frog. After you get out of your aching head and are able to look at yourself from a third-person point of view, only then should you try to solve your problem. When I did, it was the first time in ages that I really, truly felt happy with myself, because I was able to think about the way I was thinking. I realized how trivial and overblown my problem was: I was madly in love with someone but felt like I wasn't good enough for her.

It seems silly now, but at the time I was really stressed out about it. Rave and I had been best friends for almost two years and I'd been meaning to ask her out since the day I met her. I became so consumed by my efforts to seem likeable around her that I felt I was behaving like an idiot whenever we spoke. I knew that she liked me and that she would say yes if I asked her out, but I couldn't possibly ask because I knew that deep inside I wasn't being genuine with myself. To make matters worse, since I met her I had developed a rather bad case of acne. Even though towards other people I was always outgoing, happy, and expressive of my inherently loud personality, it only made me hate myself even more for having poor self-regard and feeling unhappy on the inside about my body. My mental muddle prevented me from enjoying a relationship with someone with whom I shared the same wavelength in life.

Rave was perfect for me because she wasn't perfect. She's materialistic, she dominates groups, she demands attention, and she has a huge ego. She's hairy and has awkward knees, small breasts, and muscular arms. While she never wears make-up and doesn't conform to what society tells me is beautiful, her beauty is unsurpassed by the sexiest of supermodels, the most sensuous of goddesses. Because her beauty doesn't come in a box labelled Club Monaco or Calvin Klein. Because her beauty doesn't come in a mythological image of a Viking queen. But because she makes her own beauty out of confidence and style, and I see it coming from the inside.

Which isn't to say that other people don't think she's beautiful. Au contraire. While normally people don't give her a second look, her personality demands it, and when she dresses up, heads really turn. People stare in awe as she walks by, but usually I notice them more than she does; she's more concerned with her own self-opinion than with what others think of her, and I find that *sooo* attractive.

The sexiest thing she's ever done to me was to lean over and whisper something in my ear while we were seeing a movie. It wasn't that she said she wanted me to "lick honey off of every inch of my body" or anything stupid like that. I honestly can't remember what she said, just that she had bad breath. It was so perfect. Here was someone who didn't look like one of the eight supermodels in the world, but had the confidence to seem even more beautiful than the most anorexic waif out there. While a supermodel may have more make-up on than their entire body weight, there was Rave, with no make-up, with normal clothes, breathing germs on me! She wasn't only gorgeous, she was human!

Her most attractive feature to me isn't her body or her confidence, though. It's her brain. She thinks like me in so many ways that it scares me. We finish each other's sentences with alarming frequency, we say the same things at the exact same instant, and we have the same interests. I'm always embarrassed that I can never remember her eye colour, but it's only because to see my reflection in her eyes I don't have to look at her irises, I just have to look in her head. There do I not only find all the positive things about her, but the negative things as well. I don't ask that she be perfect, but I really appreciate the way she's able to deal with her problems instead of just letting them fester inside of her. She's very forthright about her problems and I reciprocate with my own openness. It takes a lot of courage to be frank, and she can be very frank. Some people think that she's a little *too* frank, but that's where my real love for her comes in. As you already know, I'm completely obsessed by her, but as I was sitting in biology class jumping into my head from the dissection table, the one thing that transcended all of the positive things about her and my similarities with those was that she had so many things about her that were really unlikeable.

Her big ego, overbearing intelligence, anal obsession with proper grammar, and ostentatiously loquacious word usage; her brutally honest tongue, stupid jokes, tendency to ramble about uninteresting personal stories; her procrastinating nature: all these things could really detract from her personality. To other people they may have, but I realized that fateful day with the frog in my head that these were the same problems I was most ashamed of in myself! Knowing that I'm happy with myself and the way I think, how could I possibly look at the negative aspects of her personality without hating myself? I can't, and it's wonderful. She's the only person in the world whom I consider to be smarter than me, whose grammar I can correct without fear of severe reprimand, who is interested in hearing my stupid life stories, and who doesn't really mind if I ramble. Sometimes our egos clash when we're in groups and we both want to dominate, but we both realize this and end up laughing about it as we discuss our own stupidity for hours on end afterwards.

This is when I hopped back out of my head and onto the dissection table. I had finally found what I was looking for. If you want to start a serious relationship with somebody, how much time are you going to spend staring at their body compared to discussing a movie over dessert afterwards? How much time kissing or having sex compared to sharing your day's experiences and personal problems over the phone? The most important things I liked about Rave were on the inside and I saw her outer ebullience despite her nonconformity with the stereotypical image of feminine beauty. Since in almost every other respect she thought in the same ways as me, would she not feel the same about me? Wouldn't she see the real me underneath my pimpled, greasy face? Wouldn't she realize that we thought the same way instead of just thinking I was weird and awkward around her? Did I honestly think that the person I loved the most would say no to me because of the way I looked?

I asked her out. Of course she said yes, and it was the happiest moment of my life. I felt bizarre and full of nervous adrenaline, but not fearful. I knew her, and she wouldn't have judged me on my appearance. I still can't really accept the fact that I was so hard on myself and that I had such little confidence, but in hindsight I just look back at it and laugh.

I can even look back at our "going out" relationship and laugh, because it only lasted for twenty days! It felt really awkward going out with my best friend, and she broke up with me because she just didn't feel right about it. I still don't fully understand why she did, but I've accepted that she just can't explain it. I too felt awkward when we were going out, but it was the best awkward feeling I've ever had, sharing the awkwardness with the person I loved, hoping to outgrow it and become an even better friend through a physical relationship. It's ironic that since we've broken up our friendship has been better than ever and I think we're closer now than we ever were before. I still always wonder if we could be even better friends going out, and wonder if she'll ever feel the same way.

Only by getting over my poor self-esteem did I realize that if other people regarded me critically, I wouldn't like them anyway. Even if I can only realize that I'm the best person when I look at myself through the eyes of someone equally egotistical, it's a great feeling when I'm accepted by the people who see the real me. If only *YM* and *Sassy* magazines came with insecure bloated frogs drenched in formaldehyde instead of nasty-smelling Calvin Klein perfume ads ...

Teen Dating Anxiety: Guys Get It Too

Chris Mallinos, 19,
Eastern/Central

It's 7:40 p.m., twenty minutes until John is to pick up Stacey for their first date. He takes a minute to ensure that he's got all the necessities. Breath mints? Check. Extra money? Check. Car keys? Check. John is about ready to leave when he makes a shocking realization: *he is nervous.*

Contrary to what many guys would have girls believe, this scenario is not unrealistic. In fact, it is quite common. Teen dating anxiety, especially on first dates, is not just a "girl thing." Us guys get it too.

Some guys would do anything to keep that information a secret. Maybe it's a machismo thing, or maybe they just don't want to be labelled "uncool." A common myth about the teen dating scene is that males somehow instinctively know, or should know, exactly what they are doing. Included in this group of misinformed people are a lot of guys who think that they should be completely comfortable with dating, that it should come naturally to them.

It's an unlikely notion once you really think about it. How can males be expected to be confident with the dating scene without having any experience? Once guys get older, they may become more relaxed with the idea of going on a date, but as a teenager, it is not an easy thing. As far as I know, there is no in-depth course for us to take before we actually take the plunge. Since "Dating for Guys 101" doesn't exist, all knowledge and confidence must be attained through experience, which takes time.

It leaves teenagers in a difficult situation. One doesn't need to watch hours of the Discovery Channel to know that humans have some of the most complex mating rituals on Earth. It generally seems more acceptable to have the female nervous before a date. The male, on the other hand, is supposed to act as if he's done it thousands of times. It's an unfair stereotype, but it has been accepted as fact by guys and girls alike. But we are not all like the Fonz.

Rebel, Rogue, Mischievous Babe

For many guys, getting the first date is supremely difficult. Examine another scenario: A guy sees a girl at a party who he would like to talk to. She is with some of her friends so he can't go over yet. To him, approaching a female with her friends around is akin to a sailor entering uncharted, shark-infested waters. Finally, after what seems like eternity, the friends leave and she is alone. "Perfect," he thinks. "Now's my chance." The guy is about to go over to talk to the girl, but he can't. His feet won't move. What could he possibly say without making himself look like a complete fool? He tries to think of something witty, but with no luck. Ample time passes and he is still idle. The threat of "now or never" races through his mind, but it is overpowered by the butterflies in his stomach. Then, in a split second, the friends return and his chance is gone. The guy is left feeling ashamed that he has missed *yet another* opportunity to talk to a girl he liked.

The stereotype of guys being "naturals" leads many to believe that males should have no problem approaching girls. But any honest guy will admit that cold feet is something we all suffer from at one time or another. Once again, this is simply a result of inexperience and teenage self-consciousness; it is nothing to be ashamed of.

Of course, not all guys suffer from dating anxiety. There are some who really do feel at ease on a date. These guys generally fall into one of two categories. The first type of anxiety-free guy has the "I'm so sexy and cool that any girl would die to go out with me" attitude. These guys think they are God's gift to women. They see themselves as being either super-macho or super-hunks. If these guys were to read this, they would laugh, dismissing it as nothing more than the Manifesto of a Sissy (of course, their language would be much more basic). One can almost smell the testosterone rising off of these "men." Girls must understand that this is nothing to be impressed by. These guys are narcissists.

The second type of anxiety-free guy can simply be categorized as "other." They truly are comfortable with their adolescence, which is certainly a rare occurrence. No one really knows what causes this remarkable confidence; it could be some sort of divine gift, but it does exist, albeit less than people may expect. Kudos to these guys for their self-certainty in turbulent times. There is, however, a fine line between these two categories. The line is drawn where confidence turns to cockiness. The first type of guy is cocky, the latter is confident.

To be absolutely clear about this distinction, we must examine it further. When a guy does not care about how he acts in front of his date because he "can get another date whenever he wants," he is cocky. When a guy doesn't spend the day after his date second-guessing everything he did the night before because he feels that he can be himself on a first date, he is confident. When a guy brings flowers on a first date in order to impress the girl's roommates, hoping to date them too, he is cocky. When a guy brings flowers on a first date to be kind and to get the evening started on the right foot, he is confident. Caution females: do not get these two mixed up.

Males who get nervous before a date should not be ashamed; there is hope for them all (first-hand experience tells me this). Most females are smart enough to be able to identify any anxiety-related masquerades. However, if they see that a guy is nervous, I am confident they would not mock him. Girls supposedly mature faster than guys do, so we guys can be safe in the knowledge that our female counterparts understand that teen dating can be difficult.

I am no expert on the issue. I don't have a Ph.D. or master's degree in anything, so I suppose that my opinion should be taken with a grain of salt. However, I speak from experience, which is the most important credential. I don't know that much about dating, nor have I dated a lot, but I do know this: Guys must learn that it's okay to be nervous, and that they don't have to be "cool" or "hip" on a date, they just have to be themselves and they'll be fine.

It's 8 p.m., John rings the doorbell at Stacey's house, and she answers. A night of indecision and second-guessing has begun.

Roundtable

Although you're probably too busy hanging out with your friends doing fun things that will help you grow as an individual, we thought you might be a little curious about the stuff that goes on in a boy's head. So we asked five guys of different ages to tell us what they think.

Alex, Patrick, and Jordie are thirteen. Marcos is fifteen, and Marcus and Frank are both sixteen.

What do you find attractive in a girl?

Jordie: They have to be nice and all ... I'm talking about inner attractiveness ...so they have to be nice and funny and someone who has the same interests.

Does it matter if they're physically attractive?

Frank: Well ... {laughter} I think that's kinda why you want to get to know them ... It's something that draws you to them.

Marcus: If they're attractive you probably want to get to know them, but I have to be able to play with a girl. She can't be too delicate. I like girls who are strong.

Jordie: I think the eyes are important. Someone with kind eyes, or caring kinds of emotions. I know what he means about the delicate thing. It's not just delicate in the physical sense, but when a girl doesn't trust herself, you can't really have a conversation with her.

What do you mean?

Alex: Confidence.

Jordie: Yeah, confidence is important. You have to know what you have and not be ashamed of it and be able to speak your mind.

So what's "hot"?

Marcos: Someone who's attractive ... but not just that, but also the life of the party.

Patrick: Yeah. And not too much make-up. I can't stand that!

Jordie: Make-up is good to a certain extent for fashion purposes for guys *and* girls. I know a lot of guys who wear make-up and it looks good on them. And the same on some girls. On eyes and stuff ... patterns ... that looks good! But when they coat their face in layers of stuff just to hide zits—

Alex: In the summer, people who are afraid to sweat because they might smear their make-up—pathetic.

Okay ... that brings us to sports ... Is it important?

Marcus: Very definitely.

Alex: They don't have to be good at it, as long as they're into the game.

Marcus: Or willing to participate.

Frank: It shows something about them, that they're not china dolls, they're athletic, active.

Jordie: Well, it's not like I care exactly what their personal choice is in sports and exercise because I'm not a sports fanatic myself so maybe going out with someone who isn't would be just as good a thing for me.

Patrick: Well, I want them to like sports because I play hockey every weekend and if they didn't like hockey I wouldn't ...

You really wouldn't go out with a girl who didn't like hockey?

Patrick: Well ... I *would* ... but ... she'd have to be ... like ... okay ... She'd have to respect it. She wouldn't have to play it.

Marcus: I don't like the type of girls who are just, "I don't want to go swimming in a pool because the chlorine will mess up my hair ..." That's just wrong. Who cares?

Marcos: It's one thing for a girl to look good, it's another thing for a girl to worry constantly about how she looks. If you look good you should know it, you shouldn't be worrying about it ...

What is an attractive body type?

Alex: Not anorexic.

Marcus: Curves are important. Muscles.

Frank: They have to have some meat.

Would you want your girlfriend to be your size or thinner?

Marcus: I'd want to be taller ... I'd want to be bigger ... I suppose I want the power in the relationship.

You want to overpower her?!

Marcus: Well ... no! Size is just something like ... if she's bigger than you ...

Alex: You're going to be intimidated.

Marcos: You don't want to be scared of your girlfriend.

Patrick: You don't go out with a girl who can beat you up.

Alex: Hmm. A girl who can beat off the bullies.

How important is it that your friends like your girlfriend?

Alex: Not important! Not important!

Patrick: When I'm out with my friends I might want my girlfriend there, but if my friends don't like her, then I won't be able to bring her. I don't think that a girl should stand between you and your friends.

Jordie: I think that if your friends see a definite hole in her personality, and they see that she's not a good person, then you should listen to them because maybe they're right ... Maybe you shouldn't get involved in the relationship ... but you shouldn't let them decide for you.

Alex: Unless they're being totally pig-headed and stupid about it, like, "Ohhh. Your girlfriend's fat," or something. Then it's like, "Shut up! You're not going out with her!"

What's the one thing you wish more girls would do?

Jordie: Be original in how they dress.

Marcus: Be more open. More forward, more aggressive.

Alex: Ask us out or to dance to take some of the pressure off of us.

Patrick: Most people are afraid of rejection at this age. But what would happen if they did feel like you and you never knew? There should be some signs.

So you think girls should dress more originally?

Frank: Yeah. We had a dance on Thursday and all the girls wore bell bottoms and hip huggers and army tops. Why does everyone want to look the same?

Marcus: ... or those Adidas pulloff pants.

Patrick: Everyone's wearing Nike.

Jordie: Don't buy something that says Nike—Just do it. That's so dumb. You're an advertisement. Make it your own. Do something original.

Marcus: I don't think that's really a girl problem. It's everyone. It's a society thing.

Where do you think your idea of what is beautiful comes from?

Alex: Definitely the media.

Marcus: The media.

Frank: The media.

Jordie: That's a hard question to answer because if society said that all fat girls are beautiful, then ... we might think that all fat girls are attractive.

Alex: Yeah! We would! We would! Because there was a time, back in the 1930s and '40s, when larger women were more attractive.

Patrick: The society you live in totally shapes what you like.

Jordie: It's a difficult question because none of us can actually tell ... We were exposed to these things ... all of these things ... parents, friends ... the toys we had when we were small.

What about make-up?

Marcus: You should wear make-up, but we shouldn't be able to tell.

Patrick: Your face shouldn't look powdery.

Jordie: I'll always comment if a girl's make-up looks really good. People don't respect that they're doing it to look nice, and if they want to look nice, well, more power to them.

Alex: I'd prefer a girl *au naturel*. I want to like them for them!

Would it bother you if your girlfriend decided to stop shaving?

Frank: Yes.

Marcus: Yes.

Patrick: Uh-huh.

Alex: Where?

Marcos: Next topic, please.

Frank: Legs or pits?

Jordie: I wouldn't mind underarms ...

Marcus: Mustaches ...

Let's just say she decided to stop shaving her legs or under her arms. Would this bother you? We're talking about a girl you're really crazy about.

Marcos: Yeah.

Marcus: Yeah.

Frank: I'd be lying if I said it was okay.

Patrick: Yes.

Jordie: If she doesn't want to shave under her arms or her legs, it's a natural thing! It's just hair! It's not gonna hurt you!

Would you rather date a girl who's smart or beautiful?

Marcus: Beautiful.

Alex: Smart.

Jordie: Smart.

Patrick: Smart.

Marcos: Smart.

Jordie: There was a girl at my school who was really attractive, so I tried to talk to her at lunch, and then I realized she's one of the dumbest people I've ever met in my life. I'm never going to talk to her again. She's just so uninteresting. She can't go anywhere with a sentence, cuz, she ... you know ... runs out of words. I don't care if she knows the periodic table of elements or whatever, but it's more important that she's smart all around.

Is there anything that you would like girls to know about you?

Alex: If we could say what we really think without them freaking out. I also want to say that all girls think guys are so superficial and all they care about are cars and breasts and stuff. Some guys are, but some girls are, too. All they care about is pecs or abs or their clothes ... So ... before you stereotype or anything, think about yourself!

Marcus: They should be open. They should say, "I like you." "I don't like you." ... Don't beat around the bush.

So, what is your big fear regarding girls?

Alex: Rejection.

Marcos: Rejection.

Marcus: Oh, yeah.

Chapter 7

Depression

A Serious Case of the Blues

Every November I find myself with a serious case of the blues. I hesitate to call it a full-blown depression, although it can bring tears that will not cease and a sense of gloom that refuses to leave. I feel sad and lonely and unable to get off the couch.

I know it's probably weather-related; too many stormy grey days can kill a good mood in seconds flat. And it doesn't last forever, so I haven't had to take anything for it—even though when I'm in it, it feels like hell and I can't say I ever feel very hopeful about it lifting any time soon.

I am lucky. Some of my friends are on medication year round, performing a balancing act by tinkering with the dosage or trying an altogether new medicine, just to remain on an even keel.

It's not as though the sadness that grips me in November leaves me entirely alone the rest of the year. I have days of intense highs, where everything is light and beautiful and I am overwhelmed with laughter and huge amounts of silliness. And those days are inevitably matched by lows that, while not as profound as the highs, leave me reeling.

Sometimes the blues are brought on by stress. Other times they are the result of not having been to the gym. There is a definite connection for me between feeling good and lifting weights or jumping my body around during a game of tennis or in an aerobics class.

I don't think there's any one particular reason I can point to for the blues or its more serious counterpart, depression. These feelings can be brought on by many different factors. Some of them are physiological, like hormone imbalances or light deprivation. Others are centred in emotions: moving away from your friends or family, losing a friend or relative through death.

I do know some of the effects, though. There's a wide range, including the desire to sleep the days away, a change of appetite, and the wish to isolate yourself from friends and family.

If you are feeling sad or blue or depressed, you need to ask for help, because depression is a mental illness, and without help or treatment, which often involves a combination of therapy and medication, it can lead to thoughts of suicide.

Sometimes it's hard to ask for help. We all want to be able to figure out and resolve our own problems—it's part of feeling self-assured, independent. And often young people are not taken seriously when they complain of depression.

When I was a kid, the cure for any kind of sadness was sunshine. Maybe your mom tells you the same thing: "Quit yer crying and go play outside!" Most of the time, for me, it worked. Even now, the more sunny, natural light I am exposed to, the happier I am. My mom really *does* know everything!

Still, suicide is the second-highest cause of death among teens in Canada, and statistics show that 70 to 90 percent of teens who commit suicide have a psychiatric disorder such as clinical depression.

In 1997, more than three hundred young people between the ages of fifteen and nineteen killed themselves. And yet there is no specific training in schools to help teachers identify and help students who might be depressed and suicidal.

If you are having suicidal thoughts, if you want to help a friend who you think might be in danger of killing herself, or if you are dealing with your own emotional difficulties in the aftermath of a friend's suicide, it can help to call the Kids Help Phone.

Understanding how to cope with depression and talk about suicide is important in helping yourself and your friends. To assist teachers, parents, and young people, Dr. Elyse Dubo of the Sunnybrook Health Sciences Centre has helped create a video about depression and treatment. It's called *The Other Side of Blue*, and it tells the stories of five young people who experience depression and eventually get help.

The Other Side of Blue is available from the Canadian Learning Company. Individuals can order copies for $39.95. The institutional price is $195. Call 1-800-267-2977 ext. 303. Send a fax to 519-537-1035. Or order online at www.canlearn.com.

Myth:

"Constructive criticism" is important

I hate criticism. And you know what? I don't think there is any such thing as "constructive criticism"—especially since most people seem to leave out the constructive part.

When people offer to give you their "constructive criticism," it's like saying that they're going to tell you some critical stuff that's going to hurt, but you're not allowed to take it personally. Hey, if someone is criticizing your work, or your style, or your ideas in a way that is hurtful or condescending, they can couch it any way they like, but it's still personal and it's inappropriate.

I do like input, and even advice when I ask for it, or when people ask if they can offer it. But I think the only time criticism is acceptable is when the person offering it has been involved in the project or endeavour and has a stake in the outcome. For example, let's say a friend of yours recommends you to a contact of hers as someone who is worth hiring or investing in because you're talented and fabulous. Let's say you get a job based on that recommendation, but then, for no apparent reason, decide that you don't want it after all. In that type of situation I think your friend is entitled to give you some constructive criticism about your behaviour, since it reflects badly on her.

Otherwise, I think criticism, even under the guise of being

constructive, makes you doubt yourself and your projects and fear about the future.

Sometimes people use criticism as a way to motivate. They think their harsh or tough words will cause you to modify your behaviour, or take action, so that you perform better in school—after all, you wouldn't want to have to hear criticism like that again, would you? That style has always had the opposite effect on me. I find that I tend to respond better to praise than to criticism. When I'm told that I'm doing a good job, I always assume that I can do even better. If I hear that some of my work is impressive, even if parts of it could be stronger, it makes me want to keep improving.

It's fair to let people know how their criticism makes you feel. Ask them how they want to help you, and if you find there is a genuine desire to assist you in making your project better, then tell them that they need to take a more tactful and respectful approach if they really want to be of assistance.

Chrystie's World

Chrystie, 14,
Eastern/Central

I always knew I had a lot of problems for a fourteen-year-old. Two bratty sisters who annoy me constantly, my brother turning twenty-eight and still living at home, my father being an alcoholic, and my mother always being in a bad mood because of my father. I could easily say that at that age I had nothing to live for. I was always upset and I would secretly cry to myself every night hoping and praying that I would be released from this stress and pain some day soon.

I would close my eyes and picture myself in a nice place with butterflies and angels flying by, but when I'd open them I'd see homeless people and pollution and think to myself, "Welcome to the real world, Chrystie."

I would never stay in one place; I was always moving to a new town and having to make new friends. I never did fit in anywhere because of having to change everything to adapt to the new atmosphere. One year, when I finally had some friends and was beginning to fit in, I had to move and start all over again. I hated having to change myself just to be part of the "cool crowd." After a while I stopped caring about what other people thought about me, and I stopped caring about myself as well. People thought I was stupid because I was quiet and independent, I shied away from others. I never thought I was stupid until I began hearing it. I've always been very sensitive and I've always taken every little comment to heart. That's why I started believing I was stupid. Why bother trying to succeed in something if I couldn't?

I wanted to disappear from the earth so everyone would just leave me alone. The only way I could do that was to die. I'd always thought about committing suicide. I'd wanted to for so long, but I knew I couldn't take the pain of cutting my wrists or anything else along that line.

One afternoon, after having a huge fight with my parents and having just broken up with my boyfriend, I couldn't take the pain of living any longer. I was afraid to live more than to die. I locked myself in my bedroom and sat on my bed. I caught my eyes darting around my room in search of a way to stop the anger and frustration. I noticed a bottle of pills on my desk and before I knew what I was doing, I had swallowed about twenty pills. I started feeling dizzy and I felt as if I was floating with every step I took. My heart was pounding so furiously inside my chest it began to hurt. The phone rang and I began telling my friend what I had done. I hung up, and was so tired, I decided to lie on my floor. The phone rang again but someone answered it before me.

I decided to crawl to the bathroom to try and throw up all the pills I had swallowed. I had no luck with that, because I didn't know how to force myself to throw up. I felt tears pouring down my cheeks and for the first time I realized how scared I was knowing that I was going to die all alone in a bathroom. I kept thinking to myself how stupid I must be to have done this to myself. I was about ready to give up on life when I heard a knock at the door. I opened the door to see my mom accusing me of trying to kill myself. I was too tired to argue or to wonder how she found out, so I confessed.

She drove me to the hospital without breathing a word to me in the car. I could tell she was just as upset and confused as I was. I was rushed to emergency and the doctor made me drink charcoal, which made me throw up for a long time after that. The doctors asked me a lot of questions, and they wanted me to see a therapist. I did not want to see a shrink, so I lied and said that I would be fine. I know I'll never be fine after what I've done to myself.

My mom held my hand through the whole time I was in the hospital. She never let go. I realized then that she did care, and she was my reason for living. Seeing her cry made me cry even harder and made me feel worse. I had hurt her more than I hurt myself, and I could only pray that she would forgive me. I'll never forget that day, I was so scared. I abused the greatest gift a mother can give ... life.

Later on, I found out that the second telephone ring that someone had answered before me was from my friend. She explained everything to my mom. I can't help but wonder if I would still be alive today if I had answered the phone before my mom. I'm glad I'm alive, and thinking back on it is weird. I can't believe that I almost died. I think that every teenager has thought about suicide as a way out, at least once. Luckily, not all teenagers go through with it.

Personally, I think that a person has to be stronger and braver to *not* commit suicide than to try it. That day in the hospital, I learned that I wasn't as strong as I thought I was. I know that I'm finally becoming one of those stronger and braver people.

Black Flowers

Natasha Chorneyko, 12,
West Coast

My life started out well. I grew up in an Alberta city, sheltered by a loving, caring family and a lot of good friends. I was a happy, gung-ho kind of kid, always smiling and laughing, though shy, and I had a huge passion for animals and people. I was fairly chubby and quite tall, but that didn't bother me. There were too many people who cared about me that I hardly even noticed that fact. I loved life.

Then I moved a few times.

At the age of nine, my world shattered. I ended up, after sweeping briefly through Ontario as a resident, on Vancouver Island, B.C. It was a really gorgeous place, and after a few rough starts, I gradually started to settle in with my family in this new place and new school. I had to try my hand at making new friends too. I made a few bad decisions, and ended up toughening up a little, but overall, it was probably for the best.

After spending two years here on the Island, I hit middle school. And rock bottom. I was really, almost painfully shy, quiet, sensitive, tall, and more overweight than before, but I wasn't obese. I was also unhappy. Very unhappy. It had started out innocently in elementary school, quietly enough that I didn't even notice that anything had changed with me. I thought I was just growing up. Some days, it would begin to dawn on me: *I was different than the other kids.*

It was a shock and I didn't like it. This was all new for me. I rode that out for a while, being constantly hurt, downcast, and upset with everything. I began to get moody and fake sickness with my parents so I could stay home from school. Things just got worse when I didn't tell anyone. But I didn't want to believe it.

I started to skip meals in an effort to bring my weight down. I slept a little less, became more distraught, and found myself thinking very deep, black thoughts. I would constantly hide behind my waist-length hair that I always wore down, my curtain to hide from the world. After a while, I began to think about suicide.

I mostly just talked about it, not having seen its effects before, but it was enough to scare the few friends I had into taking me to a school counsellor. I talked with him and it helped a bit, but I ignored his request to tell my parents what was going on with me. I was sure I was going to pull through.

The blackness began to seep away gradually, and I lived a little more normally. Things became a bit easier, but I still wasn't enjoying life as much as I used to. I was still quiet, heavier, and almost a foot or two taller than all of my classmates. I knew there was no way to change that. I got into wearing light make-up, which boosted my confidence, and bought clothes that were more in style than my previous ones. I was going to be fine.

I survived the rest of the year, and spent a cool summer visiting old friends back in Alberta. I cut my hair up to my shoulders and dyed it auburn. I bought more make-up. Then I came back to the Island and started Grade 8.

It began once more. The unhappiness that I had experienced before came back, stronger and more potent than ever. Like the year before, it came on a step at a time, but actually more quickly than the previous time. I was in trouble and I didn't know what was going on with me.

I skipped meals for entire days and then, at a later date, often binged. This left me with a feeling of helplessness, regret, and horror. I slept only three to four hours a night, insomnia robbing me of my rest. I had trouble concentrating and became irritable and quieter than ever. I got dizzy spells and headaches, sometimes coming near to fainting. My menstrual periods stopped completely. I didn't care about the things I used to. I had lost interest in them. I started to look anemic and I accented the look by getting into dark make-up, especially eye make-up, lipstick, and nails. I spent more and more time thinking about death and dying than anything else. People were starting to notice and I was having a harder and harder time denying that anything was wrong. I *hated* my life, yet I was frightened, terrified of what was happening to me.

One day, in researching a CAPP (Career and Personal Planning) project about the teenage years on a school computer, I searched for anything that might provide information. There was a huge section on teenagers and depression.

I clicked onto it. What I found shocked me. With my heart pounding, I read article after article on depression, including a list of symptoms of a depressive. If you had three or more things in common with the list, you were advised to seek help immediately. I had nine.

Again, I denied it, my head spinning. *That couldn't be me.* So I ignored it completely. Refused to acknowledge it. It was probably just some stupid mistake. Depression didn't have anything to do with me, did it?

In the second term, things struck a really serious note. I sank deeper into a black hole, and I couldn't seem to pull out of it. It was the same vicious circle as always: hate myself, starve, get no sleep, binge, cry ... and be terrified.

Suicide popped into my head again after someone else in my town made a successful attempt. It was the older brother of a girl in my class. I got the call from a friend during Christmas vacation. I hadn't known him, but still I was dazed and felt awful for the family. But here was my answer. Suicide.

I was numb. I couldn't keep this up anymore. I couldn't take this nameless, faceless pain. No one knew; no one could help; it was hopeless. After a long, vicious day in which everything seemed to go wrong, I broke down late in the evening at home. I couldn't handle it anymore. I sobbed, feeling tired, panic-stricken, and very near to swallowing the rest of a bottle of pills. Somehow I picked up the phone and called an old friend. She listened, cried with me, and said she wished she had known, and she made me swear to tell my parents. It was the hardest thing I ever had to do.

What followed was a night of tears, hugs, sobbed confessions, and a release of pain. They scheduled several appointments with counsellors and psychiatrists, doctors, and eating disorder specialists.

The next month or so was a blur, but it seemed to drag on forever. Things actually hurt worse. I was still trapped in the darkness. However, I saw tons of professionals and they finally diagnosed me as suffering from severe depression with suicidal tendencies, social phobia, and eating disorders.

Almost immediately I was put on Prozac, an anti-depressant. It didn't change my outlook one bit. Some days, when it got really bad, I would spend hours in the hospital talking to a crisis nurse until my suicidal feelings passed. Other nights, I would sit at home crying, cutting myself with knives, and swallowing more pills than was safe—anything to make me feel better.

I wrote a suicide note and kept one copy in my room and another in my backpack. It was comforting to know that there was that option, that I could always check out if I had to. And I was pretty sure I would need it. Things weren't changing. My parents really cared and were trying hard too, but they couldn't make it happen either. I hated my life and there seemed to be no way to change it.

I needed a way out. When I occasionally attended classes, I would meet other people around the school. They were sweet, nice kids and, although reluctant, they helped me get into smoking pot and drinking. I felt better while I did these things but the aftereffects really dragged me down. I would feel burnt out and worse than ever. To pass the time I sometimes burned myself on my stomach with cigarettes. I took sleeping pills just to get some rest.

The drugs hadn't improved things and, after getting caught one day, I quit doing them. After the high they imposed, I felt more black and depressed than before. Plus, they were expensive, illegal, and addictive. They couldn't help me. Nothing could.

Being a writer, I spent a lot of time in the basement, typing out poems. All of them were dark, gloomy, and sad. However, they expressed my feelings about life. I began to print my work and copyright it. One poem in particular was a favourite of mine:

Roses
Black satin roses,
petals smooth as velvet,
dark as deepest ebony,
beautiful as death.

One sunny morning after I had printed a copy of that poem, I went upstairs to examine it over a diet pop. My mom saw the sheet of paper I was holding and, curious, asked to read it. I shrugged, "Go ahead. I don't care."

My mother had read my poetry before so she probably had an idea it might be depressing, but she took it to read. I got my pop and sat down in the kitchen, indifferent, and in a dark mood. After finishing the poem, she handed it back to me and told me: "Wait here. I have something to show you."

I was puzzled, but didn't let on. She slipped on sandals and disappeared outside, leaving me without a clue. Upon returning, she handed something to me and said, "You see this? What do you think it is?"

I stared at the soft-petaled, coal-coloured pansy in my hand. "A black flower. So what?"

"It may seem like it, but hold the flower up to the light," my mom told me.

I held it up against a lamp, blinking at the light. Against the brightness, it wasn't really black ... it was a deep, royal purple. "It's purple," I remarked, still not getting it.

"They've been trying to create a black flower for years, but they still haven't done it," my mom explained. "Don't you see it? There's always light. Purple is one of the colours of the rainbow. Do you know what the rainbow's a symbol for?" I shook my head.

"Hope," she answered, smiling. "Hope for mankind. And for you, too. You talk about black roses and death, but there is a light. You'll find it."

I kept the flower on my desk until it withered after a few days, then I pressed it into a book.

Things are getting better with me. It's been only a few months since my major low point, and I've still got a long way to go. I'm still struggling with eating, sleeping, and being at school, but the Prozac is starting to slowly take effect. I'm noticing little things here and there, things that I never took the time to appreciate before. I know I'll look back later and be glad that I stuck this out. Because after all, between black roses and rainbows, there is hope in the world. For everyone.

Maybe One Day

Kristyn Ferguson, 18,
Eastern/Central

I was watching a rerun of the classic TV show "Degrassi High" the other day, the episode about a boy named Claude who killed himself in the school washroom. I observed the reactions of all the kids at Degrassi: shocked, sobbing, confused, and I found myself thinking, "Why are these kids reacting like this? Why are they so surprised and horrified? Stuff like this happens every day." That's when I noticed that the kids on Degrassi weren't acting strangely...I was.

How could I criticize these characters for feeling the pain and grief that they felt about something as terrible as teenage suicide? I then understood that after attending Sir Oliver Mowat C.I. for the past four years, it's me who reacts improperly to suicide, and that I have come to accept it as something normal. In the junior years at my school, murmurs about suicide passed my way and I thought what a sad, painful, terrible thing it is. As time went by, and as more teenagers at my school took their own lives, the impact of the news gradually wore off until I was hardly even taken aback when I heard of yet another Mowat suicide.

Now it feels as if I may never feel the same anguish about the suicides of my fellow students again. I wonder what it will take to jump-start my heart into making me feel that break-down-in-tears feeling when I hear the word "suicide"—the death of a friend?

Mainly I just want to express the sadness I do feel for all the past and recent suicides at Mowat. Looking back at the pain it has caused friends, teachers, and fellow students, I can certainly conclude that suicide is not the answer when times get tough. Instead of "solving" one problem, it creates hundreds of others.

Some kids at my school have organized an anti-suicide group to promote community awareness about suicide and to prevent it from happening again. I think this is an excellent idea and I very much hope it will decrease my school's suicide rate. I have heard my school referred to as "Suicide High," which I think is despicable and insensitive, but I hope that the awareness group will prove to Toronto that there are people deeply concerned about preventing this horrible occurrence from happening at Mowat again.

As for me, all I want is to not think of suicide as a normal, everyday happening, but to cry the tears and experience the feelings of shock and grief if it does happen again. I don't enjoy being "used to" something like suicide and I almost envy the kids on Degrassi for being able to react and feel things as they mourned Claude's death. Maybe one day, suicide will not be a word that rolls off my tongue quite so easily. Maybe one day, I will cry again.

Self-destruct

anonymous

Sometimes, a girl just falls apart. A heavy head and sore heart, reflected in eventual self-destruction. This was my position for over five years: five years spent cutting, burning, and scraping myself apart. Self-mutilation is alarmingly common among teenage girls: arms traced in perfect scars that linger long after the blood dries.

I recall trying to hurt myself as early on as ten years old. Running over my fingers on a cobblestone street, trying to break the bones. Crushing my arms between furniture and walls to see if they would hold up. These aren't the most common self-mutilation behaviours, but I guess I was born with an on/off destruct switch.

I would be overwhelmed, and I needed things to stop. I would be in pain, but I couldn't feel it. I needed to see the physicality of my own being before I could identify with my thoughts. As I got older, I progressed to more direct forms of mutilation. Cutting, burning, or scratching the skin off my arms. Sometimes, it was like being in a trance. Methodically scraping away, dissecting myself, became soothing. At twenty-two, I understand depression. I know anxiety and panic, I know the textbook symptoms and definitions. At thirteen, I knew nothing. I knew an overwhelming fear, a spinning darkness. I was terrified—I would panic, and then I would cut. I didn't go deep enough to leave scars—just enough to see blood. Just the sight of my own blood, and the control I felt in exacting it, would ground me for a little while.

I wore long sleeves and made up stories. My cat scratched me, I fell off my bike, I scratched myself in my sleep. Sometimes I would cut my face, but I would lie about that, too. I didn't talk about it, and neither did anyone else.

When I was fifteen or so, a girl approached me in the bathroom at school. I knew her vaguely, as a face from the hallways or a hand raised in class. She, too, had scars. Deep ones, barely healed. She said something about my arms; I don't remember what. Just some acknowledgement that she knew what I was doing. Then she said something about a competition. Let's compare arms, see who has the most battle scars. I looked at her for a moment, and walked out.

Later that year, another girl from school tried to kill herself and ended up in the psychiatric ward at a local hospital. People knew about it, people sympathized. I kept my sleeves pulled down and my mouth shut. I wasn't crying out for help. I didn't want to be stopped. Hurting myself was the only way I could control the pain and fear of my own depression. Just before my eighteenth birthday, I found myself afraid for my own safety. A night with the most panic I had ever felt. I walked the streets in circles. I had to keep moving because I was afraid to stand still. I knew if I started to cut, I wouldn't stop. I ended up at a friend's house, and the next day I went to the hospital.

I didn't know what I was thinking. My thoughts were a blur. All I knew was that my head was spinning and it had to stop. The doctor told me about panic attacks, something I had never heard of before. I didn't realize how strong depression is, what anxiety can do. I just thought I was losing my mind. Over the next few years, I started to learn about feelings. I was eighteen and learning how to feel all over again. In time, the panic faded. I could feel things as they happened, so it wouldn't hit me all at once.

To this day, I still suffer from depression. I've spent over half my life depressed, but it was only in the last year that I began to understand it as a disease. For some people, depression is a response to certain triggers. For me, it's a constant shadow. I have to work every day to be okay. Just getting up and thinking clearly is a struggle. Even with medication and therapy, I still have to be careful; I have to make sure I'm taking the best possible care of myself. My mind has presented me with pain and pictures I could never imagine, but as difficult as it has been, I've come through it all.

Pain gives perspective, and my love and passions are increasingly focused. As far as I feel in one direction, I feel in the other. Seeing horror has made seeing beauty that much clearer.

Chapter 8

Drugs, Drinking, & Smoking

Lucy in the Sky ...

He bites the purple tablet in half and holds it out to me on his palm. I am sitting on my couch and he is standing above me. The others have all taken theirs, and I know I said I would try it, but I am apprehensive. I'm not sure what to expect. I have only ever been high on alcohol.

Now he's offering a sensation of something I have only ever heard described, seen in ads, felt around me, but never fully tasted. At least, that's what I think. I'm not sure because everyone's description and experience of ecstasy has been different.

Why is it so hard to decide whether or not to open my mouth and let it dissolve under my tongue as instructed? After all, pleasure has always been my goal.

I think it's because I know so little about the truth of drugs and taking something synthetic that was probably hastily concocted in someone's bathroom has me a little worried. Can I trust my friend? Can I trust his sources? The extent of my high school "education" on the subject was limited to "drugs are bad." There was no discussion about why people use drugs, or why some people become addicted. It was as though there was one typical experience that applied to everyone. The attitude about sex was pretty much the same. Except with sex, they at least tell you that there is an appropriate stage of life when you can start to try it. Alcohol is one of the few exceptions: a drug that our culture seems to think we can, after a certain age, handle responsibly. And we have recently, grudgingly, come to accept that marijuana has legitimate applications in easing the discomfort of those who are ill.

But I digress.

A few of the guests who took their hits of ecstasy before arriving at my apartment talk about going dancing, in order to really feel the rush. I am reminded of a print ad for a Gucci perfume called "Rush." The model's eyes are closed, her hair is dishevelled as though she is dancing, her head is tilted back ever so slightly, and her lips are parted. She is in the throes of ...

Advertisers have always tapped into popular culture to sell their products. Remember the HMV ad that ran in store windows over Christmas 2000, featuring a pink pill on an outstretched tongue? One clerk told me that it's "supposed to be an aspirin for relief from holiday shopping, but I guess it can be whatever you think it is."

The ziplock bag on my table has purple, green, and pink pills in it. Each coloured pill provides a different type of high, he explains.

When I ask a young friend about the HMV ad, she says, "That ad doesn't glamorize ecstasy or drugs any more than it already has been. It's just not the demonization that some want to see."

Others I talked to about it believe that HMV is "in a position to reveal some of what is true about drugs. To actually demystify some of the things we are told about it, but they don't. They just capitalize."

We can't count on corporations to reveal the truth about drugs—that's not their mission—but maybe schools could do a better job. In 1997, the Centre for Addiction and Mental Health introduced a drug prevention program called Opening Doors to be implemented in thirty-two schools across the province of Ontario. While they say that "truly effective programs are difficult to implement," they don't say how they will measure their success rate, which brings up the question of accountability and effectiveness.

Certainly the American campaign of "just say no" has been ineffective, and anti-smoking messages are largely a joke. It doesn't help that the anti-drug programs in school and in government-sponsored media campaigns ("This is your brain ... this is your brain on drugs") are fear- and not information-based.

You might expect schools to operate under the assumption that knowledge really is power: the more you know about the way ecstasy affects your nervous system, or the way pot causes the synapses in your brain to fire more slowly, or that some people are genetically disposed to becoming addicts after trying drugs even once, the better you will be able to make decisions for yourself. Instead, it's believed that a "don't ask, don't tell" policy will deter drug experimentation.

I'm not willing to accept the little purple pill. Drugs are problematic for me. I have these amazing natural highs, which, I think, is the reason why I never felt the desire to smoke up in high school. I also just met someone who suffered a neurological problem because of the amount of ecstasy he took. He lost the ability to walk for three months. He needed help just to get to the bathroom. Fun.

Sometimes we turn to substances to help us dull pain, or alleviate boredom. Researchers in the psychology department at Florida State University have found that teenagers are less likely to turn to alcohol or drugs if they are involved in extracurricular activities, like sports, where they gain a sense of personal achievement, recognition from their peers, and reward for accomplishment. No surprise, really. The natural highs that result from being challenged, successful, and rewarded are often missing when we turn to drugs or alcohol.

Masking or drowning your problems with drugs or alcohol won't change what you will eventually have to deal with. Finding rewards in artificial highs, rather than in natural ones, robs you of the opportunity to know yourself and your capabilities.

Myth:

Being a teenager is the best time of your life

The word "teenager" didn't come into popular use until the 1950s, when marketers and advertisers recognized the spending power wielded by adolescents and began to see the potential of targeting that age group. All of a sudden, fashion, beauty products, toys, gimmicks, magazines, and, of course, music were packaged and sold specifically to teenagers.

James Dean, Elvis Presley, and Marlon Brando were teen icons, and everything about being young and wild and free screamed *teenager*. Being a teenager meant having the best time of your life because you had money, wheels, and no real responsibilities—at least, that was the idea. Plus, because adults were (and continue to be) afraid of them, teens weren't really expected to follow the rules.

Being a teenager does rock in lots of ways, but for a lot of young people it can be a very difficult time, and I think high school has a lot to do with that. It's hard to explore your dreams and ideas when your energy is being poured into keeping up with the codes and categories for "belonging" at school.

And what if, after trying to find a way to fit in, you still don't? I've learned that the best thing is to turn your attention to activities where you might meet people who share interests similar to your own.

I had a reasonably difficult time in high school. I always felt like an oddball and a misfit. I didn't realize that relief would arrive in the form of university, where the sheer number of students and variety of disciplines meant I would find both a group to pal around with and an area of study that actually held my attention.

Leaving my teen years behind meant real freedom, because I stopped caring about what other people thought and said about me. I know most people hate the idea of getting older, but for me it meant that I finally got to taste the myth—the freedom from pressure to conform, the chance to rebel and chase my dreams, the opportunity to make important friendships—that I thought I'd missed when I was a teen. Considering that you're going to be an adult for many more years than you were ever a teen, it's a sweet irony.

CAN-dee?

Julia Dascalescu, 17,
Eastern/Central

Never have I seen parents recoil with such fear and disgust as when the word "RAVE" is spoken. Uttering this word in a sentence, along with "Can I go to a ...?" causes many parental units to react as follows. First, their eyes glaze over as images from "20/20" episodes haunt them. They become distracted for a minute as they hear Barbara Walters's voice frantically warning them about the evils of raves. Then, snapping out of the reverie, they rant about the corrupt society we live in that allows such events to take place. Following this, the first thing that comes out of their mouths is a slur of angry reasons why one cannot go to a rave, accompanied by foaming at the mouth and spittle.

As you can see, somewhere along the way, raves have gotten an incredibly bad reputation. And although I am not some raver vigilante, here to defend the almighty Rave and all its trappings, I also cannot agree with the hysterical crusade of parents and government officials to end the Party.

Saturday, December 4

I grabbed my glowsticks and my whistle and headed to Hullabaloo, one of the more "mainstream" raves dishing up happy hardcore, jungle, oldskool, trance, and break beats.

10:15 p.m.: I am standing in line, moderately frightened by some raver walking around in a full-size purple Teletubby costume. Nonetheless, I am quickly consoled by the fact that, after waiting in line for only ten minutes, I am inside Newz, the club where the rave is being held.

10:30 p.m.: I am now fully regretting the large Coke I drank in the car, as the lineup to the washroom is ludicrous. I wait patiently, amused by the colourful ensembles of the candy ravers surrounding me in their large pants, fun fur, and baby blue baseball hats.

10:35 p.m.: Finally. I have escaped the harrowing washroom experience (which includes flooded toilets and such), and as I am waiting for the coat check, a friendly fellow sporting a Polaroid camera asks me if my friend and I want our pictures taken. I eye him suspiciously, wondering what he could possibly want in return. I hesitantly pose for the picture.

10:36 p.m.: I am now happily holding a Polaroid picture and waiting for it to develop. Turns out camera-boy was simply trying to spread a little peace, love, unity, and respect and wanted nothing in return. It's weird how our own twisted society has made me so cynical. I thought he was going to ask for money afterwards or try to sell me something.

10:40 p.m.: With my bag checked and glowsticks in hand, I bounce off to the dance floor that has been tempting me for so long. The 240 beats per minute have everyone happy, smiling, and completely enthused. I dance around while waiting for my favourites: Anabolic Frolic & E-by-Gum.

12:30?: Must ... have ... water ... So incredibly thirsty and sweaty. Yuck. Must buy incredibly overpriced $3 water.

2:00 a.m.: WHY DID I DRINK THAT WATER????? Now I need to use the washroom that is completely over-flooded with suspiciously brown-coloured water. WHY DID I WEAR WHITE TEAR-AWAYS????

2:30 a.m.: I am now walking around with my pants rolled up to my knees, successfully avoiding the sludge that has accumulated even on the dance floor. A young, innocent-looking blond boy asks me if I want to purchase "E." Ummm, no.

2:31 a.m.: I realize I am in a room with more drugs circulating than a hospital.

3:15 a.m.: As I walk around, a candy raver in pigtails thrusts a bag of candy in my face and, in a high-pitched voice, squeals, "CAN-dee?" I decline her offer.

4:00 a.m.: I QUIT—I can't take it any more. My feet hurt, I'm covered in layers of sweat, I can no longer hear, and I'm feeling mildly claustrophobic. I retire the glowsticks and head towards the car.

Reflections on the night: I have finally figured out what raving is. It is the neo-hippie movement of the '90s. It's about people with a love for music trying to do some kind of damage control in a world of cynicism and corruption. It is about dressing up ridiculously and hugging strangers. It's about looking someone in the eye, smiling, and asking them how they are doing tonight, even if you've never seen them before in your life. After all the raves that I have been to, the thing that astounds me the most is the lack of violence. I go to clubs all the time and witness fights and aggression. At raves, there is an atmosphere that invariably stuns me. Every time somebody turns around and starts up a conversation, I think that maybe, just maybe, it's not about drugs but about peace, love, unity, and respect. Mental note to self: never wear white pants again ...

Raving Can Kill You

Geneviève Giselle Pagulayan, 18,
Eastern/Central

Approximately ten thousand kids in Toronto, ranging from thirteen years of age to their mid-twenties, are catching the craze every weekend: raves. Though they have just recently surfaced into mainstream culture, raves have been going on in Toronto for the past decade and a half.

For the uninformed, raves are weekly all-night electronic-music dance parties, which are described by police, social workers, and politicians as one of the fastest-growing and most worrisome social trends among teens.

Are teens aware of the harm raving could cause them? Could going to parties, using illegal substances, and dancing until the break of dawn possibly be bad for you?

"Yes," states an OAC at Jarvis Collegiate Institute, "but it's worth it. I'd rather live a happy short life than a crappy long one."

"I go to raves because it's fun ... the atmosphere is great! Everyone is having fun, and people dress up for them," says Amanda Finkle, another Jarvis OAC student.

When asked, many adolescents comment on the great atmosphere. Everyone seems happy, like a big family—everyone is accepted. "[Raves] are a place where you are with a family of friends which get together to bond and unite without prejudice toward one another," states Adrian Segeren, eighteen. "It's a place where frowns become smiles, where smiles become truth ...

a place where plush toys revive and handshakes become hugs."

This is one reason why the rave scene is so popular: the outcasts of the outcasts can be loved. Ravers who have the fattest pants, the best moves, do the most drugs, and have the longest partying history tend to be the most popular—it does not take much to feel special there. Everyone likes to feel special, to feel wanted, and raves are where many turn to achieve this.

Despite the rave philosophy—PLUR (Peace, Love, Unity, and Respect)—there is a somewhat hierarchical and elitist society that exists. "You dance well, you get noticed," says Jay, a former Jarvisite. "At a party, if someone isn't dressed like a raver, a lot of people feel they don't belong there. I used to look at someone's fat pants and automatically assume that I had something in common with them."

However, there are reasons why raves are dangerous. The popularity. The "love" can suck people into the scene. It can almost be compared to being in a gang. "Drugs themselves make this 'love' even more apparent," notes Paul, twenty-two.

Substance abuse is another reason why raves are popular. "[I went to parties] for the music and to escape from reality. I don't go anymore. I went because I wanted to have fun, to take drugs, to get high," admits a former raver, also a Jarvisite.

Eight out of ten Jarvis students surveyed lately who went to raves admitted that they went under the influence of drugs. One reason for this is that drugs are more available at raves than at school or at work. Upon walking into a rave, one might be offered drugs (such as "E," "crystal," "K," or "acid") several times in the first half hour.

"I think people use E because it makes you feel good. I did it the first time out of pure curiosity, because it sounded interesting," states Paul. The effects of ecstasy that attract people to use it are entactongenesis (the "at peace" or "happy" feeling one may feel within), empathogenesis (the close feeling to others), and enhancement of the senses.

"People told me that E doesn't cause brain damage, that it's safe. That's why I tried it," says a fifteen-year-old raver. This is not true; ecstasy can cause permanent neurological damage, as well as insomnia, convulsions, learning inability, and memory loss. It weakens the immune system and lowers the levels of serotonin, a chemical that aids in balancing out moods, in the brain and spine.

The lowering of these levels results in depression and anxiety. Methamphetamine (also known as "crystal," "jib," or "meth") is the drug that ecstasy (methylenemethamphetamine) branched out from. It is highly addictive, both psychologically and physically, and very popular at raves because it keeps people up on their feet and speeds them up. "It's like being really awake and nervous at the same time," explains Jay.

"[When the effects of crystal wore off] I felt hungry, then nauseous ... very jittery and fidgety and my teeth were grinding ... and when I finally came down, I was exhausted," says Jamie, eighteen. Upon stopping abruptly, the user goes through withdrawal sickness, feeling extremely tired, ravenously hungry, irritable, and depressed.

One hallucinogen often taken by ravers is LSD. People take it because it goes for five dollars, lasts twelve hours, and is definitely an escape from reality. It commonly causes insomnia, and it might release psychosis or depression, leading to irrational behaviour.

Sammy, a nineteen-year-old raver, shares her experience: "I had a bad trip once. I saw this path like Bugs Bunny ... digging a tunnel ... in a cartoon ... And it travelled over certain people, then to me. I heard a voice tell me to stand up on a path, but there was no one there. It'd tell me that it was my turn to get on the path, and when I'd try to get away from it, out of the warehouse, and walk forward ... I couldn't. I could only walk sideways ... I broke down and started to cry."

"I'm never going to do acid again ... I had deep bad emotions, remembered things I didn't want to," says Paul. These experiences, called flashbacks, are common to acid users. A flashback is the replay of an intense emotional experience in the user's head, such as the death of a loved one, the moment of discovery that one is in love, a past traumatic event, or even the trip itself.

One of the most dangerous drugs available to ravers is ketamine, referred to as "K." "[I use it because] it makes me feel detached from the rest of the world, living in a happier space," says Jaime. With ketamine, consciousness, memory, perception, and motor activity are all disassociated from each other. Veterinarians commonly use ketamine as a cat tranquillizer. K can be highly addictive (depending on the user). It can also cause brain damage and trigger psychosis, seizures, depression, and other neurological and psychological diseases. "K is fun, but I'd never do it again. I'd rather drink if I wanted to feel that way, plus it is safer," states Paul.

"I think it's worth it to go sober, because you still have fun," states Gaby, Grade 11. "I go sober. I've never tried any drugs ... I'm afraid of trying it ... I have other things more important to me," says Amanda Finkle.

Even attending raves sober can be dangerous. At the Effective (a production company) rave this past August, a teenage girl was found raped. Someone slipped a drug called GHB (gamma hydroxy butyrate) into her drink and she was sexually assaulted.

In the rave scene, there is a big movement against the use of GHB, the killer drug known as the new date-rape drug ("roofies," or rohypnol, being the drug of choice commonly used for date rapes). GHB is also known as "liquid ecstasy," for in dosages of only 0.5 millilitres it causes feelings of relaxation, inner peace, and happiness. Taking only slightly more can cause nausea, vomiting, diarrhea, headaches, confusion, dizziness, seizures, comas, and breathlessness. When mixed with an alcoholic drink, chances of overdose and death are greatly increased. "[GHB] made me feel like I was really drunk, drowsy, disorientated ... then I felt sick and threw up," notes Kari, a nineteen-year-old raver and a first-time user.

The most obvious reason that raves are dangerous is the mere act of staying out all night, which is unhealthy. The body is not only deprived of a good night's rest, but it is also overworked (ravers tend to stay up on their feet, dancing for hours) and deprived of quality water. The water bottles at raves range from $1.50 to $3.00, and a body that dances and sweats profusely needs more than just one. As a result, ravers fill up the bottles in the washroom. Owners of venues sometimes turn off the water supply, resulting in the dehydration of many ravers, and the lack of water for those on ecstasy can be fatal.

Up until two years ago, raves happened in warehouses, where there would often be no running water, no washrooms, no medical aid, no fire extinguishers, fire alarms, or sprinklers, insufficient exits, and hazardous materials stored on site. When the police caught on, they started shutting them down due to the lack of a permit. Raves are now legally allowed to happen only in aboveground, rented spaces (such as the International Centre and the Toronto Congress Centre).

Still, they are problematic for many reasons. Police and politicians continue their mission to shut down the scene due to factors such as noise disturbance, increased drug use among teens, health and safety risks, and corruption of youth.

My Mother

Julie Gourley, 10,
West Coast

My mother smokes, drinks, and does drugs. While I was in her stomach, she did drugs, the result of which is that I am allergic to drugs, alcohol, and smoking. If I ever do any of these things, I could get addicted and die. I am also very emotional. If I get in a fight with someone, I can become very sad or angry and lose control. I'm emotionally challenged, that's what I call it.

Me and my mom used to hang out together. Sometimes she would not come and she would be hours late. I hate waiting. One time when I was younger I sat outside on a little bright green chair and sat there all day long waiting for her to come and she never did. After that my parents would make me go and watch TV or go play with my best friend across the street, Raphael Magaro, who comforted me when I was sad.

One time when I was three and my sister was seven, my mom left us alone at home when my dad was not living with us. My sister took care of me and I love and cherish her for that. My mom went to a bar to get drunk and do drugs. When I was little, I asked my mom what she was drinking and she said apple juice. I asked her if I could have some and she yelled at me and said no. When she left the room, I tried some. It was beer.

One time I fell down the stairs and I was yelling and screaming and my mom was on the couch and she did not even look at me. Sometimes she used to play loud music and lock herself in her room and do drugs and when she woke up, she would come out and she would be a mess and she would sleep in her clothes. My parents are divorced now and they never talk, they have a very bad relationship, and they don't like each other. My mother never once paid child support and she used all my dad's money and used all the money on my dad's credit cards and she now has a drug debt, which she rarely pays. I'M VERY MAD AT MY MOM. I don't go on visits with her anymore. I don't know much more because my dad and my stepmom don't think I'm old enough. I'm ten years old and in grade five.

The Young and the Breathless

Jennifer Schoffer, 18,
Eastern/Central

Many teenagers are very curious about trying new things, and would even risk their own health to find acceptance by others. This curiosity makes them vulnerable, especially to one of the most preventable deaths in the world, and that is death from smoking.

Rebel, Rogue, Mischievous Babe

Smoking among teenagers has risen to extreme levels through the years and is increasing. Studies show that 85 percent of smokers began to smoke before the age of sixteen, and more than half are females. Teenagers who do smoke run the risk of becoming lifelong smokers.

Users will begin to notice immediate physical effects, like wheezing, worsened asthma, and shortness of breath, as well as an abnormally high heart rate and a lower tolerance for exercise. These conditions will eventually get more serious with continuous use over the years.

Everyone knows that smoking is a proven killer, so why exactly are so many doing it? Teenagers do it because of peer pressure and the need to fit in, convincing them that they look cool doing it. Others feel that it provides a sense of increased energy or stimulation. It can reduce tensions, or give you pleasurable feelings often accompanied by a sense of well-being. The main reason why people do it is because they are simply addicted to it. The reality is that each time you smoke a cigarette, it is costing you five to twenty minutes of your life.

All cigarettes contain nicotine—a drug that's more addictive than heroin, cocaine, or opium. Over four thousand chemical compounds make up a single cigarette, including many cancer-causing chemicals, ammonia, and formaldehyde. These poisonous chemicals are found in paint thinners, pesticides, gasoline, nail polish remover, and embalming agents used to preserve dead bodies.

Second-hand smoke is a killer known to cause many forms of cancer. A non-smoker breathing second-hand smoke is being exposed to the same four-thousand-plus chemicals that a smoker is. Exhaled tobacco smoke contains stronger concentrations than the smoke that goes into a smoker's lungs, which is being filtered, allowing fewer chemical substances to affect their bodies. Second-hand smoke is harmful, and the more that is breathed in, the greater the risk of a heart attack, stroke, lung cancer, and respiratory problems.

When teenagers first begin to smoke, they never intend to get hooked, but they do, and it is so hard to stop. Studies of ex-smokers show that their risk of dying from smoking-related diseases lessens with each year of abstinence. No one ever said that quitting smoking was easy—that is why those who are going to quit have to really want to do it. Don't ever get discouraged because, in the long run, you will have more money, energy, and better health.

What Could Have Been

Meghan Roy, 17,
Eastern/Central

I keep asking myself what life without you will be like, except that I can't seem to find an answer. I always thought that you would live forever—I never even imagined that something like this could happen to someone as special as you.

I suppose when you're a child, the idea of someone so close to you dying seems like an impossible thing, but here we are. You might not survive, but we have to try to survive without you. I still remember you calling me your "little turkey," but now you might never call me your "little turkey" again.

I'll never forget how all of us grandkids would pile into your truck and drive up the street to the corner store. I remember how we used to sing "You Are My Sunshine." Every time I think of that song, I can't help but smile and cry. What will get us through your sickness are all the good memories that we all have of you.

I am glad that I have a grandpa as good as you, and I only wish that you had listened to me when I said smoking can kill you. I might have been only a child, but look how right I was. I hate having to visit you in a hospital room, listening to you cough and seeing you with an oxygen mask because without it you cannot breathe. I hate how you look so helpless just lying there in that bed.

The family is trying to be strong, but it is so hard to be strong when you know what you might lose. I wish I had broken more than one of your cigarettes, because now they are taking you away from the people who love you the most.

I want people to read this. I know that many people in school have no sympathy for what other people go through, and I am not looking for sympathy. I just want to show how much pain smoking causes. If my grandpa had never smoked, he would not be lying in a hospital bed. My family would not be trying to hold back the tears, because there would be no tears. I know that smoking is a game to some of you, but guess what? It is a game that is gradually going to kill you. So go ahead and puff away, but just remember that with every puff you take, you move closer to a hospital bed.

I will never smoke because I am experiencing first-hand the side effects of smoking: I might lose my grandpa forever. The pain of seeing my grandpa in a hospital bed is far greater that any criticism I might get for writing this. I hope that this true story will make at least one person quit smoking; it would make all the difference to me.

In memory of my grandfather, Mr. Melvin Earl Carson.

Chapter 9

Friends

Through Thick and Thin

When I was fourteen, my mom used to tease me about being in love with my best friend, Lori. She said we had all the symptoms. We would walk to school together, had practically all of the same classes, ate lunch together, walked home together, and then talked for hours on the phone after dinner.

My mom said she couldn't figure out how we could possibly have so much to talk about every day. "Must be love," she said.

It's true. It was love. Although I never really told her, Lori was the first person I ever felt deeply connected to. We understood each other.

We talked so much because, honestly, there was so much to talk about. We didn't spend every minute talking about guys, either. One summer month we spent all our time reading about the painter Gustav Klimt, how he believed that the female form is superior to everything, and how in almost all of his paintings there are babies and crones mixed in with the beautiful women, in order to show the different stages of life. I don't even know why we became so obsessed with his work, except that my aunt had sent me a postcard of *The Kiss*, a painting by Klimt, and we couldn't stop looking at it.

I don't know exactly why Lori and I found a connection that was so quick and easy. Maybe it was because we were misfits in a school full of very beautiful, popular girls—we were thrown together because no one else would eat lunch with us. Or maybe it happened when we noticed that we shared a lot of the same opinions in class.

Whatever the reason, it was the beginning of a kind of love affair of the mind that I've since learned is unique to being fourteen. As I've gotten older and busier, there's simply been less time to just hang out. Where there used to be endless weekends and summer days to pore over magazines and swim at the rec centre, now get-togethers with friends need to be pencilled in in advance.

I guess my friendships with girls were kind of more special, more deep before I hit fourteen because, up until then, we hadn't really noticed boys. Things change when boys come into the picture. Instead of talking to your girlfriend for hours, now you're talking to the guy. It's not as though the intensity is transferred from your best girlfriend to the boy you adore, it's just that this whole other side of you feels butterflies and gets excited. Maybe it's him, maybe it's hormones. Either way, the feeling is hard to ignore.

Lori and I went through that. She got a boyfriend, and for a while she disappeared. I moped and waited and made other friends. I didn't resent her for not wanting to spend all of her time with me, I just missed her a whole lot and I wanted her back.

Mostly, I missed talking to her. I could hang out with other girls for company, and we did have lots of fun together doing things, but I didn't know anyone else with as many opinions as Lori. I also didn't know anyone else who liked to argue as much as she did.

Ironically, it was her argumentative and contradictory nature that brought about the end of her relationship. Her boyfriend just didn't like having to defend his position on music—their main topic of discussion—all the time. "I think he thought I was always picking on him," Lori explained over Slurpees one afternoon. "I just wanted to know why he was so into ..." I can't really remember the rest of her sentence. I wasn't paying attention. I was just thrilled to have her sitting on the curb next to me.

I haven't figured out whether it's possible to be really good friends with guys. If they're straight, there always seems to be one person holding out some faint hope that the friendship might develop into something romantic. I guess the basis of all friendships is attraction, so it makes sense. My female friends are funny, intelligent women—qualities I find irresistible. With guy friends, though, there just seems to be a tension that makes it harder to relax, since they almost always want to be your boyfriend, your big brother, or your dad.

Some of that tension can disappear when your friend is gay, but he's still a guy, and there really is a difference in the way that guys and girls get along as friends.

Guys or girls, making friends doesn't come easily to me. I have lots of acquaintances, but sometimes I feel as though I just missed that handbook "making time for friendships." Over the last few years, though, I've made a conscious effort to spend time with people. It was actually tough, because I have always picked loner activities, like reading, over hanging out with friends.

I have made some great friends over the last few years—people who let me arrive late for dinner, friends who didn't get upset if I had a change of heart and decided to stay at home and read instead of going out with them. They've been very cool. And each time I did make it over I had such a good time that it became easier to make the commitment to see them. It became essential to show up on time, because those friends became important.

Friendships can empower you. Good friends will support your plans and schemes, take your side when the world is coming down on you, and get excited about sharing ideas. On the other hand, getting too dependent on the reassurance and acceptance of your friends can leave you feeling a little off kilter when you have to go it alone. I like spending time on my own because it's important to be able to separate yourself from your friends in order to know that your opinions are not entirely shaped by *their* feelings and ideas.

Your friends should make you feel good about yourself. Sometimes mine do and sometimes they don't. I've had friends who have disapproved of my romantic involvements. Occasionally, you will need to stand up to your friends and tell them to stop criticizing you or your choices. Friends who are loyal often believe they have a right to comment on your love life, especially if they sense something is amiss. You need to decide when to listen and when to tell them to back off. True friendships have an quality of unconditional acceptance.

When we criticize other people, without realizing it, we often focus on the personality traits in them that we really don't like in ourselves. If a friend is giving you a hard time, her criticism might say more about her and how she feels about herself than it does about you. If she criticizes you for being too flirtatious or girlish when she prizes a certain reserve, does that make you feel bad about yourself? If so, you need to tell your friend how you feel, and point out that you are probably friends because of your differences and not in spite of them.

Picking friends is an art. Your friends can exert a tremendous influence over the decisions you make about school, travel, dating. They occupy a special place that puts them in a position of power. And you have power over your friends. You can encourage them in their pursuits, and you can share your ideas about your hopes, dreams, and desires in a way that might make them look at their own in a new light. Being a good friend means being aware of your motivation when giving advice. Good friends recognize that we look to each other for approval and guidance, that we soar when our friends believe in us, that we are fragile and require that advice be given gently and kindly, and that we are stronger together if we are good to each other.

Myth:

Girls are catty and not supportive of each other

Some of the things I love most about my girlfriends are the way they listen and make soothing sounds when I'm sad or upset; the excitement they express when good things happen; and how protective they seem to become at the first hint of meanness from a boy or strife at work.

None of that means that we don't compete against each other, or at least compare our goals and accomplishments. We do. It's natural. After all, we became friends because we share similar traits, including ambition.

The myth that girls are catty and always jockeying for top-banana designation undermines our ability to support one another, because it creates fear and mistrust. There are all kinds of people who will try to put you down because they feel inadequate about themselves, but not good girlfriends.

Penned Pals

Kelly Turnbull, 12,
Prairies

When your friends consist mainly of your brother's nine-year-old classmates, one of their siblings, and only two or three kids your own age, you can get pretty lonely. It's important to have friends or you grow up to be a freaky, antisocial bully magnet. I do have other friends, but they're more the type of people who are nice to you until a popular kid strolls by and then you're just the scum on their shoe.

However, the number of friends I have now is like the population of Toronto compared to a year or so ago. To cope with the loneliness in the path of my life, I would draw cartoon characters and they would become my friends. I got so much practice at drawing that I can now draw almost anything and while I was doodling Loch Ness monsters in the margins of my Math notebooks, my cartoon characters were evolving off the pages of my diary into comic strips and full-page cartoons.

My original cartoon was called "The Cyber Mutant Guinea Pigs" about two superhero guinea pigs. I still have the first comic that I drew of them on a piece of loose-leaf paper where they battled mutant soap scum.

The cartoon that I currently draw is called "Squirmops" and is often mistaken for Pokemon. It is abut Cinder the puffpom and his trainer, Jaggret, Brainstorm, and Doggett, Dagget's twin sister Jannice, and Fuzzy. The bad guys are Alisa, Raven, Chi, B.B.Q., and Maun, and eventually will include a character based on me, named Norbert. I know, I know, Norbert is a guy's name.

Norbert is basically a way for me to link myself with my cartoon characters. Even though they aren't real, sometimes my creative mind takes over and convinces me that they are really nonfictional people who go everywhere with me.

My comic actually did help me become more social because it's not every day that you can watch someone draw little pictures of a hundred and fifty-four little monsters that could never exist. Some people come to me because they want to meet the person who invented the Squirmons cartoon that they can read in the school newspaper. All that I can say is that while I cherish my friends, pencils and paper will always be there for me.

Kelly Turnbull

Staring at the Sun

Amanda Henry, 18,
Eastern/Central

It was March 23, 1999, when I walked through the doors of Mount Sinai Hospital. I took a piece of paper from my pocket that read "11th floor, Room 1110." When the elevator doors opened, I stood there, frozen, face to face with the intensive care unit.

Paralyzed with fear, I started to look for Room 1110. As I approached, I did not know what to expect. I slowly pushed open the door, I saw her, and my blood went cold. I walked up to the bed and saw my best friend lying there, motionless. The surgery had been eighteen hours long. Numerous tubes, supported by metal IV stands, were draped across her every which way, from both sides of her body: a feeding tube through her nostrils, a tube in her throat to enable her to breathe, and another connected to her bladder. I couldn't bear to look at her. I closed my eyes, and it all came rushing back to me.

It was a cool day in November 1998. I was waiting outside my house for the bus to get to school. Then I heard someone yell my name from across the street. It was my best friend, Anjanette. I was surprised because she had been up north for a while and she had come home early. Still overjoyed to see her, I ran to her. As I got closer, I could tell by looking into her eyes that something was wrong.

We embraced and she started telling me about her trip. Then her tone got serious.

She mentioned something about the numbness that she had below her lip. I remembered her telling me about it months ago. She had gone to get it checked out and the doctor had said that it was just some nerve damage, nothing to worry about, so I couldn't understand why she was bringing it up. Then she hugged me and started to cry. Through her tears, I heard her say, "It is a tumour. The doctor said it's a tumour, and we don't know if it's cancerous or not."

I froze, and then I cried. We stood there in the middle of the street, in each other's arms, and everything else just disappeared. Nothing else mattered. From that day, things were never the same. We later found out that it was cancer, and it was growing rapidly along the side of her jaw.

The next four months were a blur. Anjanette started to undergo weeks of extensive radiation treatments. The confident and strong girl I once knew was starting to wither away. My once fit and statuesque friend started to drop pound after pound, until there was tightness in her face, her eyes were inset, and the bones in her hands and elbows and knees started to jut through her light-brown skin. The girl whose beauty I had once adored and marvelled at was now shedding hair by the handful. I felt at times that radiation would destroy her. She survived the treatment, but her battle wasn't over yet. She had to go in for emergency surgery.

At this point, I felt as though I was trapped in a never-ending nightmare. My world was starting to crumble. She had always been the strong one. Whenever I was weak or in need, she was my rock. As kids, we'd always pledged "Together forever!" No matter where we'd go or what we'd do, we would do it together. Yet now, she was the one in need, and I was supposed to be the strong one.

We were so close, and yet so far apart. My jokes were only a temporary distraction, my hugs merely a diversion from the loneliness. Some nights she'd fall asleep and I would just hold her in my arms until morning. Still, nothing could ease the pain. I could not change the fact that fate might tear her away from my life at any given moment.

Little things in life seemed so insignificant. I started asking myself why it had to be her and not me. I wanted to know why. She was only eighteen. It just didn't make sense. I lay awake all night just praying, thinking, and then praying some more. As I watched the early-morning sun rise in the distance, I thought about life, friends, family, loved ones ... I thought about how life was so short and our time here was so precious. It's the little things that we do for each other that make all the difference. The time goes by too quickly to spend it in any other way than loving and appreciating the time spent together.

Suddenly, I felt something. I opened my eyes and her hand was holding mine. Once again she was my rock. Right then, I knew, everything was going to turn out just fine.

Letter to a Boy

Angela Kostenko, 19,
Eastern/Central

I know you don't believe me when I tell you about it here. I know you don't want to hear about it, and I know you think that life is so much better where you are. But I love it here. You love the concrete jungle and can't understand why I'm sick of it.

I should tell you about all my dreams, but it's been years since I've told you about my dreams. And even longer since you've understood them. My dreams aren't the kind you get when you go to sleep at night. My dreams are the kind I think about when I write letters to Lisa and Laura and random zine girls you've never heard of. My dreams are the kind I get when I walk alone in newly fallen leaves at seven in the morning on my way to class. My dreams are the kind I get when I sit on my big windowsill at night and see the stars shining in the sky. These are stars you can't see in your city, they are overpowered by bright lights and skyscrapers. I don't have anything against your bright lights and skyscrapers, but I happen to like stars (and big trees and fresh air) better.

I don't know your new address. If I was there, in the city, I could find you. It wouldn't be hard. I'd know where to look, and where to go ... but as it stands, I'm not in the city and I don't want to go there. I don't want to see you again. The last time I was called "pretentious." With my laptop under my arm and my animal-friendly shoes and my political T-shirt. I was on a date with a girl. That was "pretentious." Excuse me. That's just who I am.

You sit in coffee shops all day. You get money sent to you every month. Don't call me fucking pretentious. You went to Toronto to find yourself. I could have told you what you'd find before you left. I saw it in your eyes when I met you five years ago. I saw it in your eyes when you walked into this city, my old city, my old home. I saw how excited and anxious you were. I saw how beautiful you thought the shiny, vaguely happy hipster people were. You don't know what you're missing here. Here the people are giggling, running, happy, and crunchy. You'd laugh at them. They smell funny. They're strange. They're crazy. Well, yeah, so what. So am I. And I'm glad they're my friends.

When I told you I was queer, you told me that I was pretending, being trendy, trying to fit in. If you saw me here, you'd know you were wrong. You'd see the girl I like, the girls I make eyes at across the club or coffee shop. She could kick your ass, but she wouldn't. I would, maybe. If you were here, you'd see this has nothing to do with being trendy. I go to a trendy concert, and leave early to watch a musician in a closet-sized bar with sweaty, smiling, dancing kids. I've started dancing at concerts. I found out that you don't anymore. I guess that's because the kids in the concrete jungle don't dance at shows; at least they didn't when I went there.

I thought you would never turn out to be like "those people" ... the kind who sneered at me. Hell, the people who who sneered at you, once upon a time. I thought one day we could sit around talking about respective girlfriends. Wondering out loud how we came to know each other. I thought we'd have a special friendship, and I guess we did for a while.

I want to tell you how horrible you made me feel when I was fifteen and depressed. You told me I was pretending. I almost proved you wrong. You almost killed me, in an indirect sort of way. I remember what it was like at fifteen. To care so much about what you thought. About to prove to you that I wouldn't lie.

I want to tell you how I still miss you sometimes. But how I feel guilty for that. And how I don't want you to have that power over me anymore. I don't think about you much, but when I do, I'm sorry for all the things I never said. I'm sorry I never told you I loved you, and I'm sorry I never told you how much I hate you. Right now, right then.

I remember when you laughed because I wanted to move to a crunchy, hippy university town. I remember you telling me I was selling out. That's just the way I felt about you when I saw you sitting in a coffee shop three months ago. I spat words under my breath. You were wearing $200 black pants that were faded to look used. You were wearing leather you swore you'd never wear. You had a notebook balanced on your knee, you were drinking $5 coffee, and you had a new haircut. When I tried to ignore you, you grabbed my hand and sat me down. And I chatted for a moment. My date was getting our coffee and cake. You asked me how I was; when I started tell you how I was feeling, you interrupted with your own life, your own stories, your own problems.

When I finally got in a word, you laughed at my university choice, you frowned at my choice of orientation, you said, "That's so passé." You told me I changed. You changed, too. But you know what? I don't care.

You should see me dancing alone in my room to Dar Williams or the Need. You should see me making eyes at cute girls across dance floors, and blushing when the studliest one asks me to dance. You should see me reading, highlighter flying. You should see me typing this letter right now. I'm listening to crunchy hippy music. You'd disapprove, but maybe next time you won't force me to sit across from you in a coffee shop, even for five minutes. And when my date came and put her hand on my neck, you frowned, looking noticeably uncomfortable. And when she pulled my chair out for me, you made some comment like "I thought you were a feminist" ... I smelled the coffee on her breath and I forgot you were sitting there.

I don't know if I'll ever forget you, or the things you meant to me. But that doesn't mean I still like you.

Love, Angela

Friendship

Natali Chin, 18,
Eastern/Central

As I was surfing the Internet the other day, in an attempt to finish my English ISU, I stumbled upon this quote, from Ralph Waldo Emerson: "It is one of the blessings of old friends that you can afford to be stupid with them." That was when I got sidetracked from my studies and began to think of all the stupid things that my best friend, Sherri, and I have gotten ourselves into over the years. Then I also laughed out loud because I realized how true that saying is, since she is the only one that I can act that stupid around, without her thinking that I'm in desperate need of help from a mental institution.

I remembered the day Sherri and I found ourselves acting very nostalgic in a coffee shop. Like two old retired ladies, we had begun to reminisce about the way we were years ago. Oddly enough, our travel back through "memory lane" was induced by a Backstreet Boys song that we had previously heard in the car. The song seemed to remind us of our embarrassing "New Kids on the Block days" back in the '80s. Even though we might deny it now, there was a time in our lives when we were both crazy about that group. So crazy that we even made up our own dances to their songs and swore that she would marry Joey McIntyre and I would marry Jordan Knight when we turned eighteen. (Boy, were we stupid and naive back then!)

It must have been weird for the other people around us to hear two teenagers joking about the "good old days" and how we missed our carefree childhood, as if we were elderly. Nevertheless, for about four hours we talked about everything under the sun—from the "Barbie Soap Operas" that we made up, to the time when we went to camp and I got so hyper from the candies we'd smuggled in that I would even laugh at the joke "Why did the chicken cross the road?"

To add to everything, when she and I were ordering our coffees, we began to fight over who would pay the bill while we teased each other about embarrassing moments that only the both of us knew about each other. The cashier, who was also Sherri's boss, began to laugh and she gave us this look as though we were truly crazy. She then asked us how long we had been friends, and in perfect unison we said, "Sixteen years." At that moment, it hit me that we had known each other for almost our entire lives. Sherri was more like a sister than just a friend. Fortunately, our friendship was so strong that it had even survived the time she moved to Stouffville, when we were ten or eleven.

I think the cashier noticed the bond that Sherri and I had right away by the way we interacted. She told us that our lifelong friendship deserved free coffees. That was just one of the many rewards that our friendship has brought us. However, the greatest reward is that I know I will always have someone who believes in me, cares for me no matter what I do, and, most importantly, accepts me for who I am, without wanting to change anything about me.

As I look deeper into our unique friendship, I am reminded of the time when I first knew that we would be best friends forever. This poignant moment occurred when I was in grade eleven and I was extremely ill in the hospital for weeks on end. I was so ill, in fact, that my parents would not permit anyone to visit me, for fear that my friends would catch what I had, or that they might make me worse. Sherri was the only one who would call me constantly just to see how I was, since my condition made her worried sick that she might not see me ever again. She then decided to come anyway, because she so desperately wanted to relieve some of my pain by keeping me company and lifting my spirits. It is that kind of compassion that helped me get through my illness, and other things in my life, like the time she stayed up with me almost all night on the phone when she heard that one of my friends had just died. She has never let me down, no matter how difficult or impossible the circumstances. We are always able to tackle and conquer hardships, as long as we do it together, and that's why our friendship has managed to last so long.

Now that university is quickly approaching, and many friends are going their separate ways, Sherri and I will not. We will be starting a new stage of our lives as we always have: together.

Chapter 10

Jobs

Minimum Wage, Minimum Satisfaction

I had my first summer job, making $3.25 an hour, when I was thirteen. I was a telephone sales person for the Shiners' Circus. It wasn't a lot of money, even back then, particularly after deductions, but I was just looking for something to supplement my allowance and to keep me in Slurpees and bus fare to the beach until school began again.

During one of my shifts, I got into trouble for talking. It was worth it, I guess, because I found out that the dialing finger in the row next to me was making $3.45 an hour. Boy, was I peeved. As far as we could tell, the only reason for the disparity in wages was that she had been there longer—yeah, like a whole two weeks. Back then, I didn't really know about minimum wage, or the ten-minute break I was entitled to take every four hours, but I knew that that was just plain wrong. I didn't say anything to the "team leader" about the difference in wages, though; I wanted to keep my job.

The desire of young people to make money, working at almost any job, is why companies are able to exploit workers. It's why multinational fast-food chains get away with subjecting young people to unsafe working conditions, few if any benefits, and irregular hours.

Corporations know that most young people are seeking short-term summer employment or part-time work during the school year, and so do not have the time or know-how to organize a union or fight for their rights. Unions were created to protect workers. Their power lies in negotiating on behalf of the group. Unions can ensure that employee-employer contracts detail hiring and firing practices, wages, hours of work, and health and safety regulations. Job security and wages are generally higher for unionized workers than for those who do not have union representation.

Low-wage jobs tend to fall to workers who lack education—and this problem is not unique to young people. Many adults get stuck in dead-end jobs because they do not have the skills or education to secure a better salary. Although that link becomes pretty obvious when you're older and have been in the workforce for a little while, it's not that clear when you're still in school. I went to school with guys who dropped out as soon as they got their first taste of the power and freedom of earning their own money, even if it was at McDonald's. Some of the others who left school for dead-end jobs did so because they didn't receive the kind of guidance or information they needed from parents or counsellors about programs that might have been of interest to them, when the more obvious choices of doctor, lawyer, and dentist didn't appeal.

Of course, even qualified professionals face problems getting work. In Canada, many doctors, engineers, and other professionals are denied work in their field because their education and training has taken place abroad and so is not recognized here. This is a problem that mainly affects new immigrants. Although there has been much criticism of this practice, especially since we are experiencing a shortage of doctors in Canada, particularly in rural areas, nothing has been done to change it. Critics have said that this practice is intended to ensure that there is always a pool of workers available for low-wage, low-skilled work.

I'm not sure if you've noticed this, but interest in a certain field is often contingent upon whatever program happens to be popular on TV. If "ER" is getting the big ratings, then it seems everyone wants to work as an emergency room doctor. Throughout university, a lot of my friends talked about becoming lawyers. I'm sure it's because they were watching "L.A. Law," and I think a lot of their ideas concerning what it meant to be a lawyer had to do with the way the profession was portrayed on that show. "L.A. Law" lawyers were always in court defending an important cause, or making a brilliant speech. Plus, they drove fabulous fast cars and made piles of cash. Those of my friends who did become lawyers talk about the piles of cash they are making, but they also say that they rarely get to see the inside of a courtroom, because most cases are settled out of court. And they barely have a chance to spend their money because they work eighty to ninety hours a week on cases that are a snore.

A well-paying job can't guarantee work that is interesting or challenging.

I think the key to finding work you love is to try a bunch of different things. Make a list of the most exciting work you can think of doing—be limited only by your imagination—and then start asking your parents, your friends' parents, and your teachers for any leads or contacts they might have in those areas. More jobs are landed through connections than by answering ads. And there is a tremendous amount of power in taking action. It means you give yourself the chance to decide what you want to do, rather than letting someone else, like a parent or guidance counsellor, pick for you.

Once you've pinpointed a person to contact in your field of interest, call and ask about volunteering, or an internship. Finding your passion requires putting yourself in the right place, for the right things to happen to you.

The great thing about being young is that, hopefully, at least during the summer, you have time and fewer financial responsibilities, which means greater freedom to follow leads and learn more about what you like and what you're good at. If you live at home, you probably don't have to worry about rent just yet, so you have the luxury of volunteering, or taking an unpaid internship. While it's easy to criticize people for sticking with jobs they hate and not following their passion, sometimes the reality of having children, a mortgage, and other financial obligations can make it nearly impossible.

Although I'm not a huge fan of unpaid work, it does have lots of benefits. For some reason, when you work as a volunteer, you are often given the chance to do work that is more interesting and comes with more responsibility. Perhaps that's because, even though you may not have all of the qualifications for the job, the fact that you are willing to volunteer your time speaks volumes.

The other decision you will need to make at some point is about who you want to work for. During my first year of university I worked as a waitress in coffee shops, breakfast joints, and even a bar. The tips were good, but I felt the need to own my labour. I decided that it was important to put my energy towards something that I owned, rather than giving it away. I think part of that need came from a desire to understand how a company works in its entirety, rather than simply being slotted into one section and never fully understanding how my role affected what other people in the business were doing.

So, in my second year of university, instead of getting a regular job, I applied for a $3,000 student venture loan and started a crêpe stand. I filled the crêpes (they're like thin pancakes) with ice cream, covered them with fresh fruit, and sold them at summer fairs and festivals across southwestern Ontario. If it didn't rain, I made a killing. If it did, I lost my shirt. I ran that business every summer until I graduated.

Operating my own business certainly meant knowing every part of it, largely because I was *doing* every part of it, from mixing the batter at night to making sure that a freezer and an adequate amount of ice cream and fruit would be ready in the town where I'd be setting up that weekend. It was also loads of fun. Given the number of hours I put in, I might have made more money working for someone else, but the experience of developing an idea into a business, writing a business plan, applying for a student venture loan, hiring an employee (usually a willing boyfriend), and then making sure I had made enough money to pay back the loan before the start of the school year, while also having enough leftover for books and tuition, gave me a good idea of my strengths and skills.

When you learn that your work is your life—that it is used to define who you are, that it is a means to create things, to shape things, and to have an impact on the world around you—it becomes pretty clear that you'd better make sure that you're doing something you love, regardless of the perks or the pay.

Myth:

Success requires sacrifice

Success is defined for us by our parents, teachers, peer group, the government, in ways that usually relate to wealth and position. But how do you define it for yourself?

The more specific you can be about your definition, the easier it will be to achieve it. For me, success used to mean making a lot of money, until I learned that "a lot" is a vague concept, and that it's entirely possible for me to do all the things I want to do by making a dollar figure that is less than I imagined. I also didn't know that being successful for me would mean creating things, and contributing to society. Those intangibles are learned only when you begin to do things and see how they feel. Your ideas about success will probably change as you begin to experience what it's like to work in a corporate environment, as an entrepreneur, in a small firm.

I think success comes from doing work in an area that engages and stimulates you.

Tuna Warp

Lauren Kirshner, 18,
Eastern/Central

Friends: Welcome to the Tuna Warp. No, scratch that. Welcome to the Salami and Cheese with Oil and Vinegar Warp. Feel this deli meat angst, ladies and gentlemen. I beseech you to climb inside my underwashed uniform and feel the dank wetness of a worker who quit two weeks ago, and now I bond with this stranger through his perspiration. I would gladly shake your hand, only mine is swathed in a filmy latex glove, which is encrusted with Warp bits and pieces. But allow me to tip my cap to you, in a meagre submission. I am your Warp-maker. Hello!

"What the hell is a Warp?" some emaciated troll asks me from the other side of the counter. He is wearing overalls with no shirt. His nipples are covered with Band-Aids. Everything is warped. I no longer wonder.

"It's a typo. It means WRAP. We make WRAPS here."

"You guys should learn how to speak English," he drawls. "I don't know what this fuckin' country is coming to. No one speaks English anymore. They need to get all these aliens out."

Yes, yes, aliens. I imagine his mottled nipples, severed off in some demented Fascist ceremony. I do not want to make this man a Warp. I do not let bigots enter the Warp.

"Gimme a cheese and tomato one. I'm in a rush."

Rebel, Rogue, Mischievous Babe

The monkeys in the kitchen go to work. There are five cooks in the kitchen. Each wearing sterile white gloves fit for a laboratory, and filthy shirts. I ache with the irony. One monkey slices open the bread, the other passes him some mustard.

"Dijon or sweet?" is of course the next phrase in my lexicon.

"I don't want any mustard at all," he howls.

The monkeys scrape the bread on the counter. Mustard smears everywhere. One monkey cleans his ear and produces from it a yellow, rock-like substance that resembles heroin. He passes it to a monkey who subsequently passes it to another monkey who then douses it in mayonnaise and adds it to the Warp.

Up at the front, I have given the sadomasochist his change. He is wearing roller skates. He rolls around the floor and returns. We stare at each other dully. A monkey lumbers towards me. He has been in the basement eating. You are allowed one Warp for every five-hour shift. He has now eaten his allocated Warp and there will be no more for Gord. His self-tattooed arms grapple at my waist.

"You're too pretty to work here," he coos. "Come down to the basement. I want to show you something."

Images of kindergarten show-and-tell flood back to me. I recall a blond boy named Matthew who was six when I was five (and I thought he was so old) who, during nap time, would expose himself to me while we nibbled on pilfered graham crackers. If only real life were so easy.

It has been seven minutes and the Warp is still in its embryonic stage. The cheese is AWOL and the monkeys are scurrying around the kitchen. They are angry with me.

"Did you bother to ask if he wanted American, Swiss, Cheddar, or Provolone?" they hiss at me in unison. "You could make this a lot easier for us."

He is rolling around again. He strikes me as the Cheddar type. They are always passive-aggressive and posing as benevolent when they are in fact psychotic.

"Give him Cheddar," I command. "The boy will eat Cheddar."

I am sweating in the cap. I fear that I may be emitting an odour. No one would care. I take comfort in that. The Monkeys are wrapping the sandwich. They argue as they do it, all speaking different languages. Somehow, they understand enough of the profanity to get the gist. Pablo, an Indian sailor from Bombay, wants to use twine to tie the sandwich up. He brags that he can make over two hundred different types of knots. Pete, the Russian would-be cowboy, tells him that the only knot he knows how to make is a slip-knot.

"With that I would tie you to the ceiling," Pete says darkly.

Pablo ignores him. He launches into a speech, a sort of contest he likes to play with his colleagues.

"Name any coastal country," he says.

"Borneo," Gord replies.

Pablo pauses and strokes his chin.

"I don't believe in my heart of hearts that Bor-nayo is coastal. I will refer to my nautical atlas tonight."

"New Zealand."

"I have been there four times. Each time with a shipment of exotic pine nuts and saffron."

"And mail-order brides," Gord says. He scratches his tattoo of a buxom brunette. It is so old that her face is blurred now.

"I've been to every coastal country," Pablo brags. "Every last one."

I ding the bell. This is hell. I have to tell the Ministry of Health that this place ain't so swell. In the smoked turkey is hair gel. It is my hair gel, I confess. I wear that gel to tame my irate Mediterranean tresses. Now the Warp is ready. They pass it to each other and one minute later it reaches me. I hand it to my man. He says nothing. He is displeased at the time it took. I should have said, "Would you like a nipple with that?"

Now Tuna Warp is empty. The Monkeys read comic books, smoke cigars out the back door, make long distance calls to Iran and Bolivia, and attempt to access naked women on the Internet. I am tired. I have served one person today, and now I am fully exhausted, prisoner in this fast-food miasma. Now I must go and clean the toilets. I have made the equivalent of two dollars so far today. I can buy two chocolate bars, one fare on the subway, or half a rat at PJ's Pet Centre.

PLEASE, when I die, embalm me in the meat trio, which consists of mortadella, salami, and prosciutto. Let me pay homage to these humble blue-collar roots. I am often told that from simple beginnings rise charmed lives. Let me be the phoenix that rises from a mound of salad dressing and meat scraps. I will wear a cape of scrap salami sewn together like Joseph's. I will look back on this time in my life and revel in my tolerance and bad judgment.

Friends, my vocation beckons. Answer the call. You know you are hungry. For food? For passion ... so am I. Join me next time and let's do the time Warp again.

What's the McDeal with McDonald's?

Anna Kiil, 17,
Eastern/Central

Have you ever wondered, as you sank your teeth into a juicy Big Mac, special sauce dripping down your chin, guilt creeping into your head, what it's really all about? No, I don't mean the Meaning of Life, I mean McDonald's.

Ever worried about what you've been eating all these years? Ever wondered how anyone could work behind a cash counter, serving greasy fast food while wearing a purple visor with the big golden arch on it? Ever ask yourself, "How exactly do they make me a whole meal in, like, two minutes?" Many people do ask themselves these questions, but most of them frankly don't give a damn. They say, "If it itches, scratch it," "If it tastes good, eat it," and "If you really don't know what the hell it is, EAT IT ANYWAY!"

There are over 21,000 McDonald's restaurants in 101 countries around the world. They sell about $30 billion worth of fast food every year. They train more personnel than the United States Army. Their business has grown so much that any person in New York City can walk to a McDonald's in four minutes.

So what's the real McDeal? One issue is the food itself. When asked what she thought of the food at McDonald's, Julia Ford, a grade twelve student at Jarvis Collegiate Institute, said, "The only thing I'd ever eat over there are the fries. The rest of it is pretty gross." The quality of food is a matter of opinion, but some things remain factual. The new Deluxe Filet O'Fish sandwich contains 510 calories and 20 grams of fat. A crispy McChicken Deluxe has 530 calories and 26 grams of fat. One Big Mac burger has a shocking 587 calories and about the same amount of fat as the McChicken Deluxe. And for those of you who enjoy washing it all down with a shake, each of these beverages contains 377 calories. This isn't to say that the occasional McDonald's binge is a sin, but if the restaurant continues to grow in popularity, we may find the clothing industry doing a bit of altering to accommodate our big McButts.

McDonald's has recently been doing some alteration of their own in an attempt to improve the quality of their food. As of now, fries sit under heating lamps until they're served, and burgers are popped into microwaves. Right now, buns take twenty-four seconds to heat, and hamburgers take eighty seconds to fry. They've almost devised a way to heat a bun in ten seconds, and they're working on a method of cooking a hamburger in the same amount of time—all of this to serve the customer more efficiently. (And if a ten-second burger seems a little unnatural to you, THAT'S 'CAUSE IT IS!)

Some of our fellow students at Jarvis have even worked at McDonald's. Judy Huynh, a grade twelve student at the school, feels quite differently about the food after having been a McDonald's employee. When asked if working behind the scenes at the restaurant changed her opinion about the food, she said, "Uh, yeah! I never eat there anymore ... it's disgusting!" Who better to hear it from than someone who actually had to serve the food to people, knowing how it was made?

Because so much of the food sits around so long that it eventually has to be thrown out, they're trying to find a way to keep it fresh longer. (Finally, something that might benefit the environment.) New holding cabinets are being designed to store cooked chicken and beef patties so that they will keep for twenty minutes. This will save the company money on wasted food (their main concern), and at the same time cut down on the unfathomable amount of garbage produced daily.

However, the McDonald's restaurant chain has created more severe problems than the stale hamburger. In 1997, a group of activists in England published an anti-McDonald's pamphlet that contained a list of accusations about the company. A trial was held, and the judge ruled that the accusations were unprecedented except for a few. One was the cruel treatment of animals. Before they are slaughtered, pigs, chickens, and cows live in small cramped cages in rooms without sunlight. Footage was found of the slaughtering process, in which many chickens had their throats slit while they were still conscious and died unnecessarily slow deaths. Almost three years after the trial, McDonald's appears to have shown no effort to improve this situation.

Another charge that McDonald's was found guilty of was the manipulation of the minds of children through advertising. (This might not be as shocking as the chicken thing, but it is still interesting.) The judge agreed that their advertising technique exploits young, impressionable children who have no control over these ads that target their desires. They then pressure their parents into purchasing McDonald's food and toys (found in Happy Meals) and, in turn, raising McDonald's profits. The corporation uses the vulnerability of kids to make a buck.

Remember when each McDonald's would have a sign outside with a big yellow arch and a notice telling you how many people they'd served? Once the number rose to 99 billion, they stopped counting. Their business has grown to a dangerous size. Beautiful European cities have been blemished by tacky McDonald's franchises. Paris now has one under the Eiffel Tower. Not even India has been spared.

There are a few things to think about as you decide whether or not to go to McDonald's at lunch, or at any other time as a matter of fact. As I see it, you'd be supporting a restaurant that a) serves pretty low-grade food; b) doesn't give two *$%*s about the animals it uses; and c) probably got inside your head when you were young to try to tempt you to eat their food. But the most important thing to think about is that you'd be supporting a corporation that is slowly teaching the rest of the world to be wasteful. They are subtly teaching the world the fast food culture: to appreciate quantity, and not quality. McDonald's is creeping into all corners of the world, showing people how to be like "real" North Americans. Is that what we want? I'm really asking you!

Who's Grace?

Carly O., 19,
West Coast

I passed by a smooshed-up coyote in the middle of the road. I can usually tell how my day's going to go by the morning drive.

Unaware of how brave he was being, my first customer darted into the restaurant before I had a chance to finish my morning coffee. After a sleepy conversation, I filled his cup for the third time and passed him a crushing look of bitter jealousy. Another wounded coyote!

I work in a small independent restaurant on the outskirts of White Rock, British Columbia. During the week the place is filled with landscapers, car salesmen, and the wealthiest upper-middle-class white seniors. These people all carry a certain "dying to be alive" air about them that makes my heart ache. They don't know they're dying. They don't know there's a whole other world that passes them by hourly. Often I find them rude, inconsiderate, and in an overall blind state of mind. I have adopted a low tolerance level. Not too healthy, though.

My restaurant is filled with an eclectic collection of old and young blues, jazz, and rock & roll memorabilia. The walls are plastered with

the faces of real musicians, the ones that play music for love, not for money. From the wailing voices of AC/DC and Tom Waits to the brutally honest vocalists—Elvis Costello and the Art Kane Jazz School of Harlem—the place is filled with an appreciation for life through music. In the background, through the music, I can hear an air of strong voices and brilliant words that's enough to knock you on your mind's ass.

I don't know how I got here. In the service industry, I mean. I hate people. That's probably not fair—I often tend to get carried away judging people too quickly. The way someone walks through the door, the way they expect me to dote on them, even how they ask for a glass of water. I've developed an "I could kill in one breath" look. I only use it when necessary. I'd hate to know that my waitress is passing her judgment on how I react even before words are spoken. However, I'm not entirely unfair. My surly service is reserved for the mindless schmucks who don't know the difference between asking for something and ordering something.

The morning drives when the sunrays are streaming down through massive rain clouds—I find it difficult to be so hard on customers. I extend them some small talk, short enough not to be a bother to either of us, just sufficiently tolerant to make both our days a little smoother. Every customer's lines are different; you know the ones who are willing to interact.

My customer-server relationship has caught me off guard on several occasions. "Don't lick a metal pole in the middle of winter." Something has to be said for a relationship built on bitter service. I wish people tipped on quick banter rather than on how quickly and gracefully I placed their food in front of them. "Enjoy"—is that what they really want me to say? Or would they rather have some quick-witted remark on how they lusted over their coffee and eggs? "Enjoy!" I find it more obnoxious when a waitress says that. What does she mean? Enjoy the food, enjoy the atmosphere, the music, why don't you just sit and relax, drink your coffee and eat your eggs and enjoy watching my ass as I fetch you a glass of water to wash down your breakfast. Just leave the tip on the table, come back soon; maybe next time you can bring the wife and kids.

My job is easy. I suppose anything is easy when you do it for a long time. The job of running back and forth fetching customers' requests, smiling insincerely, grows old very quickly. So maybe on a day when I reach the crest of the highway where all I can see is a blanket of fog covering the ocean as far as the horizon will take you, I'll step back and breathe. Perhaps I'll catch a glimpse of a customer who's worth more to me than "How 'bout the weather?"

An older couple walks into the restaurant, smack dab in the middle of a lunch rush. I offer up the most sincere *"Good afternoon."* The gentleman smiles politely, the woman says nothing. After attending to other needy customers, I make it back to the old couple's table. The woman stares at me like I've aggravated her pissy mood. They order. I bring food to them in less than ten minutes. Wasn't I fast enough? She doesn't understand that it actually takes time to cook food. I should serve it raw next time. They leave, unaffected by me. They are gone, leaving me with a dollar fifty-nine and a strong urge to kill. The next person I see is going to pay with more than money.

A couple of realtors slide into a table at the back of the restaurant. I acknowledge their presence but take time bringing them their drinks. A minute later they've ordered and continue to talk about a slut with big boobs they were watching on TV last night. I bring them their food. One man claims he ordered something he didn't; we argue. He's a liar. I walk away, and under his breath, but loud enough for me to hear him, he mumbles something about "fucking bitch ..." I don't turn around and continue walking.

Bea walks in the door. She comes in every Thursday at one o'clock. I know her order. She gets her hair done every week, then comes to the restaurant to get herself a sandwich. I like her; we have good small talk. Her daughter's getting married on the weekend.

Mr. Johnny, the realtor, stands up at the other side of the restaurant, gives me a snap of the fingers, and hollers louder than the bustle of the rush, "Water." I turn around quickly so I won't have to look at his crusty face. It's one of those moments when I wish I was in the old west with a six-gun holster around my waist. I would take him out right then and there.

I take him his water, laced with enough poison to kill even all his nose hair if he inhaled it. He doesn't drink, too busy yapping his flappy lips off. He pays and leaves me five something in a tip. I suppose I was to feel guilty for having the right to kill. Bea sits staring blankly at me, refusing to acknowledge how the realtor has treated me. I ask her if she wants a glass of water while she waits. I go to the back room to get it. She should be dead by the time she gets home. My poison gives me a ten-minute grace period. I love grace.

Strawberry Picking Should Be More Fun than This!

Christine Phrakaysone, 16,
Eastern/Central

The summer break from school presents an opportunity for most children to go to camp, swim, play, and have some fun with their friends, but not all kids can afford to have such carefree days in the sun. At the age of ten, Kham was waking up at 6:00 a.m. to get ready for picking vegetables at a farm in Ontario during her summer break from school. She would hitch a ride with her uncle and aunt, who also work on the farm. Her work day ended as late as 8:00 in the evening.

Kham is not alone. The Farmworker Justice Fund in the United States estimates that 300,000 to 800,000 youth work in the fields. There doesn't appear to be a great deal of research or statistics on migrant farm workers in Canada, but according to Stan Raper, the Canadian co-ordinator for the United Farm Workers, 10,000 workers are brought into Ontario every year as transient farm labour. Canada gets seasonal farm workers from Costa Rica, Africa, and other parts of world that condone shipping seasonal farm workers to Canada upon approval from the provincial and federal governments.

In most parts of Canada, except for British Columbia, it is illegal to organize farm workers. Raper says that farm workers make less than minimum wage and have no employment standards or workers' compensation. Two years ago, about 1,000 farm labourers from Mexico and the Caribbean worked in the fields and greenhouses of Essex County, down by Windsor.

There are 3 to 5 million farm workers in the United States, and women and children under the age of fourteen represent 38 percent of that population. In 1974 it was made illegal for children under the age of twelve to work on any farm with the exception of family-owned farms. A twelve-year-old working on a farm needs to have parental consent.

Charles first tried picking vegetables on a farm in Windsor when he was sixteen. He says, "My parents' friends asked me if I wanted to go. I thought it was a lot of money—$500 a week. There was free housing and no experience required, so I went and took my best friend with me." The farmer wanted him to stay for two months—he lasted three weeks. Charles's day was similar to Kham's. He would wake at 5:30 a.m. and finish picking at 6:00 in the evening. He usually harvested corn and cucumbers.

"When you start working, you don't see the other end of the row, until you get halfway," he says. "I never managed to finish my row. I was a beginner. I don't know how other people did it—they'd go to the end of the row and come back past my row," he says. Like Kham, he was also paid by the basket, which weighed 15 to 20 kilograms when filled. Small cucumbers were preferred because they are easier to make pickles with. "If the cucumbers are too big, you make ninety cents a basket," Charles explained. "If they are an average size, you make a dollar-thirty, and if they are small (7 centimetres), you make two dollars." On average, you can make six dollars an hour by picking corn. Not only do some labourers harvest, they might also plant, package fruits, cultivate, or stake and tie the crops.

There are between seventy and a hundred workers on the farm that Kham harvests for. The children who come with their parents or relatives range in age from ten to sixteen, and the adults are in their thirties or forties. Upon arrival on the farm, "You pick what they tell you to pick," Kham says. She picks sweet peppers, tomatoes, peas, or pencil beans, depending on the season, earning $1.50 for a single basket. "If you're lucky, you make fifty dollars in one day."

Kham comes from a family of seven. Her mother has limited use of English and takes care of her younger siblings at home. They do receive social assistance; unfortunately, it is not enough. Therefore, Kham and her sister go to earn extra money to help pay for bills, food, clothing, and school fees and supplies. She can afford to buy the produce that she picks, but only because she is living in

Canada. The same isn't true for farm workers in the United States. Most farm workers can't afford to buy the very crops they pick.

Kham's older sister started picking when she was fourteen years old. She earns close to $500 a week because she is a fast and experienced picker, having worked the same farm for two summers. Kham is paid on a piece-rate basis—the more baskets she fills up, the more money she earns. Kham picks tomatoes for the first half of the day, then moves on to something else. Rain from the night before makes picking difficult; even though she wears boots, the mud reaches halfway to Kham's knees. Charles says, "I've never seen my feet get so wrinkled in my life," referring to mornings when it rained and his feet would be soaked in mud for hours.

Kham wakes up at 3:00 a.m. to travel to London, Ontario, with her aunt and uncle to work on another farm. She sleeps in the back of a truck. "There's a lot of people on the truck, so there's no place to move." Her mother picks not just produce but also dew worms that are used as bait for fishing. From 6:00 p.m. to 8:00 a.m., she collects about five hundred worms per can, and the amount of money she is paid depends on the boss's mood. Sometimes she receives nine or ten dollars, or fifteen dollars for two cans. She says her work is "cold, too hard, no good." There are times when no worms appear, so the three-hour journey is made in vain.

When asked to describe a typical day on his farm, John Jakes, an asparagus grower, says, "There's no such thing." Yet he explains that his workers, ranging in age from eighteen to thirty, begin at 6:00 a.m. He says that you can hire sixteen-year-olds, but you "normally don't hire students because they should be in school." In hot weather, picking ends eleven or twelve hours later. How the day goes "depends on how much asparagus there is to pick. You can't control the weather. When the weather makes the harvest grow, you have to harvest it. When workers don't make any money, growers don't make money."

Even if that's true, workers who are parents don't make enough to support their families. Lombardi says, "Most farm workers are living below the poverty level." That is because the average salary in the United States for farm workers in $7,500 or less per year. Most of Jakes's workers are paid on an hourly basis, from $6.85 to $8.00. Jakes says, "Poor workers don't make minimum wage." A family working together has the advantage of earning more money than one worker who earns minimum wage.

In the United States, wages of farm workers have decreased 53 percent since 1985. According to the United Farm Workers, wages for workers could be increased by 50 percent if the price of a pint of strawberries were raised by only five cents. The United Farm Workers are "organizing a parallel campaign to build support among consumers and retailers" and "they are asking consumers to pressure retailers to sign a pledge supporting basic rights for strawberry workers. To date, they have been quite successful. Retailers representing one quarter of the supermarkets in the United States have pledged their support. In Canada, A & P and Safeway have joined the campaign." "Basic rights" means having clean water to drink, toilet facilities, and adequate medical insurance and housing conditions. These are rights that we should all have, yet many farm workers are denied them.

Having basic rights is not the only matter of concern for many workers. The housing is awful, according to Charles. He says he lived in a "rundown house" about "fifty years old which had never been repaired." He says, "I was living under the toilet, which meant that with each flush, a horrible stink would permeate through the room. There were urine stains on the mattress. Whenever you turned on the tap, you would see brown water with mud coming out." He had to buy water at the supermarket, and, of course, food was not provided. There was a stove to cook on, a broken television set, no heating, and no air conditioning.

At the San Andreas labour camp, near Watsonville, California, workers pay $500 for an apartment with two bedrooms, which doesn't even have windows. Three hundred and fifty labourers crowd into forty "suites," but hundreds more come when harvest work is available, which caused tuberculosis to spread among tenants one summer.

Other labourers are not lucky enough to find labour camps or other affordable housing and are forced to sleep outside or in their cars. The living conditions do not prevent farm workers from performing their back-breaking job of picking. They simply need money to survive. Charles says, "Farmers don't run farms, they run people." The treatment from farmers can be downright rude and abusive. "They don't treat you right," says Kham of some other farmers. "If you pick it [vegetables] wrong, they don't pay you. If pencil beans are too short, they scream at you." Kham mentions racism and stereotyping and the way that the bosses spoke and acted, which communicated ill feelings towards Kham and her family just because they are poor.

Kham's older sister's knees have turned rough, hard, and black from crawling to reach the fruit. She often has nosebleeds, and an aching back and muscles. She endures extreme pain every night. Normally, when she returns home from picking, she is so exhausted that she just climbs into bed hungry. Her fingers are stiff and raw, and the sweltering heat from the sun causes her skin to peel and her face to burn, even though she wears long-sleeved shirts and a hat. Kham herself saw a man faint while picking because he was dehydrated. Injuries and health problems caused from bending and stooping, or from climbing ladders and stretching, will last a worker's lifetime.

According to doctors, children who perform hard labour suffer from low weight and stunted growth. Farm workers are seldom covered by workers' compensation or have disability compensation benefits or sick leave. They can be fired for missing just one day of work, so they put off getting medical treatment for any illnesses until they become serious. Workers suffer from falls, heat stress, dehydration, and pesticide poisoning. 300,000 workers are poisoned by pesticides each year. What's more disturbing is how employers of only eleven or more farm workers were only recently ordered to provide drinking water and toilet facilities. Why did it take so long to realize that those working in the fields need basic necessities in life such as water and washrooms? Shouldn't these things be provided automatically without any question?

Paying farm workers a fair wage is perhaps the first step needed to ensure that children do not become labourers, working next to their parents. Lombardi says that "if parents have enough income, they won't have to enlist the help of their children, who would be able to attend school and get an education, rather than working in the fields." As well, Lombardi points out that "enforcement agencies need more funding in order to crack down on farmers who do use child labour."

And 85 percent of fruits and vegetables need to be hand-picked at some point. Considering the arduous and honest work they are doing, you would think that workers would receive reasonable wages to provide for their children, that they would be treated fairly, and that drinking water, sanitary working conditions, and decent housing would also be made available.

Farm workers, the people who actually pick the vegetables and fruits we consume, deserve our respect and gratitude, but more than that, they deserve to be paid fairly for their hard work.

Chapter 11

High School

High School Hell

High school had to be one of the crummiest times of my life. The effort it took to fit in and not be noticed, so as not to be marginalized, teased, or taunted, was exhausting. I wasn't very successful at blending in. I never had the right clothes, or hair, or whatever. I was one of the misfits.

The unspoken truth about high school is that it's not really a whole lot like real life. Think about it. The institution is supposed to simulate some distorted kind of reality where, for eight hours every day, you are surrounded by a bunch of people you hate, who probably hate you. If you had the choice, would you go to a job every day where you were hated?

Also, in the outside world, the people who are given opportunities to succeed are generally the ones who don't blend into the background. Instead they're the ones who have something to say that might be unusual, or provocative. That's not how the system's set up in school, though.

And then, to top it all off, what you learn is confined to a strict curriculum, and you are judged by your ability to regurgitate it. Of course, that's no surprise, since school was created in the early nineteenth century to produce good little workers, not free-thinkers. The only reprieve from this is getting a good teacher who has a broader notion of education and doesn't want to stomp the sparkle out of you. They do exist, and you're lucky if you get one.

Still, unless you are home-schooled, or lucky enough to attend an alternative school, you will probably spend a significant amount of time in the institution, so it makes sense to find a way to survive it.

In the movie *Hurricane*, boxer Rubin Carter, who was wrongfully convicted of murder and sent to prison, explains that we must learn how to "transcend the places that hold us." Okay, it might be a little harsh to liken prison to school, but the advice is still useful. By disciplining himself not to need anything, not to desire anything beyond that which he could have while in prison, Carter was able to survive and serve his time. But is this all you can expect from your school experience—something that you'll survive, with some remnant of your free spirit intact?

Early on, even before we set foot in a school, we are taught to bide our time and wait our turn. We are told not to ask for too much, or question why things are done a certain way. And yet young people are restless; they find it hard to wait, to be quiet, to listen. And you are hated for it, probably because you notice and try to reject the constraints of getting along, of not disrupting the status quo, when the rest of us have learned to grin and bear it.

Raging against the machine can be like beating your head against a brick wall, leaving you feeling powerless and insignificant. In talking to young people in the confining and enforced arena called high school, I've been taught many ways of dealing with that hollow feeling—the one that makes you feel as though you could put your hand through the middle of your centre and come up empty.

It sometimes manifests itself in me as a hunger. I eat cookies, and french fries, and fish, but nothing satisfies. And then I recognize that the hunger is something I can't satisfy. It's some other kind of emptiness I feel.

So, I go shopping.

Swept along by the maddening crowd probably looking to fill a similar void, I traipse home with lipstick, dresses, shoes, but no relief. They soothe for a while, though, these goodies, for at least as long as I can bear to play dress-up.

And then, after weeks of wondering, wandering, and spending, something triggers it. A book, a stranger, an unexpected letter. I am reminded how to transcend the emptiness, or at least my need to fill it.

I don't have any one method to banish the blahs or to instill courage. In fact, I have a terrible memory, which is why it takes so long to remember how I did it the last time. But, if it helps, here are some of the methods I seem to come back to again and again and again.

Sometimes I'll make a collage of all the things I dream about doing. I list all the places I want to go: every place on the planet. I call friends who remind me to look ahead and to have great expectations rather than worrying about the here and now.

Other times, I revisit passages from books or stories that have stayed with me. Seeing the words and hearing the way they feel and sound in my mouth gives me proof of the existence of beauty when life seems ugly.

If none of this works, maybe just ask yourself what it means to you to be magnificent in your life. For me, it always means taking at least a small risk. I believe that "fortune favours the brave." It has also been said that "the gods only go with you if you put yourself in their path and that takes courage." Maybe it won't make you appear magnificent in other people's eyes, but who cares, as long as you're fulfilling your own idea of magnificence?

The other thing that we don't learn soon enough is that school can be a good resource. It might not nurture your interests very well, but if you start asking your guidance counsellors and teachers and librarian about how you can participate in exchange programs or work study programs, you might be able to take advantage of some of what it offers.

School can be what you make of it. So, if you have the motivation to start a newspaper, or to organize a roster of speakers who can come in and talk about their work, or their lives, you might be inspired by the sheer energy you have to organize, assemble, and share. Better yet, you will probably be blown away by the stories you hear.

However you manage to get through school, even if it isn't the most rewarding place for you right now, take heart. Although you might not hear it often enough, high school really can be hell.

Myth:

It's character-building to finish what you start

At the end of my first year in the Radio and Television Arts program at Ryerson Polytechnic University, I contemplated quitting. I hated it. It just wasn't for me, and I couldn't imagine slogging my way through another year. I was already working in the industry and I had a degree in English Literature. I decided to talk to a number of people I respect to seek their advice about quitting or continuing.

While most people said I should follow my heart and instincts, the advice given to me by one of the older women I was close to at the time was "plug your nose and finish what you started." I was taken aback. The dread I felt at hearing her words made me physically sick. But I didn't stop to question her advice or why she felt so strongly about it.

The nice thing about advice is that you don't have to take it. And the good thing about talking to lots of different people is that they give you plenty of options.

I decided to listen to myself and to another friend of mine, who told me that learning was about "sitting at the foot of the prophet," and that if I didn't feel as though I was really gaining knowledge in this program, I was wasting my time.

So I quit, but I didn't tell anyone. I didn't even tell my parents for six months; I was so concerned about their disappointment. I had disappointed my dad by telling him years earlier that I didn't want to pursue law because journalism was for me. I was a scholarship recipient. I had moved from Vancouver to study in this program. Plus, I still hadn't fully accepted the fact that quitting isn't failing.

One of the best ways to see if something is for you is to try it. I did, and now I can cross journalism school off my list of things to explore.

I suppose what I'm saying is that when you are confronted with a difficult decision, trust your instincts, ask for advice from people you respect, and remember that abandoning something that's deadening to the spirit can only be a good thing.

Another Brick in the Wall

Lauren Kirshner, 18,
Central/Eastern

The fact was that I was spending far too much time in the school washroom writing inane graffitti on the door of the wheelchair-accessible stall. I would quietly evade such tiresome classes as math and American history and stealthily creep down the linoleum halls, black magic marker tucked into my pants pocket ... I found more boredom enclosed in those dank bathroom walls than on page three of a past failed grade ten math exam. Girls held huge pink powder puffs to their faces and pressed tawny powder onto their youthful freckled skin with the sensuous instincts of Mae West. Fourteen-year-olds pranced around in high heels and tight jeans complaining of their boyfriends' adulterous ways and the favourite track on the new 'N Sync Album. Feeling excluded, I pulled out a crusty old Chapstick and pressed it to my parched lips. The faucets rolled their eyes at me. "Don't even try to fit in," they chided. "You act like a geezer and you're only seventeen years old."

This was true. High school fit me like OJ's supposed black leather glove. I had no interest in being on a schedule. I had fantastic dreams of being a teenage editor at *The New York Times*. The facts that I had never been published and had difficulty punctuating a sentence properly were completely ignored. My high school days were filled with evasion and with adulation for a bevy of has-been punk rock stars who now resided in methadone clinics. I was lacking a purpose. My school made me squirm with unease. I hated the long endless halls. I hated the hours my eyes would stare fixedly at the clock, just waiting for the bell to ring so I could zombie-walk to my next class. "Where is your homework, Lauren?" was a common question teachers asked my alien gaze, which had once resembled a high school student. At first I made up creative responses. I fabricated notes of excuse. Time passed and my ambition grew stale. I simply shrugged my shoulders, feigning a street-smart "I don't give a rat's ass," and simply told them it was not done and the chances of it being done were less than zero. I was such a stupid and lost idiot.

Please do not misunderstand. This is not a condemnation of the cookie-cutter high school formula. I happen to know a great number of fine people who have come out of huge high schools who will soon become cogs in the wheel, as will I most likely. That is our purpose in the world; just ask Huxley. But I was not functioning. My keenest interest was watching Jenny Jones and investigating the hidden lives of albino strippers. I did not want to work. AM I LAZY? AM I? This frightening thought plagued me. Laziness is a sin, I knew that. This mantra had been pounded into me from a very young age by my toiling European family. I needed to make a change. I bought some false eyelashes. They were spidery and chocolate brown. They fell off at the Spadina subway station two days later. Obviously my change would have to be more drastic. I investigated being turned into a giant grasshopper by calling the Metro Toronto Zoo. "Hello," I stuttered. "My name is Gregor Samsa and I was just wondering if you could help me ..."

I needed a new school. I returned my textbooks to their rightful owners and saw my guidance counsellor. LET ME OUT OF HERE, I mumbled continuously like a moron. I was desperate. My heart and loins longed for open pasture, a school where I could sow my wild oats while learning about world domination and fascism. Have you thought of an alternative school, I was asked. Images floated through my mind. My interpretation of alternative schools was dark rooms, walls covered with tapestries, and cushions everywhere. I imagined an opium pipe being passed around while Anthony Robbins motivational tapes hummed drearily in the background. Smiling at this epiphany, I said, Yes, please sign me up.

Not for the very first time, my initial vision was incorrect. The teachers at these schools were real. They were teachers, not yoga gurus. There was work, and lots of it. But there were no classes. I was free to scamper in and out at will. This both ignited me and made me feel suddenly very responsible. No one here was going to hassle me about whether or not my homework was completed. Here I was my own boss. It was sink or swim. So I began to swim, a pitiful dog paddle ...

Four months later I am about to graduate from high school having earned my final two credits from an alternative school. When I think back to my initial thoughts about what it would be like, and in turn, the responsibility and freedom I was allowed to work with, I believe the change I made was one of the better decisons of my short time on this earth. Finding an environment with such an intimate nature and such a wide array of people made me savour my last few months of true teenagehood. So I threw my big magic marker in the garbage. I had no time for graffitti diversion, and for godssakes grow up, a nagging voice said in my head. You can vote and drive—you have no time to scrawl your silly messages on the wall. One last one, though, okay? If you hate school, move. There's light somewhere at the end of the class-evasion tunnel.

My Decision

Leah Pagels, 15,
Eastern/Central

One day when I came home from school, tears were falling down my cheeks. I had received terrible marks on my report card. The highest grade was a C+. I had given up and stopped really trying at school. When my mother saw me crying, she asked me what was wrong. Tears streamed down as I showed her the envelope. My mother looked disappointed, which made me feel worse. We sat down and she calmed me down to a few sobs. I started to complain about my music teacher, whom I despised. The pupils at school constantly harassed me. I did not fit in.

Then my mom said something so astonishing I still don't believe it. "You don't have to go back there if you don't want to." I was shocked, but happy, too. My mother was suggesting I take home-schooling! It did not take me a moment to decide. I said, "Okay!"

My mother had not expected me to say yes and was suddenly as nervous as I was. We discussed it and decided that we would try it out until I got to high school, which would be the following year. I am still taking home-schooling and do not plan to stop. April 2, 1996, was my first day of home-schooling and the first day I started living.

I now look back on myself and my old (so-called) friends. I wore black Adidas track suits (which I hated and still do) and black lipstick, and I had started smoking. My friends also smoked and they did pot and drank the occasional beer. (This was the norm for eleven- and twelve-year-olds.) Now they don't have any communication with me and they call me a "geek." My new friends now are home-schoolers. They don't smoke, don't do drugs, don't get drunk. And they most certainly do not judge me by the way I dress. I dress how I want and that's the way it should be. They are thoughtful, polite people, and I enjoy their company.

At the beginning of home-schooling my parents asked me what I wanted to do. I said I wanted to get a babysitting job and buy a horse in a year! I am happy to say that just two weeks ago I bought a beautiful horse named Kalao.

I'm making my dreams come true, and I believe I can do anything that I want to. I have honestly learned more in the past six months then I ever did in my eight years of school. So I conclude by saying: "Home-schooling Rocks!"

A Day at the Fair

Kristin Foster, 18,
Eastern/Central

Rebel, Rogue, Mischievous Babe

As we neared our destination, the stream of bodies became more and more dense, all of us flowing past the heavy glass doors. Some chattered with their friends; some remained silent; some just struggled to keep up with the surge. All headed down the hallway towards a long series of escalators, which carried us farther and farther into the earth ...

No, I'm not talking about the descent into Hell, although it probably isn't very different. The atrocity of which I speak has a longer name, which evokes terror in the fresh, innocent faces of youth and parents all across Ontario. It is the Ontario Universities' Fair, and it comes every year to the same place: the Metro Toronto Convention Centre, also known as the Netherworld, or Hades! Okay, so I'm kidding, but I could have sworn the greeters had pointy tails and pitchforks.

They handed me a pale purple brochure with the logos of the universities on one side and their own huge logo emblazoned on the other. It read: "Ontario Universities' Fair: Your Future Today." In the words of the immortal Joey Russo, "Whoa!"

First of all, the word "future," as defined by the good folks from Webster's, means "that is to be or come; of days, months, or years ahead." I like taking my time. My future, as far as I was concerned, was not going to be making any important decisions that day, and reading that did not make me feel good. I hadn't even crossed the threshold and already my brain was pounding from the pressure.

Taking a deep breath, I continued my arduous trek into the belly of the Convention Centre. Brightly lit and buzzing with excitement, it seemed to scream "GIVE ME YOUR MONEY!!" the same way Oliver Jewellery screams for Granny's diamond engagement ring at three in the morning from your television set. "Friendly" university experts stood eagerly at the sidelines ready to pounce with handbooks, magnets, temporary tattoos, pens, stickers, nifty tote bags, and more information than you can cram into one science class with Mr. Bunsenburner. Now *that's* scary.

We began at McMaster and ended up at Lakehead. Along the way, we stopped everywhere: Queen's, Windsor, U of T, Guelph, Brock ... I even had the outlandish idea to consider the Ontario College of Art and Design. Ha! Let's just put it this way: they have an entire pamphlet in six-point type explaining the admission process. I whipped out my official plastic OCAD magnifying glass to read it. Not a good sign.

Of course, all of the informative handbooks featured goofy-looking "students" hard at work, taking a break, smiling for the camera, eating tasty cafeteria food and such. To quote the character Cher from *Clueless*: "As if." We all know those students lucky enough to live in residence are in their rooms crying about their deadlines and chugging Pepto Bismol because that Jamaican beef patty, the only thing on the menu they could afford for breakfast, didn't go down well. I'm surprised they don't sue the universities for misrepresentation.

In the end, I left the building with a headache, a sore throat, and enough paper to insulate a bungalow. I can't describe how incredibly frightening it is to be growing up, especially right now when tuition is rising and the employment rate is not. I've begun to see a therapist named Breyer's All-Natural Chocolate Ice Cream. He makes it all right. And as far as the whole "Your Future Today" thing goes, I say this:

"Fight the future! Fight it!"

Say Hello!

Kathleen McMenamin, 18,
Eastern/Central

Okay, here's my message. The next time you're sitting in the cafeteria at school or in your classroom, look around you. You're probably surrounded by some of your friends, your clique. Now look past your friends to those you're not so familiar with. Look especially for those in your grade, and now be honest—DO YOU ACTUALLY KNOW ANY OF THESE PEOPLE? Other than your circle of friends, who else do you talk to?

Think about the ridiculous barriers that exist between us all. Be honest with yourself again: have you ever wanted to talk to or get to know someone, but hesitated because they don't fall under the same damned social standing that you do?

If not, that's great, the school needs more people like you, but if you have felt this hesitation, listen.

If you think you can't talk to someone who's more "popular" than you, get over this negative self-image and say hello next time. You'll find that they're not the snobs they might appear to be. Maybe you'll see that they're just as afraid of straying from their clique as you are.

Now, if you think you're too cool to say hello back, just open up that narrow mind. The barriers that exist between us exist because we fearfully create them on both sides.

Knock them down, and you'll soon find that there are some pretty awesome people outside of your clique. Give people a chance, no matter how intimidating it can be. Be braver and stronger than most and, dammit, say hello.

Chapter 12

Bullying, Violence, & Racism

Bullying

For me, school and bullying always seemed to go hand in hand. But that doesn't make it acceptable or tolerable. Bullies undermine and destroy confidence. They build themselves up by putting others down. Bullying is about power.

Learning how to deal with the bullies means developing strategies. It isn't a bad idea to know how to protect yourself. But bullying is something that you can't just ignore, hoping that it will go away, or something you should face alone. Most of the time, it won't. You need to be able to assess the situation in order to know when it's time to walk away and look for help. And you have to decide when and how to confront the bully, which might require reporting the incident to teachers, your parents, even the cops.

In most schools, there is a zero-tolerance policy towards bullying, which means that bullying is never acceptable, no way, no how. Your teachers and the principal have an obligation to make the harassment stop. Ask them for help. It is their job to provide an environment that is safe for you. They want you to be able to attend school without fear of any kind.

When we picture a bully, what we usually see is the big guy who roughs up a little kid until he hands over his lunch money—every day of the week. But bullying can take many different forms. Sometimes it's physical—and both boys and girls are the aggressors—but sometimes it can be something more subtle. Any time you feel that someone is pushing you to do or say something that makes you uncomfortable, it might be a case of bullying, and you should feel free to talk about it with your parents, teacher, or principal.

Girls might bully other girls by making comments about clothes, body, hair; and boys seem to bully girls by making inappropriate comments to them about sex or their bodies. At a time when you're probably already feeling a little unsure of yourself because of the enormous physical changes you are undergoing as puberty comes crashing down on you, this type of bullying can crush your self-esteem. Bullying in this way is also a kind of sexual harassment.

It is not okay for a guy to comment on your body. It is inappropriate for him to snap your bra strap or yank at your tear-away pants. The idea that "boys will be boys" is one that too often allows young men to threaten young women and get away with it. When this happens, you need to tell someone in a position of power that you are being bullied and sexually harassed and that you need help to make it stop. School officials are obliged to help you. But if, for some reason, you feel that your plea for help is being ignored, you should go ahead and call the non-emergency number. The service is not just for extreme cases; the officers who answer the calls are there to help you learn how to resolve cases of harassment.

If you are being bullied, it is really important to ask for help in order not to choke down the anger and hurt you are feeling. Our bodies are pretty good at telling us about our emotional health. Headaches and stomach aches are often symptoms of other problems, and they are your body's way of screaming for help. Early on, I noticed that I always developed a sore throat if I didn't speak my mind or say what I was feeling. Now when I get a sore throat I look at situations in my life in which I probably need to confront someone, and I find a way to do that. My throat almost always feels better when I do.

According to a study called *Take Action Against Bullying*, in British Columbia "an incident of bullying takes place [on average] once every seven minutes and usually lasts about 37 seconds." I'll bet 37 seconds never felt quite so long or so harsh. I know that the pain of bullying often comes from its cumulative effect, from physical blows or cutting words striking again and again, but even one incident of bullying can leave you feeling punctured.

If you are being physically assaulted at school or in your neighbourhood, there's no way that you should just let it slide, hoping to prove to the bully that you're tough and not a snitch, to get on his or her good side. You should report this to an adult immediately and make sure that steps are taken to resolve the problem as soon as possible, so that you can be safe and comfortable. If it's a girl who is assaulting you, it might be harder to convince the adults to take the problem seriously—there is still a tendency to think that girls are "sugar and spice and everything nice" and couldn't really hurt anyone. Wrong. You should never have to put up with physical violence, from anyone.

And what do you do if you are being taunted and teased by a bully? Sometimes the best response is no response at all. Bullies want to get a reaction from you. If you show them that their words have fallen on deaf ears, they will probably go away. And this next bit of advice might sound a little strange, but it too can work. Let's say a bully teases you about being fat. Instead of getting upset, in a very nonchalant way just say, "Yeah, so what?" and don't say another word. But if you're feeling that you really can't walk away without saying anything more, then try something like, "Yeah, so what? You're ugly and you smell and you're stupid." And say it with conviction.

Bullies can have an effect on us, no matter how strong we are, because we are all vulnerable to other people's words and idle comments. If you are feeling miserable, there's no need to suffer. If you don't think you want to confront the bully and tell him or her to stop, you must report that person. I know the belief is that it will only make the situation worse, but being pushed around and made to feel inadequate is about as lousy as it gets. Let the bully know that you will not be intimidated, that you are not afraid to demand help and an end to this insufferable treatment. Bullies count on your silence. Learn to push back because, guess what, bullies don't go away when you leave school.

Bullies can take the form of bosses, friends, lovers who want to keep you down or keep you in your place. Whenever someone intimidates, insults, or undercuts you, you can be sure that you are being bullied. Learn how to identify and deal with this type of behaviour early on. When you understand and identify behaviour that is unacceptable, it becomes easier to name it and call the person on it.

People who believe in their self-worth do not put up with bullies.

Friends, siblings, people who care about you can sometimes try to bully you into doing something, or they can make you feel as though a choice you have made is somehow wrong or inappropriate. Most of the time if you can calmly say, "I don't like to be bullied and you're bullying me," the people who care about you will be shocked. No friend wants to believe they are capable of being a bully. Usually, they will apologize.

Schoolyard bullies or bullies at work probably need a tougher approach. You need to remain calm, but you also need to say, "Stop trying to bully me." Pushing back means matching their level of aggression.

Sometimes people in positions of power use bullying as a way to remind you of their authority. You need to call them on that behaviour, too. Let them know that you won't be cowed, or threatened, or made to feel bad. Bullies at work count on your silence, just like the bullies at school. They think that they can intimidate you because there is no record of their behaviour. If you find you're having a problem at work or school that you can't easily resolve yourself, keep a journal of the occurrences. It will help you substantiate the inappropriate behaviour of your boss or co-worker, if you find you need to seek help from outside sources.

You spend a lot of time at school, and you will find that eventually your work will become a huge part of your life, too, so take steps now to make those places safe, welcoming, and worry-free.

Myth:

You must be doing something to provoke the bullies

Bullies don't need much encouragement. After all, they're called bullies because they tend to pick on people who are weaker or somehow vulnerable.

Increased school violence has meant that bullying is no longer treated as a normal part of growing up. Instead, teachers have taken a more serious approach to complaints of bullying: they call in the parents, and experts in conflict resolution, and in some cases the police.

Even so, victims of bullying are sometimes treated as though they asked to be bullied—maybe because they didn't ignore the person who was taunting them, or because they complained and so "aggravated" the problem.

It's hard to stand up to a bully, and, as a friend once told me, if you can't get rid of the person who is bothering you through strength of character alone, it doesn't mean you are weak.

As you get older, you'll notice that bullies don't disappear. They come in the form of bosses, colleagues, even boyfriends or girlfriends. It still doesn't mean that you asked for it or have to put up with being bullied.

Fish Boy

Leah Culver, 12,
Eastern/Central

They call him Fish Boy.

Why? Because of his personal hygiene and his appearance.

One girl teases him constantly and others close to it. Nobody wants to touch his tests that the teachers give us to mark because they are afraid that they will catch something. On his locker people write mean sayings, swear words, and "FISH BOY."

I have teased him, not because I don't like him but because I have been drawn into doing it by other people. I can't say I dislike him because I don't know him that well.

He lives with his foster mom and is not rich. He seems poor, but that's the way people have labelled him. I can't blame them, though, because he does look dirty sometimes and wears the same clothes day after day.

He has on and off friends at school who tease him when they are not his friends.

Nobody wants to stand by him or his locker. He gets some good grades, but most of them are not very good. He is also a teacher's pet most of the time.

I feel really sorry for him and am trying not to tease him, but the peer pressure is so great that I sometimes can't help doing it. I think that most people do it because they are afraid of what others will think of them if they don't. They want to fit in. There are really only two people that say they truly hate him, but still they don't know him very well. Those two people are the ones who tease him the most. I tease him because of what people will think of me and to fit in, but I'm trying not to care what other people think of me. I'm a Christian and try to do what is right for God, but it is not always easy. At youth group we talked about strong holds, and I guess this is one of mine.

He hides his hurt I'm pretty sure. I think teasing and bullying is wrong, but it is very hard not to do, especially if it is always happening around you at school.

What I'm trying to say is this: If you tease people, stop to think how this makes them feel and how it affects them. Then, think about why you spread rumours and say unkind things to them and about them when you don't even get to know them. And if you are being teased, then I will tell you this: Everyone is their own special person whom God created and loves. God is not making this happen to you to punish you, but this will happen to everyone in life at some time. We are to love one another as He loves us.

I hope you will remember this story the next time you tease or bully someone, because it's hurtful and you never know how deeply it can affect someone.

Rebel, Rogue,
Mischievous Babe

On the Lookout

Amy Miller, 17,
Eastern/Central

Do you ever have the feeling that somebody is watching you out of the corner of his or her eyes? I have been there; I know exactly what it feels like to be stalked. There are many ways in which a person can be stalked. It does not have to be in person. You can also be terrorized on the phone or by e-mail.

I received an e-mail last year from a boy who goes to Laurentian High School. He said he knew who I was and that he had my phone number. I was petrified when I read this, as his name did not ring a bell. I replied to his e-mail, telling him that I had never heard of him before and promptly blocked him out of my e-mail.

A few days later the phone rang. It was a boy who claimed he knew me. He phoned me non-stop and would get mad whenever I had to go. I finally came to my senses and had his number blocked from my phone line. I have not heard from him since.

Sometime last year, late one night, I was coming home from a friend's house on the bus. I was alone and sat in the back. A man in his twenties came onto the bus and sat beside me. There were so many seats to choose from, I was wondering why he had sat next to me. I started to get a little worried because he tried to make conversation. He was asking where I lived, how old I was, if I had a boyfriend. I was thinking how stupid I was for sitting at the back of the bus, so I moved to the front so that I would be nearer to the bus driver. A few minutes later, the man came and sat in the front of the bus.

It was almost my stop and I was terrified that he was going to follow me home. I wanted to tell the bus driver, but I was afraid that this stranger would hear me. My stop was next; I rang the bell and started to get up. The bus driver gave me a look as I was getting up and I noticed that the man was standing right behind me. As I got off the bus, the man tried to follow me. The bus driver stopped him and asked where he was going. He said that he lived in the area, but I knew that he didn't. The bus driver asked him if he had been drinking; he said no. The driver then made him stay on the bus and said that he was going to take him back to Baseline station. I was very relieved that the man did not get off the bus, and very thankful to the driver.

I do not know what I would have done if he had not made the man stay on the bus. If you ever take the bus home alone (especially in the dark), please, sit in the front of the bus and be very careful. You never know what is out there.

Stop Abusing Me!

anonymous

It all started on a night when Mom was in the garden. I was sitting on the couch with a family friend reading a book when he put his hand down my pants and started feeling around my vagina. Usually, I'm a very outspoken person. I believe that if you've got something to say, then say it. But for some reason I could only say, "I'm thirsty, I want some milk." I went and got a glass of milk, but when I came back he was still there, so I lied again. This time I said, "Just remembered I have to do my homework."

As I walked up the stairs, my mind swirled in confusion. That night I didn't sleep well. I would wake up in a cold sweat from a repeating terrible dream where all I saw was red closing in on me.

After that first time, it kept happening and happening. To me it felt as if, up until that point in my life, I had been walking on firm ground, and then without notice I'd plunged into a mushy, squishy, deep mud puddle.

It has been about five years since that first time, and about a year ago I told my mother. She was pretty cool about the whole thing (not that she didn't care).

Now, I'm in the middle of taking this guy to court so he can get what he deserves. Everyone is very supportive and encouraging. It's not easy, but at least it's the end.

What I would say to anyone who is being assaulted is TELL SOMEONE! If that someone doesn't believe you, keep telling people until someone does believe you. Second, tell your abuser, "NO! STOP

THAT! I DON'T LIKE IT!" Finally, until you can get help and make the situation stop, avoid being alone with the person abusing you.

The good thing about telling someone is that you get the help you need and no one thinks you're weird because we all know about these things happening.

I hope that by reaching out, I have been able to make at least some of you feel less alone. You're not alone.

No *Is* No— Taking Control

Veronique Lafleur, 17,
and Marlene Morency, 17,
Eastern/Central

Translated by Nancy Forster

Has a group of guys ever made you feel uneasy just by the way they look at you? Kind of like they could jump on you at any minute? Do you know how to handle a situation like this? This type of incident frequently happens, so we formed a group to get together to talk about it.

After a couple of meetings, the group thought we should create a play about harassment and violence. The tickets sold out right away, so we knew a lot of people wanted to know about this issue. We also wanted to expose this issue to as many people as possible, yet we knew that we couldn't do that through the play alone.

With the help of some of the staff at the Montreal youth centre Head and Hands, we produced a video. The play and the video are called *NO IS NO*. Each one of us has experienced a violent situation and we wanted young women to know that they are not alone. It is not always easy to avoid relationships that are manipulative, abusive, or violent, but we think that if you recognize the many shapes of aggressive behaviour then you can either make it stop or find out why you continue to put up with it.

In our video we talk about the different faces of possessiveness, jealousy, and emotional abuse, and how in romantic relationships we can be persuaded to believe that these are forms of love. We also tried to incorporate ways in which young women can respond to this type of behaviour so that they can begin to feel they are in control.

Taking control

- If you want to make the other person stop what he or she is doing, you have to say exactly what you want. Make the point in a very direct manner.
- Look the person in the eye and use a firm tone of voice.
- Use sentences that begin with "I," as in "I feel," "I don't want to," "I refuse to."
- Stay calm. Don't attack or insult the person.

If you have been in a violent situation, don't blame yourself. Ask yourself why it happened and think about how you can protect yourself in the future. Remember, you're not alone. If we stand up for ourselves, we can be strong together.

Racism

The first time I experienced racism, I was thirteen. My parents had just moved to Surrey, a small suburb outside of Vancouver. Today, Surrey is quite multicultural, with lots of East Indian and Asian people, but back then it was predominantly white and redneck, which has to be just about the worst combination when you're a kid and brown.

Although I was sometimes harassed while walking home from school, or during trips to the mall, most often I was hassled on school property.

At my school, I would often find myself swarmed, threatened, or called names. And every so often I could count on some guy's heavy textbooks being smashed against my chest. I got the message. Not being white meant not being protected, or strong, or even just left alone. After a while I began to hate myself for not being any of those things.

I guess that's the irony of racism. Unless you have someone who can tell you that the problem is not with you—that you don't smell, and that the colour of your skin doesn't make you less worthy of respect—you can begin to believe that the problem lies with you and not with the perpetrator of the abuse.

School can be a dangerous place for both the mind and the spirit. The racism at my school was crushing. It was also so widespread and out of control that it proved useless to seek help from teachers. I didn't really find a way to cope with it, except to develop eyes in the back of my head.

My older brother, who was a grade ahead of me, was often in fights after school. But he was kind of a tough guy, able to fight back with a destructive fury, so I think the bullies learned to leave him alone. My brother did look out for me, but I couldn't expect him to be there all of the time.

Those were scary days, and yet we still did the things that teenagers do. We still went out at night. My brother's friends were all white, so there was at least a cloak of protection there.

My parents, as adults, were also subject to racist attacks, though mostly verbal ones, and they soon decided that our safety lay in leaving. We moved back to civilization, which was only a thirty-minute drive away.

It took me a long time to feel safe in my skin again. It took me a long time to relax and to know that people were not staring at me, or whispering about me, or laughing at me because of the colour of my skin.

Racism exists for lots of reasons, even though those reasons are hard to imagine, especially when you believe you're totally lovable. I gained some relief and perspective on the subject when I read a psychology text that talked about the notion of "the other." Although we don't consciously think this way, somewhere in the back of our minds we harbour a fear of the unknown, the "other," the person or group of people that is simply *not like us*. The "other" threatens us and so it has to be destroyed. When we come face to face with people who represent the "other" to us, we feel justified in putting them down, taking away their power, shunning them.

For example, the Russians were believed to be the enemies of the United States because they believed in Communism, which was threatening to the American capitalist system. The Russians also set themselves up in competition with the U.S. space program, which immediately made them spies and a threat to American security. When the Cold War ended and the Berlin Wall came down in 1989, the Americans no longer knew who to identify as their boogeyman, so they began to replace the Russians with the Muslim fundamentalist enemy.

Having an enemy that you can see and destroy means that your fears of being annihilated or displaced as the authority figure, or the dominant race, can be assuaged. It also means that when things go wrong, there is an easy scapegoat to point at.

In parts of Germany, young people who are frustrated by the lack of jobs and opportunities are being recruited into the Nazi movement, whose leaders wrongly point to Turkish immigrants as the cause of their problems. By telling these young people that immigrants are responsible for their frustration because they take all of the good jobs and deplete the country's resources, they give them a way to feel better about their situation.

You can't always rise above racist slurs or attacks. It requires more than just strength of character to recover from racism. Living in a multicultural and cosmopolitan city rather than an isolated suburb has helped me feel safer. And because the racism I encountered was largely at one school and seemed like an anomaly during my teenage years, I understood that the entire world was not racist and that my experience in Surrey was more of an exception than the rule.

Still, violence, physical or emotional, whether it's in the form of racial harassment or bullying, takes its toll, and if you've been on the receiving end, you might need help in dealing with your anger and fear. You might also consider talking to a counsellor who can help you navigate your way out of feeling bad about yourself, because racism—and this is its goal—can make you feel as though you are somehow deficient, less than a person.

The most important thing to remember is that you don't want to give racists power over you. By accepting that you're not good enough, or that you will always be slighted, you will curb your desires and dreams in order not to be hurt or rejected. In a way, that's what people who are racist want you to do. They want you to buckle under and disappear.

I Can't Buy Lysol ... Why?

Carmen Daniels, 21,
Prairies

Where I grew up, inner-city drugstores are prohibited from selling Lysol, disinfectants, and basically all other cleaning agents to Indians. How many people know this? That it's up to a sixteen-year-old part-timer barely out of the tenth grade to discern whether or not somebody is going to use the product for purely escapist reasons? Or maybe it's left to the better judgment of the forty-five-year-old full-timer whose realm of reality only extends as far as the automatic doors.

Society takes a huge leap forward with the growth of such things as Native cultural training for city police officers or Native agencies reaching their summits and recognition within communities, and then takes two—@#!$—ten gigantic leaps backwards, by keeping people down and feeding stereotypes; because feeding them is a whole lot easier than actually facing, battling, and conquering them.

It's easy to typify those Cree neighbours next door as nothing but drunk, rowdy partiers. The slum neighbours next door who have nothing better to do than go to Bingo and party on the weekends and who engage in their fair share of beer brawls and petty crimes. The rest of the week, they sit around on their rickety, broken steps, staring with blank unregistering faces onto their unmanicured lawns overtaken by quack grass and nettles. Over the fence—over on the other side—the grass is always greener, the lawns are always perfect, and you're never allowed to play with the next door neighbour's kid because—what? She has blond hair and you don't? Because she wears lace and you wear terry cloth and corduroy? No. Because the parents say no. And the parents are always white. Oh, I mean right.

Could we regress any further? I've already had a hard time at the drugstore today. How many times do I have to prove that I'm an Indian with really dirty floors?

Same Difference

Maya Krishnaratne, 17,
Eastern/Central

"She's different," a little boy said about me in preschool. The words stung like salt on a fresh wound. They cut through my naive, young heart like rusty, old razor blades. It was at that moment, that one very clear moment, that I came to see the harsh reality of my life. I was indeed different. I was unlike everyone around me, and I was Sri Lankan-Canadian. Who could have known that preschoolers could be so cruel? Even at that young age, I began to believe that although we are all flesh and blood on the inside, our physical appearances dictate how we will be judged. It was then that I began a search I am still continuing today: a search to figure out where I belonged.

My brown skin had never been a problem until then. My dark hair and dark eyes had not stopped me from being happy and animated. Yet I was suddenly shoved into a separate category. I was a minority. As I faded into the shadows of my white peers and succumbed to the taunts and stares I seemed to receive from "the majority," I was lost in a world of which I clearly thought I was not a part.

The world had suddenly become an unfair and unwelcome place, and that made me want to crawl into a hole of nothing and just cease to exist. What was once the joy and pleasure of a jubilant girl was now just a forced smile and a tear-stained pillow.

I'm not that same little girl I once was. I've grown up and learned to face the consequences of being a Sri Lankan-Canadian and a minority. I still hurt and my heart still aches with the memory of that little boy's words. However, I have also come to realize something else. No matter how many people refuse to believe it, no two people are alike, at least not physically. Therefore, we are bound together universally by something much stronger: our differences. We each have a million distinct dimensions, but when we recognize our differences it unites us in a paradoxical kind of way. It is our diversity that brings us together. No matter what social class we belong to, what political stand we take, religion we believe in, race we are, we all qualify for membership in the group, which stands out more prominently and more remarkably than any other: the human race.

Chapter 13

Creativity & Work

DIY

I was in New York a couple of weeks ago, sauntering in and out of a few of the trendiest shops on Ludlow Street, when I spotted little white T-shirts with felt girls sewn on the front. Very cute. Very fashionable. Very DIY. And then, I saw the price tag: $75. Are they joking?

I *know* someone had to sew the simple blue and orange felt pieces in their assortment of triangles, circles, and oblong shapes to make these girl figures ... but $75?

Yeah, it might have been the store I was in. New York's Lower East Side is becoming more fashionable and less bargain-basement, but that was still a hefty price to command for what would essentially take a little imagination and some cut-and-sew skills. Heck, you could even glue those figures on with fabric glue, if you didn't feel like sewing.

I guess, like everything, DIY has been fully co-opted by the marketing and merchandising machine. The naive "handmade" look has been lifted from the hands of people who just want to make stuff for the sake of creating and entered the world of high fashion.

I suppose it doesn't really matter, because sewing stuff is all about personal expression. Your nifty ideas might get copied and sold in trendy stores, but that doesn't exactly diminish the pleasure you find in making things for yourself or your friends.

When I was about thirteen, my friends and I all went through a phase of wanting to sew our clothes. We would see things in stores, quickly sketch the pattern in the tiny notepad covered in stickers that each of us carried in our vinyl purses, and then search Fanny's Fabrics for the material. My friend Laura was the best. Laura was the only one who could really could make little tops and skirts. But since almost everyone's mom could sew, we usually persuaded them to finish our creations.

Even though I knew I couldn't sew, let alone follow a pattern—honestly, are all those pieces of brown paper necessary?—I didn't give up. I wanted to know what it felt like to make something of my own design, so even though my mom would tell me that spandex or stretchy material wouldn't move through her machine as easily as cotton, I'd just push the stuff through anyway. It went in looking like a flat piece that would join the other flat piece but came out knotted and covered in uneven thread glitches.

Still, it was much better than what my older brother did. I guess the "make stuff" bug had infected him and his friends too. One summer, while my mom was away at work, he and his buddies hauled my mom's sewing machine down to the basement and attempted to sew a canvas sail for the sailboat they were building. My mom had a regular sewing machine and not the industrial type needed to sew thick canvas sails. They ended up breaking all her needles and then the machine. Boy, was she steamed.

The desire to create things should never go ignored. You don't need to justify the stuff you make. You don't need to sell it, or give it away, or show it to anyone. If you're lacking inspiration, one of the most fun things to do is to hang out in an art shop for a couple of hours just looking at all of the neat supplies. My art supply forays have led to clay sculptures of feet and hands, a series of pastel postcards that I sent to friends in the mail, quick-tie sarongs, and rings made from fimo.

The ability to create something—high- or low-tech—is reassuring, don't you think? Making stuff, taking pictures, writing stories, and trading zines nurtures the imagination. Sure, there will always be slicker shirts, jewellery, and artwork around that you can buy, but even manufacturers know the value of things that are made by hand. If something is labelled "handmade," you can be sure you'll pay a lot more for it.

The other thing about creating stuff is that our society values people who can make things, even if they don't always reward them financially. In 1998, the average annual income for artists was $6,500. I'm not kidding. Still, the innovator, the creator, the artist all carry a special status in our eyes. They are creative beings who can build the things they envision, while the rest of us can only purchase them.

I recently went to an architecture exhibit and there was a video about the work of Frank Gehry, featuring his magnificent building for the Guggenheim Museum in Bilbao, Spain. The thing that struck me about Gehry's buildings was his playfulness and his desire to experiment with materials. The Guggenheim, like much of his work, is inspired by his love of the sea. The shapes he uses, the colours he tries to capture, the way the light reflects inside and out are all the result of the architect letting his imagination run without restraints.

The ability to take your vision and place it on the landscape in a way that complements and enhances the environment, and possibly people's lives, is a unique talent. To actually believe that your ideas can translate into visions that other people will admire and respect takes courage. We often leave that job to the "creators" in our society, and they become our artists, our visionaries. Although we all have the ability to create, and build, and inspire, only a few of us will actually pick up the tools we need to make things and see what will come.

Are you one of those people?

Myth:

You can't have everything

"You want to have your cake and eat it too." "Don't ask for so much." "You need to learn that there are limits to what you can have."

Those are just a few of the things our parents, teachers, sometimes even friends tell us. Maybe they tell us not to want too much because *they* didn't ask for enough. Or maybe it's because if you only ask for a little bit you won't be disappointed. Or maybe it's because they think in a kind of poverty consciousness—they worry about not having enough instead of believing that their needs will be met and surpassed if they can be open to prosperity.

The wide-eyed five-year-old will ask for everything and believe she can have it. We are quickly taught to want things in moderation. And while that's not exactly a bad thing, it can stop us from reaching for more, make us fearful that we'll look greedy or impossible to satisfy.

I should make it clear that by "everything" I don't necessarily mean something as obvious as having the wealth of Bill Gates or a glamorous career that takes you around the world or the perfect "Brady Bunch" family. I'm talking about great big globs of excitement, and joy, and happiness. "Having it all" for you might mean that you find pleasure and a thrill in having all your material needs met, satisfaction in the work you're doing, happiness in your personal life. Oh, it does sound like a lot to ask for, doesn't it? It's not. It's just that so few people believe that it is possible or even okay to expect it.

I used to believe that you could have everything, just not all at once. I thought that having a great career meant sacrificing my personal life. I imagined that having a family would mean giving up my work. Now, I think it's a question of balance, and of asking for help rather than trying to be superwoman, like Mom, and simply knowing and believing that it is possible.

It's not safer to believe that you can't have everything. You're not keeping yourself from disappointment, because you will inevitably meet people who *do* have everything, and you'll wonder why they got so lucky. It's not luck. They chose to believe they could have it all. Will you?

No-Budget Publishing

Anna Humphrey, 21,
Eastern/Central

When Audra Estrones first dreamed of starting a magazine, she wanted it to have a Canadian voice. She wanted it to be educational, as well as fun. She wanted cross-country circulation and a frequent enough print schedule that it would keep up with the news. She also wanted to be able to publish it within a very limited budget. In short, she wanted the moon.

No newsprint, no copyright, next to no money, and, most importantly, no limits. The somewhat-underground world of no-budget online magazines (commonly referred to as "e-zines") is thriving. "I'm a big fan of magazines in general," says Audra Estrones, creator of *Marigold* (www.marigoldzine.com), a relatively new Canadian feminist/girl e-zine.

"I feel they have a huge ability to impact popular culture. We believe the most absurd things, because we see them again and again in magazines. We believe that only about thirty people on the planet are pretty. We believe that we need to know about the home life of that dude who won $1,000,000 on that show where you can win $1,000,000. It is totally bizarre."

Audra's original dream was to start a feminist print magazine with all-Canadian content. "I wanted it to be fun and informative at the same time. I also wanted it to be able to come out often enough to contain news, and not have it be outdated by the time the reader got it. In a male-dominated, corporation-run, zillion-dollar publishing world, what's a girl with a small budget and a big dream to do?

"It totally became clear when I wrote an article about the rapes that happened at Woodstock '99," remembers Audra. "The same article appeared both in a print magazine, called *Velocity*, and in *Hissyfit*, an e-zine. In *Hissyfit*, a bulletin board forum was set up to discuss the article ... I probably got about twenty e-mails from women, letting me know how they felt about what I'd written. The print magazine? Well, it went under. I needed no further persuasion: e-zine it was."

Hundreds and hundreds of young people, from hundreds and hundreds of home computers, are learning about the low-budget power of Internet publishing, and, just like Audra, they are creating magazines that are more than just pictures or pages of articles. In a very real sense, they are creating communities. "The site is 40 percent political rally, 60 percent slumber party," says Audra of *Marigold*. By this she means that the site has become a place where like-minded women can meet, share or debate ideas, and just basically "hang out," in a virtual kind of way. The inclusion of bulletin boards where readers and writers can post messages and discuss relevant topics means that, unlike in print magazines, nobody has the last word. Readers have as much authority as writers, and everything is open for discussion.

And curiously enough, in the world of e-zines, young women seem to be taking the lead. "I can't think of many boy e-zines," says Audra. This comes as a pleasant surprise considering that a number of pervasive stereotypes are still kicking around. For one, there's the assumption that men and boys have more computer knowledge than women and girls, and then there's also the idea that publishing is really a "man's field."

A search using the words "feminist zine" or "girl zine" will bring up a list of over 5,000 sites, which in itself is proof that girls are making their mark in the Internet publishing world. Some of the most popular girl e-zines can be found on Chickpages server sites (www.chickpages.com). Chickpages offers templates for zines (great for beginners) that you can plug pictures and text into. While Chickpages is geared specifically towards young women, there is also a wide array of server sites for both males and females: tripod.com, angelfire.com, and geocities.com are all user-friendly and completely free sites that provide templates for beginners.

However, in the case of *Marigold*, as with many quality e-zines, money is still an issue. Online magazines are business as well as pleasure. Signing up for a domain name (in other words, signing up to get your own "dot-com"), as opposed to using a free server site, has its advantages. For one thing, it simplifies your URL (the site's address), so that readers can remember easily where to find you. Since e-zines generate income by running banner ads, and not all servers permit this (especially not the free ones), it's important that e-zine editors with profit in mind shop carefully. Server costs can vary, depending on how many features are offered. For example, some might not offer the software necessary for interactive bulletin boards.

Profit aside, though, most important for Audra has been the opportunity *Marigold* has provided to meet and bring together Canadians who otherwise might never have had the chance to exchange ideas. "I never used to know any ex-Mennonites who have pet flying squirrels and run a record label in B.C.," says Audra, "or postmodern feminist chicks working in anarchist libraries in Manitoba, or lesbian writers in tiny communities north of the Arctic

Circle, or anyone north of the Arctic Circle, for that matter!"

While *Marigold* and other interactive e-zine communities continue to grow, linking readers and writers across the country and around the world, it's beginning to seem as though Audra might get that moon after all.

A sampling of e-zines

vagabunda.com: This site refers to itself as a grrrl geographer zine. Its focus is on backpacking, road trips, and other affordable travel, all with a feminist slant.

breakupgirl.com: This zine claims it is "saving love lives the world over," and it provides an array of advice about how to get over him and get on with it.

equity/today.org: This site offers a wide selection of articles by young people on the issues of racial bias and discrimination.

fametracker.com: This e-zine is an interactive take on the grocery store check-out tabloid. Devoted entirely to celebrity stuff, this site defines itself as "A Farmer's Almanac of Celebrity Worth."

How to Make Your Own Website

Giselle DeGrandis, 16,
Eastern/Central

Some like to paint, some like to write, and others, well ... they like to build. The Internet is my preferred medium, and building websites—my creative outlet. I have built a place where I can say whatever the hell I want; where everything reflects my interests, my likes, my dislikes, and my hopes and dreams. (Parents: this is why I'm online every waking moment!) And the best part is that no one can see me, and I can't see them! Wanna build your own mental sanction? Here's how:

Choose a topic that interests you (that's who this place is for, right?) and collect some info on it.

1 Get hooked up to the net! Sign up with an ISP (internet service provider) that serves your area. If you are planning to spend lots of time online (like me), opt for an "unlimited access" plan because it won't charge you by the hour.

2 Borrow a book from the library on HTML (Hypertext Markup Language; you'll figure out what it is soon enough). I recommend the *The Project Cool Guide to HTML* by Teresa Martin and Glenn Davis. If you don't know even basic HTML, you can't do anything. Seriously.

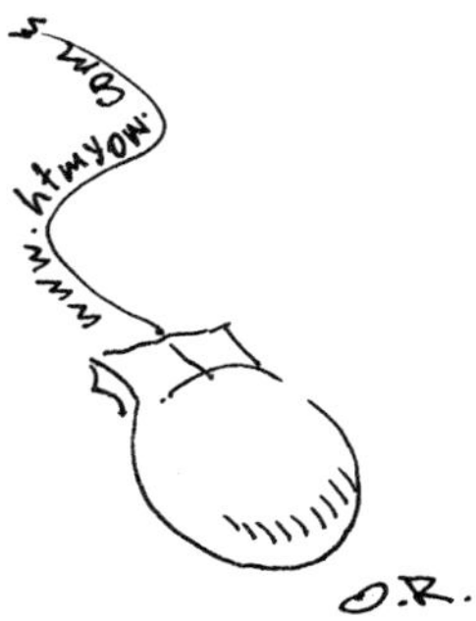

3 Register to get a free website space at a place like Geocities (http://www.geocities.com) or Angelfire (http://www.angelfire.com), which conveniently each have their own editor and file manager. If you find that you need more room for your site, you can always purchase a web space from a number of online companies or through your ISP.

4 Do lots of browsing to get ideas. If you find a really nifty trick on someone's page that you want to simulate (don't copy stuff; people get mad) on your own, then click "View" on your browser's toolbar and scroll down to "Page Source." This will show you the page's HTML in full, and you can then find the code you need within it (if you look for a while).

5 If you still need some help with your site, visit an online HTML guide or ask the webmistress of your favourite site for some pointers. There are lots of friendly people on the net.

6 Finally, work on your website day and night until it's absolutely splendid! Add a nice background, some attractive graphics, meaningful links, and lots of good reading content. Next, give your site a catchy title, and then register to have it listed in a big directory like Yahoo! so you will get lots of visitors.

7 Now the best part. Gloat to all your friends about your website, and allow them to behold the fruits of your labour. Make them jealous that they don't have a site too. And this is really annoying: update your friends on a daily basis about how many visitors your site has had (the larger the number, the more impressive!).

I think this quote from *Project Cool* nicely sums up the website experience: "What you do with your Web space is limited mostly by your imagination and the time and effort you put into building it."

So what are you waiting for, girl? Get building!

Construction tips:

- Redecorate your site whenever you feel like it; there is zero mess and zero cost.
- Make sure that you aren't taking copyrighted images and text from other people's sites. I know this may shock some of you, but there are (some) rules online.
- Choose tasteful backgrounds for your pages. Don't make your visitors blind (unintentionally). And make sure your text shows up on top of it.
- Don't go overboard on Javascripts (they make pop-up text, blinking colours, and other fun stuff) because it's just plain tacky, and it takes hours for the screen to load.
- Check your spelling! It's disappointing to find errors on really well-designed pages!
- Don't reveal your name, address, or phone number on your website, because you never know who's going to be looking at it.
- Update it often to keep your site interesting (and visitors returning).

9 to 5 (On How to Produce Your First Play)

Olga Ryabets, 16,
Central/Eastern

"The subway depresses the hell outta me," says dramaturgist Kelly Thorton, "all the 9 to 5 people ..."

It's enough to cause anxiety. That is partly why I'm here, downtown Toronto, ten minutes late, trying to find out how to escape the monotony in life. For this I'm meeting Kelly, who works at the Canadian Regional Theatre, and Franco Boni, a big part of the Buddies in Bad Times theatre company.

Ever since the school production of my first one-act play, I have been obsessed with getting produced elsewhere. And I refuse to wait twenty years for a chance, either. I want it now. So buttons get pressed, an interview is arranged, and here I am, getting the answer to my question—how does a seventeen-year-old get her work on stage in the third-largest theatre city in the world?

Once I ask this, Franco and Kelly almost simultaneously announce that drama festivals are the way. Franco was the previous year's organizer of the infamous Rhubarb Drama Festival in Toronto. Kelly is organizing it this year. I get suspicious—this seems like a shameless promotion. But once I hear more about the festivals, especially Rhubarb, I become convinced—it very well may be the best way to start out.

There are many festivals in Toronto, such as the Sears Drama Festival, or the Factory Theatre's "The Works," which happens in May, and, of course, Rhubarb. This last one appealed the most to the unemployed, high school me (the fest is completely free). Founded in 1976 by Sky Gilbert, Rhubarb is a yearly February showcase of one-acts by writers of all kinds. This time around, Rhubarb organizers dedicated part of the fest to playwrights under twenty-one.

The process is simple—you submit, and the judges read everything and pick the works to be produced. If you make the cut, you are provided with the space, publicity, stage manager, a director, actors, technical crew, and any tech stuff you might need. All free of charge. You even get $100 or so as prop/costume money. If this seems too good to be true, take a look at the criteria for choosing the work.

When asked about it, Franco and Kelly had a very unified opinion. "We look for originality, risk, and unusual vision."

KELLY: "There are plays that get produced in Canadian Regional [theatre], but not in Rhubarb." All that's new, alternative, fresh is what strikes home here. Plus, Rhubarb has a solid audience and a no-criticism policy, taking the fear out of experimenting. Anything else? "I look for honesty in a script," says Franco. That and the half-hour time limit.

At this point, I thought it appropriate to ask how Kelly and Franco started in the field themselves.

KELLY: I was in kindergarten ...

FRANCO: No, really, the first thing we both did was Rhubarb.

Next, I ask about the difference between older and younger writers. Apparently, young people have more edge and honesty, and are "brutally aware of the world around them." "They don't know how to lie," says Kelly. Both she and Franco note the "humanism and raw voice" of early works compared to the "censored, stylish technique" of an experienced playwright. At the end, however, "we're all just trying to deal with who we are," adds Franco.

With all that in mind, I am excited and relieved to not wait until I'm thirty-seven for my "big break."

It can happen now. And not just to me, but to anyone else who is afraid of computers and cubicles.

Rhubarb is only one of the countless opportunities out there—all there is left for me now is to create something brilliant. Kelly insists that theatre (like any other art) is an addiction. I agree 200 percent and ask my final question.

ME: Why do you do what you do?

KELLY: We're MAD!

She laughs like she is, and I think to myself that madness is the reason anyone does anything worthwhile in this world. I look at my watch, thank Kelly and Franco for everything, and take off to beat the rush-hour traffic—at 5:30, the subway depresses the hell outta me.

So You Want to Be a Music Star?

Alex Ribera, 15,
Eastern/Central

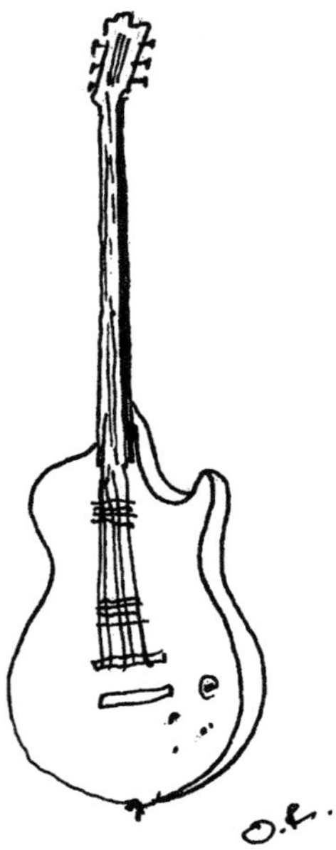

At first, I jumped at the opportunity to write this piece about what it really means to thrive and survive in the music business today. My interest stems from my love of music, and my craving to know how those who make their way into the spotlight in the music industry get there and what they have to sacrifice along the way. Someday (yes, even after writing this article), I would like to make a living as a musician. However, I feel I must confess that while collecting all of my research, I lost the drive to write this article that I started with. I only regained that drive while I was jamming on my guitar and singing at the top of my lungs one day. I was reminded of why I had been so willing (even enthusiastic) to exert all this effort to write what is basically a research paper. I love to experience music. Almost all of the musicians I listen to, the ones who give me inspiration and make me appreciate all different kinds of music, have had to work in, with, and through the music industry. You might find this article very technical and a little pessimistic at times. However, after conducting many interviews with different people, I believe that this article gives a true representation of what the music industry is all about.

To begin the process, your first step is to record a few of your pieces on what is called a **demo tape**. This demo can be sent to club owners, along with your press package, so that they can decide if they want you to play at their club. It is also used if you are later looking for management, or when you want to appeal to a label to come and hear you play at a club or other venue. Having a demo tape is key because none of this will happen without a demo tape first.

So now you ask, how do I make a demo? You have two options. The first, and cheapest, is to go to your phone book and start calling all the local music stores to find out which ones rent out what is called a four-track, and how much they will charge you per month, including microphones. This equipment will let you record four separate tracks—for example, one voice, one harmony, one guitar, and one piano track—and then overlap them.

I called up a local music store in Toronto and was told that to rent a four-track for a month would cost $40; adding their cheapest (poorest-quality) microphone would be an extra $15. If you decide that you'll need more overlapping tracks, then you will have to rent an eight-track. There are two main types. Analog records on a cassette, and the equipment can be rented for $155 per month. Digital records on to a hard disc that you can later lay onto a cassette, and it gives better-quality sound. The equipment can be rented for $210 per month. You might even want to consider burning your own CD.

Twenty-two-year-old Emm Gryner, one of Canada's newest and most promising young female artists, told me that her first songs were recorded on a four-track that she had borrowed from the music department at a school. A few years later, she was able to record in an actual studio in L.A., because her brother was working there at the time. And that is your second choice, the professional studio. However, unless you know someone who can get you some free time, this can be very expensive, because not only are you paying for the time you use in the studio, you are also paying for a technician, someone who can mix and adjust tracks for you. When I called a local studio, they told me that, depending on which studio you used, it would cost between $255 and $305 per hour, including the technician.

I was given some advice about studio recording from Terry Humphreys of Alternative Management. She said a mistake frequently made in the studio by new bands is that they try to record all of their material. If you can afford to get some time in a studio, you should try to record your best three or four tracks at most. That's all it takes to get someone's attention. Once you have your best demo, you have access to opportunities that you didn't have before.

Before you go and invest in this demo tape, know that there are other ways of exposing your music and opening yourself up for some criticism. Volunteer to perform at school, university events, community centres, and small fundraisers. Lots of people say that your family can be the toughest audience you'll ever get. Also, meeting with other bands or performers who are a little further along than you is a good way to expose yourself to different styles of performance, and it will give you a chance to see the way the audience reacts to certain gestures from the band. Jamming sessions are also a lot of fun and a good way to expand and explore your original pieces in a new form. The other reason to connect with other bands is because later on, if you are touring and you know a band that is working that city, you might be able to crash at one of their houses. They can also give you their personal opinions about working with certain labels, managers, and agents.

Earlier on I mentioned sending your demo tape along with a **press package**. A press package is what helps give people an idea of what you or your band is about before they hear your music. A press package should include the name of your band or solo act, a detailed description about the kind of music you play, and who your main influences are. You should also offer some background information about you, and this can include the details of your musical training, your experience playing with other bands, and how you evolved as a musician to come to this point in your career.

The point of having a press package is that it will expand as you grow professionally. As you play for more and more audiences, you will begin to be noticed and talked about. Any reviews, clippings, or information about the venues you have played go into your press package. A photograph is also an important part of your press package. Many people wait until they can have a professional photographer take the shot because it is important that the image of your style of music come across in the photo.

A beautiful example is the press package of D.N.A., a young woman who plays incredible piano, as well as bass, and sings her own material. When I met her in January, she gave me a copy of her tape and her package, which then consisted of only two sheets of paper. The first tells me that she began studying piano at the Royal Conservatory of Music when she was five, that her pop influences came from such bands as The Police, and that she played with a few different bands before she ended up at university, where she got her Bachelor of Fine Arts degree, specializing in composition and performance. It also tells me in great detail about the original style of her composition, using a few different genres of music to describe her eclectic sound. Her "D.N.A." symbol decorates the page in a large font flowing vertically and separating the few paragraphs from a moody shot of her that takes up about a quarter of the space. The second page is simply a photo of her with her title underneath, as well as her business address and phone number.

Steven Tennant, vice-president of artist marketing at Universal Records, explained to me that a **manager's role** is somewhat like that of a mother. Managers get to know their clients personally and are in charge of showing them the ropes. They are expected to advise their clients on negotiations and business decisions, especially when discussing contracts with record labels. Also, it's crucial to know that the people at a record company who have to sort through the thousands of tapes received every year will not listen to unsolicited demo tapes, only those that come through a reputable manager. There are a few things to keep in mind when looking for a manager. The first is that there are good managers and there are not-so-good managers. It's important to ask around. You might want to consider working with a manager on a trial basis. If, after a certain period of time, either of you decides that it's not working out, you can go your separate ways, with no hard feelings. Before you think of hiring a manager, though, you should consider whether you are ready yet to take that step. Really, you only need a manager when you can no longer handle things yourself.

Terry Humphreys of Alternative Management told me that a common mistake a band will make is to get a manager for the wrong reasons. Sometimes the band feels stuck because they don't know what their next step should be in running the business. And sometimes they are just lazy and don't want to do the work themselves. Terry's advice is simple: ASK FOR HELP! Call up a manager or another band you know and get some advice. A good manager won't take you on if they know you aren't ready. Remember, the manager needs to make money, and until you've got a band together that is willing to work hard and get things started, your manager will have nothing to work with. You've got to make the effort first.

When I first interviewed Steven Tennant, I didn't understand that there is an important difference between a manager and an **agent**. He explained that an agent is in charge of booking you into clubs and other venues. In large agencies, hundreds of agents work for many different clients.

Another term you should know is "**A & R**," which stands for Artists and Repertoire. The **A & R** people are the ones who come out to see you play. They represent a record label and are there to decide if they think their label should risk investing money in your act. If they do think that and get behind you, they then have to go back to the label and try to convince a bunch of people in higher positions that they should take a chance on you.

You have probably heard of bands whose only dream is to be signed to a **record label**. Many people think that once you are signed you've made it as a musician. This is not so! It simply means you have a lot more work ahead of you. A record label works a bit like a bank. It makes a deal with you to produce an album or albums, which it might support with videos, tours, marketing, and so on. The label take care of the expenses, but it also gets paid back first. You do make a certain amount from your live performances, but until your record has sold enough copies to make back what the label invested, you don't make a cent from record sales. Contary to what you might think, the bands you see on MuchMusic aren't all going to be taking home big cheques at the end of the day—not until the label has made its money back.

There are advantages and disadvantages to working with an independent label ("indie") as opposed to one of the majors (Universal, Sony, EMI, BMG). I learned a great deal while speaking to Peter Hardman of Outside Music, an indie distributing company in Toronto.

- A major label can invest more in you, taking your album further.
- The smaller indie labels can afford to spend more time with you and pay closer attention to your progress.
- If your first record is made on a major label and it falls on its face, it's not likely that you'll ever be picked up by other major labels.

Linda Dawe, a radio promoter at Music Solutions, a promotions company, is a woman with an incredible wealth of knowledge about many aspects of working in the music industry. Knowing that she represents Roch Voisine, who is already signed to a major label, I asked her why he would need a **radio promoter**. "Well, the Mahones and Roch Voisine have what's called pressing and distribution [P & D] deals with BMG and Universal respectively. Those deals do not include promotion and marketing. What we do is work in conjunction with the sales teams at those major labels. Then we report our promotional activity to them, and they report their sales activity to us. And we make plans and promotion ideas together."

Dan Broome of True North Records gave me zoodles of good advice, ranging across a wide variety of topics:

- Start with your local fan base. If you can't win a crowd in your home town with your music, don't take your band on tour across Canada.
- Tell the club promoter that you can bring a crowd of twenty-five to fifty people—that will give you an edge when you're lining up your first gig.
- Out of every twelve albums produced in Canada, one is a hit, one breaks even, and the rest never make a dime.
- A record deal is essentially nothing more than a loan.
- Do you want riches, fame, the whole deal? Because the likelihood of that happening is very, very, very much a long shot.
- Don't work with producers who won't come to see you perform first or be at a rehearsal so that they know what kind of sounds should come across in your recording.
- Just because A & R people agree to come see you doesn't mean they will do anything with you. Remember, coming out to clubs is their job.
- Before you go into a meeting with A & R or anyone else from a record label, know what your next step is and what you want to happen with your material. And don't forget that thank-you note—you want to make sure they remember your name.
- You can't guess what the next craze will be—who could have predicted *Stomp*, or *Riverdance*? Or Ashley MacIsaac making fiddle-playing popular?

And here are some points from many of the different people I interviewed:

- On taking voice lessons: "It forces me to get inside and access certain feelings, which makes a lot of those lessons like therapy."—D.N.A.
- "Don't invite industry to hear you play until you've got your road legs [experience playing live]."—Terry Humphreys of Alternative Management

Conclusion

Yards and yards of soft pink material are gathered on the floor around me. I've been trying to wrap my sari for the better part of an hour. Sullen and uncooperative, it refuses to hang with any measure of grace. I am in India and the women here dress in beautiful, colourful saris when they attend parties.

I start again, twirling it around my waist, and tucking a little of the silvery border into my petticoat. I try to stay calm even though I am feeling overwhelmed by the fabric, by the thought of still having to fix my hair, find my shoes, and be out the door in fifteen minutes. I try to remember what my mom told me about creating plenty of small pleats in the front, which will cause the whole thing to hang elegantly. Sure, mom.

Staring into the full-length mirror and seeing the mess of silk around me, I am not sure if I'll ever get this thing on. Forget poise and elegance—I'd just be delighted to keep my sari from slipping off at the slightest yank. I need my mom. Some things never change.

I do finally get enough safety pins in at the right places to hold it all together. I'm now thirty minutes late and the two-minute walk up the little hill to the tuk tuk stand, where the yellow and black taxis that can swivel 180 degrees in the tightest corners line up, seems ridiculously far. I hitch a ride on the back of a motorbike instead. In India, the traffic is mind-blowing. There are lanes, but if it's faster to drive in the wrong lane, or into oncoming traffic, no problem. The roads are not reserved solely for cars or bikes either. Bullock carts, ownerless horses, dogs, pigs, fruit sellers are neck and neck with two-ton lorries and '50s-style Ambassadors. Major arteries sometimes come to a standstill because a farmer is leading his herd of oxen down the middle of the road. And as for country roads, well they're as good a place as any to thresh wheat.

Riding sidesaddle on the back of a bike in my flowing pink robe is quite thrilling. There are no helmet laws; people favour garlands of flowers for protection instead. For almost every second I am on a bike with the wind and the pollution and the noise from the thousand cars, trucks, bikes careening around roundabouts and coming far *too* CLOSE, my life passes before my eyes. I know that at any second I could die. Yet, day after day, I still climb on the back of my friend's bike and assume everything will be alright. I wonder if it's simply serendipitous that I should be in India, now, when I am required to write the final chapter of this book. Perhaps it really needs to be written here, in the place where my great-grandparents once lived, in the place where the river Ganges cleanses and transforms, where tolerance for all faiths, practices, and beliefs exists, and mostly the place where freedom from the constraints of the external world is gained by self-study. I didn't come to India seeking anything in par-tic-u-lar. I'm not here for spiritual enlightenment or mysticism, or to seek out my ancestors, or because I'm running away from anything. Yet being here, surrounded by temples and mosques, palm trees, and big-eyed lizards that live indoors, has altered something in me. I will have been here for two months by the time I leave. Hopefully, by then I'll be able to distinguish between the subtle and perhaps fleeting changes and those that will be more significant and lasting.

India places behaviour under a microscope. Seemingly innocent acts can be misconstrued as glaring statements of defiance or poor judgment. Being female in India requires constant vigilance over your actions. At first, having to constantly think about how the things you do might be perceived seems like a very repressive and antiquated way to live. And I believe it has its faults, since it does, for some, lead to a closet full of skeletons and a pile of guilt. But there is, at the same time, something important that happens if you shift your perspective slightly and see that these family and societal requirements and constraints can have the positive effect of helping you to consider your behaviour and its consequences. Zeroing in on the process you use to make decisions will help you develop better judgment and ultimately enable you to make enlightened choices. Of course, you don't need India to learn how to recognize the impact of your actions. You simply need to become acutely aware of your motivation for picking a particular course of action and the impact that action will have on your life and on the people you care about.

India is a very unusual place because there is a kind of unpredictability that comes with the difference in the perception of time here. When I finally arrive, upset with myself for keeping my new friends waiting, I am shown into the drawing room and left there to amuse myself for half an hour while they finish prayers and grab their purses. India is like that, I've learned. It's not hurry-up-and-wait. It's more like, "Why hurry?" Pacing on the platform waiting hours for a train to arrive is nothing to get upset about here. People routinely arrive late or not at all, often with little concern or notice. It's not that they're being rude either. It's just that there's plenty of time to do everything and there's no need to get angry if your expectations and plans are thwarted. Everything happens, after all, according to God's will, whether you're Muslim, Hindu, or Jain. And, ultimately, the charm of India is that something or someone interesting will come along, just as you're peering down the tracks wondering how long the train's been gone.

This nonchalant attitude towards keeping a schedule and being on time is quite different from that to which I have grown accustomed at home, where we are all always hard-pressed for time. The lackadaisical approach to time in India has forced me to view the routine in North America that rules our lives as a strange and demanding wheel. The North American routine leaves little room for chance encounters, days spent sleeping under a monsoon sky, or great activity because someone or something has inspired action. I know that in North America the wheel runs and then runs us over, until part of the weekend is spent exhausted on the couch preparing for our next go around. When I return, I will try to keep some of the pleasure of simply being in a place and not worrying about how much there is still to do at my desk.

When we finally arrive at the party, it almost resembles a scene Renoir would have painted. Women in beautiful saris dot the grounds, a rowboat normally moored at the edge of the bank has drifted to the middle of the lake, and the sun is the colour of marigolds.

I wonder if while skimming through these pages, hopefully being drawn in to read, relish, and reflect on at least a few of the stories and myths, you feel the beginning of some subtle shift in yourself that illuminates a truth or possibility you hadn't yet discovered. It is a lot to ask, but words and feelings are powerful that way.

> I looked and looked—astonishing!
> (Only a rare one hears me sing!)
> The earth shot backwards to the sky,
> An elephant fell in an ant's eye,
> Mountains flew without a breeze,
> Souls and creatures climbed the trees,
> In a dry lake the waves lashed,
> Without water, waterbirds splashed.
> Pundits sat and read the law,
> Babbled of what they never saw.
> Who understands Kabir's rhyme
> Is a true saint to the end of time.
>
> —Kabir

Special Thanks and Acknowledgements

Karen Hanson championed the idea for this book all the way to the top. It's her baby as much as it is mine. Nicole Langlois challenged, questioned, and helped make the book better in every way. Down to the last pages and days, it wouldn't be here without them. A special thank you to the interns at HarperCollins, including Chantel Guertin and Liz Kribs; to Penelope Jackson for her brilliant insights and amazing skill and talent as a musician; to Gill Richardson for her twisted sense of humour; to Rachael Pleet for her help with the prototype cover; to Alicia Glavac for creating the perfect art for the cover; to Olga Ryabets for many of the extremely skilled illustrations within these pages; to Roy Nicol for his patience and fabulous page design; to Catherine Marjoribanks and Stephanie Fysh for their careful work; and to Anne Mandlsohn, Sheyfali Saujani, and Rona Maynard for their support and friendship. Every girl should be lucky to have a brother like Shane and fabulous guy friends like Eduardo Pussar and James Campbell in her corner. Of course, Naseer Hashim, whom I love and esteem greatly, is more thrilling than any 007 dream. There are quite a few people at the *Toronto Star* who I'd like to thank for their faith and wisdom, among them are John Honderich and John Ferri for believing in me, Haroon Siddiqui for mentoring me, and Mary Deanne Shears for being such a terrific role model.

The biggest thank you belongs to the many hundreds of young women I've had the privilege of meeting over the past seven years. Your enthusiasm, willingness to write, fantastic ideas, and incredibly sweet letters and e-mails made the magazine and book possible.

P.S.

I'd like to know what you think of this book. You can email me directly at: sharleneazam@hotmail.com. And don't forget to check out the websites for both *Rebel, Rogue, Mischievous Babe* and *Reluctant Hero*:

www.rebelrogue.ca   www.reluctanthero.com

—Sharlene

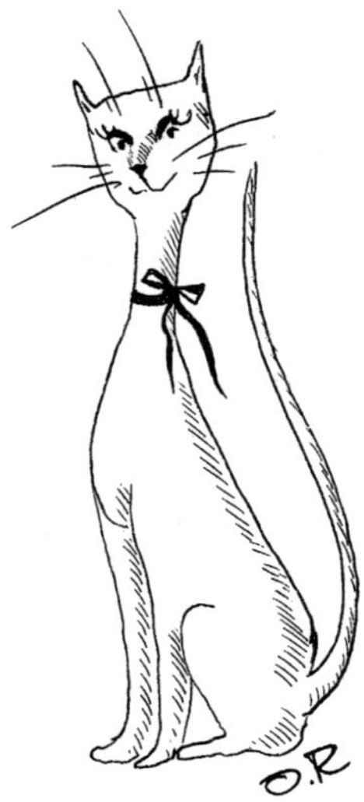
O.R